Next Level Virtual Training

ADVANCE
YOUR
FACILITATION

DIANA L. HOWLES

PRESS

Alexandria, VA

ATD Press is an internationally renowned source of insightful and practical information on talent development, training, and professional development.

ATD Press
1640 King Street
Alexandria, VA 22314 USA

Ordering information: Books published by ATD Press can be purchased by visiting ATD's website at td.org/books or by calling 800.628.2783 or 703.683.8100.

Virtual Trainer Capability Model © 2022 Howles Associates LLC. All rights reserved.

Library of Congress Control Number: 2021952824

ISBN-10: 1-953946-03-8
ISBN-13: 978-1-953946-03-4
e-ISBN: 978-1-953946-04-1

ATD Press Editorial Staff
Director: Sarah Halgas
Manager: Melissa Jones
Content Manager, Learning Technology: Alexandria Clapp
Developmental Editor: Jack Harlow
Production Editor: Hannah Sternberg
Text Design: Shirley E.M. Raybuck
Cover Design: Rose Richey

Text Layout: Kathleen Dyson

Printed by BR Printers, San Jose, CA

Contents

Preface: "The Night Before Training"

by Diana L. Howles

'Twas the morn of a weekday,
When throughout virtual space,
Each learner logged in,
With anticipation on their face.

They grabbed cups of coffee,
Clicked their join link with care,
In hopes their facilitator,
Soon would be there.

And I in my home office,
Nestled snug in my seat,
Dressed professional on top,
But in yoga pants with bare feet.

My producer joined too,
With a ring light in tow,
Settling in for virtual training,
Musing how it might go.

When more rapid than fire,
From across the globe, they all came,
We welcomed them onscreen,
And greeted them by name.

But then to my surprise,
There arose such a clatter,
I checked the participant panel,
To see what was the matter.

We heard dogs barking, adults talking,
Kids screaming down the hall,
I asked learners to mute,
To be less distracting for all.

They turned on their cameras,
But their silhouettes—how shrouded,
Their headroom—too spacious,
Their backgrounds—so crowded.

They posted chats, clicked reactions,
Raised virtual hands at will,
But when I asked a discussion question,
I heard crickets; all was still.

Then what to their wondering ears,
did they hear,
But my producer and I saying,
"Breakouts are near!"

Away to their breakouts,
They tried to join in a flash,
It worked on the third try,
Which was quite the mad dash.

Learners brainstormed on whiteboards,
With colleagues so dear,
Then returned to the main session,
To debrief with good cheer.

But then to my astonishment,
What did my bewildered eyes see?
I lost my internet connection,
No one could hear me!

I hurried to network settings,
Heartbeat racing—what was wrong?
It looked like an outage,
But I didn't know for how long.

I texted my producer,
To forge ahead without me,
Found the hotspot on my phone,
And reconnected with plan B.

But the end of virtual training,
Had finally drawn near,
And my producer and I realized,
There was nothing left to fear.
We wanted to learn from these lessons,
Take our training to the next level,
Because that would be something,
In which we could revel.

So, close whiteboard,
Clear annotations,
Tidy desks where we sat.
Close poll results,
Stop screen sharing,
Post evaluation link in chat.

And I heard learners exclaim,
As they smiled real cute,
"It's a good thing we read lips,
'cause you're . . . still on mute!"

Acknowledgments

As the popular proverb reminds us, it takes a village to raise a child. Naturally, it also takes a village to craft a book from scratch. I would like to thank my treasured village for their contributions to this project. To begin, my deepest gratitude goes to the amazing virtual learning clients with whom I have worked over the years. You inspire me daily, and it has been a true privilege to work together in virtual space. Special thanks also to Huw Newton-Hill, Dean Stewart, Kelly Eno, David Gering, Vanessa Dennen, Kari Word, Ömer Arslan, Katherine Dalland, Kim Huettl, Michael Sitte, Laura V. Page, and Melissa Albrecht for their input, contributions, and willingness to share their expertise and work experience. As always, I am grateful to Michelle Sanders for her beautiful graphics. Special thanks also to Heidi Gering, Dawn Dorning, and Kailey Gering for their willingness to assist with illustrative examples.

Additionally, I am grateful to the virtual training platform vendors who graciously granted permission to share screenshots of their products. They include InSpace, Zoom, Adobe Connect, Webex, and LogMeIn. A special thank you to Matt Pierce at TechSmith Corporation, Kortney Clark at SkillPath, and Articulate Global for generously allowing us to showcase their work and/or products. Finally, much gratitude is extended to Michael @relaxdaily, whose lovely piano music played in the background for most of the writing of this work: youtube.com/relaxdaily.

I am also indebted to the entire ATD publishing team for their tireless efforts and exemplary commitment to quality. I am especially thankful to my exceptional editorial team. To my talented editor, Jack, thank you for continuing to challenge me at every stage to improve the manuscript. It is because of your expertise and experience that I have learned much about clarity, consistency, and coherence. To my production editor, Hannah, your enthusiasm for the project and your professional excellence are truly inspiring. Thank you for making the final product immeasurably better with your thorough and thoughtful edits. To my content manager, Alexandria, thank you for believing in this project and believing in me from the very beginning. Your championing and constructive feedback have been invaluable.

Most of all, I extend a heartfelt thank you first and foremost to Les, Karra, Casey, Susie, Lowell, Thomas A., and JJ, without whom this book could not have been written. You are my heart, and your support has been my constant companion, sustaining me throughout this exciting endeavor.

Introduction

"I keep on making what I can't do yet in
order to learn to be able to do it."

—Vincent van Gogh, artist

The year was 2000. The large financial organization I worked for had recently purchased a new web conferencing platform. I was a corporate trainer at the time and remember being amazed as I watched an IT colleague demonstrate how it worked. She showed us how real-time collaboration and communication was possible from anywhere, anytime. Later, my manager suggested this could be a way for us to connect remotely with field staff, train internal staff, and educate external customers. I began using the platform to train employees and customers, and presented on the technology at company conferences to showcase what was possible. As a seasoned in-person trainer, I found this fresh online medium fascinating. It may have been the combination of technology and multimedia, the fact that it was a challenge, or the novelty of it all, but something deep down in me seemed to intuitively know it could be a game changer. Simply put, I was hooked.

And now, more than two decades later, I still find the live online learning medium exciting and brimming with possibility for greater innovation and opportunity. I strive to challenge myself to continually improve, with frequent reminders to step back so I can view things in new ways, discard what doesn't work, and eagerly build upon what does. It's also exciting to watch modern virtual training tools rapidly improve. We are fortunate to have many more affordances than we did before.

A Brief Virtual Training Case Study

Recently, I met with a new US client via video call to learn more about their organization, and how I might assist. They had requested a virtual training class on professional online presence for all their employees. Some staff were local and worked from home and in the office, while others worked out of state. More than 95 percent of their customer meetings were online, and many were on camera. As we talked about key concepts we could address, the organization's leaders and staff management assured me they would have conversations with staff afterward about key principles that could be incorporated into their development plans. Because this organization already used Zoom, we decided to deliver training via this platform. A week before the session, I met with my client contact to ensure our shared technology was working as expected. The following week, my client—who also offered to play the producer role— logged in early with me to ensure all was working correctly so I could post a welcome in chat, prepare my whiteboard, pull up supporting visuals, check the quality of my audio, frame myself on camera, and be ready for participants to join.

As the training program began, I was intentional about creating a welcoming environment and mindful of the energy I was projecting. Knowing enthusiasm takes a hit online, I tried to generate twice my normal energy level. At the same time, I was strategic. I knew the reasons behind what I was asking learners to do each moment and where I hoped it would lead the group at large. For example, I helped learners warm up their participation in a fun and easy way. I asked them to post in chat what footwear they were currently wearing (such as barefoot, slippers, socks, or shoes). Behind the scenes, my real intention was to ensure everyone successfully posted a chat. Once they did this, I knew they would be much more likely to chat again during the forthcoming substantive learning activities, primarily because they had already done it.

Throughout the virtual training, I was also intentional about being conversational and using a natural inflection in my voice to create more interest. I customized the session by offering examples from the organization and using their business lingo, which I had learned during the preliminary calls. When they divided into small breakout groups, they were able to critique and apply some of the key points of online presence that we had discussed.

I listened carefully to what participants said and spoke their first names aloud when connecting back to their previous comments. I genuinely complimented their insights and verbally rewarded their contributions to encourage more of the same.

At one point, I paused to ask a specific question so participants could stop and think. No one responded initially, and some silence followed. However, knowing the value of giving learners space to think, I waited several seconds more, and sure enough, a learner came off mute to share her thoughts, and then more shared after that. By the end, the participants had joyfully discovered what they didn't know about what they didn't know. Going forward, leadership agreed to hold follow-up conversations with staff and incorporate takeaways into development plans as part of their ongoing performance review discussions.

In this example, you've read about the wide range of opportunities available to virtual trainers to engage participants as well as the diversity of capabilities required to create the most effective learning experience. All of this and more will be covered in this book.

The Joy and the Rise of Virtual Training

Part of the fun of virtual training is that although you thoroughly prepare ahead of time, once you go live, anything can happen. This is part of its adventurous nature. Because of this, flexibility is key. For instance, during the session you might need to adjust your original order of content, remove an activity on the fly, add something relevant you think of in the moment, speed up a bit because you're falling behind schedule, or extend chat time because the rich discussion is going so well. Regardless, live online learning is an adventure that certainly benefits from preparation but must also be approached with openness. In this way, it truly becomes a unique journey between you and your learners as it unfolds in real time.

Although live online training has been a credible delivery platform for more than two decades, it experienced widespread adoption during the COVID-19 pandemic. In 2020 and 2021, when many employees from global organizations worked from home, virtual training platforms and web conferencing use skyrocketed. According to an ATD research report, 92 percent of the more than 430 organizations surveyed identified health, safety, and travel concerns from the pandemic as the top reasons for using virtual training platforms. Nearly all surveyed had converted some traditional classroom training to virtual training during the pandemic (ATD 2021). Millions quickly adopted technologies to support synchronous training across time and distance. Not only could employees now work from anywhere, but virtual facilitators could also train from anywhere. Zoom, for example, became one of those widely adopted platforms. After completing its first quarter, Zoom predicted annual revenue of $4 billion for fiscal year 2021, which was up approximately 50 percent from 2020. And when the pandemic first began, Zoom's revenue quadrupled from 2019 to 2020 (Liedtke 2021).

As organizations continue to embrace hybrid work models, their reliance on video conferencing and virtual training platforms for professional development remains. Suffice to say, online learning and virtual training are here to stay.

Next Level Virtual Training

Just as organizations scrambled to manage the transition to working remotely during the COVID-19 pandemic, so too did talent development functions. They were required to manage the shift of their in-person learning and development offerings to virtual. This meant trainers, facilitators, and educators needed to quickly learn or relearn some basic virtual training skills to keep their programs running and their customers learning. Often, they were looking for guidance just to keep their heads above water. Because we no longer live in a world where workplace training occurs 100 percent in-person, talent development professionals cannot settle for novice skills. To continue to best serve their organizations, learners, and customers, they will need to take their abilities to the next level.

So, what does it mean to go from basic to the next level? There is a difference between going through the motions as a virtual trainer and truly excelling by doing your best work. To guide professional development toward excellence, this book introduces you to the Virtual Trainer Capability Model, which identifies eight areas of expertise for the top virtual professional. Working toward proficiency in all these skills represents the full range of what it means to facilitate at the next level. Skill mastery in only one of these areas is not sufficient.

Who Should Read This Book?

Maybe you have been facilitating online for a few years but are now ready to move beyond the basics. Or perhaps you are familiar with available tools and virtual platforms, and you want to learn how to hone your craft even more. Do you find yourself asking, "What can I do to develop my live online facilitator skills?" "How can I be a more effective designer for virtual training?" "What other skills do I need?" "What else do I need to know about being a modern facilitator in a hybrid work environment?" or "What does a virtual trainer's development path look like?"

If you professionally facilitate live online learning, this book is for you. You might refer to yourself as a virtual trainer, a live online facilitator, a synchronous educator, an online adult education instructor, an instructional designer, a learning experience designer, or something similar. In this book, I use both *virtual trainer* and *virtual facilitator* interchangeably. Developers, evaluators, and producers of virtual training or online adult education will also find this helpful.

This book intentionally goes beyond the basics. Much of the existing body of work on the subject addresses the foundations of virtual training such as what virtual training is, its key features, how to make the business case for adopting virtual training, how to select a platform, how to transition from instructor-led to online learning, how to set up your workstation, tools and exercises, and how to prepare participants, facilitators, and producers. These excellent contributions have established a solid foundation and body of knowledge for the profession. Now there is a need to modernize and provide a framework for professional growth that builds upon and goes beyond what is currently written on the topic.

How Will This Book Help You?

This book will teach you how to advance beyond the basics of virtual training and online synchronous instruction. In doing so, it introduces a capability model for synchronous facilitators, applies learning experience design to live online learning, provides an in-depth chapter on how to develop on-camera competence as a virtual trainer, and addresses the dos and the don'ts of combining on-site and online learners in hybrid training classes.

Importantly, this book is more about actionable tips, techniques, and strategies, rather than the technology itself. Technology changes, but solid principles for how to use it do not. I've personally used many platforms over the past decades, including PlaceWare (which later became Microsoft Office Live Meeting), InterWise, HorizonLive, Elluminate Live!, NetMeeting, Macromedia's Breeze Meeting, Digitell, RingCentral, Blackboard Collaborate, Microsoft Teams, GoToTraining, Webex, Adobe Connect, and Zoom. Most platforms share common tools. Regardless of which platform you or your organization uses, you want to keep yourself up-to-date and do your best to leverage the affordances of each platform.

As virtual trainers and educators, we experience how deeply rewarding it is to help learners journey toward that aha moment. In a similar vein, it is my deepest hope that this book pushes you further than you thought possible, and you are inspired by new ideas that then trigger new ideas of your own. Take and apply the nuggets that resonate with you to help you tune and polish your craft.

Chapter 1 introduces you to the Virtual Trainer Capability Model, which identifies eight key areas of expertise. It is intended to serve as a framework for your professional development. These areas of expertise are:

- Experience design
- Environment shaping
- Online facilitation
- Facilitator presence
- Technical fluency
- Dynamic engagement
- Agile troubleshooting
- Evaluating impact

Chapter 2 focuses on the first virtual training capability: experience design. This skill set challenges you to approach the design of virtual training as an overarching experience from pre-class assignments all the way to post-class follow-up. You will learn how to include target learners in the design process and collect their valuable perspectives on course design. As learning designers, you also want to create learning experiences that integrate all the learning dimensions: cognitive, emotional, social, and behavioral.

Chapter 3 describes how to cultivate a successful virtual environment that is conducive to learning. To do this we focus on the second capability:

environment shaping. Facilitators must build community by leveraging the social experience dimension and creatively sourcing ways for learners to connect and discover shared commonality. Just as facilitators shape learning environments, so do environments shape learners and their overall online experience.

Chapter 4 delves into strategies to take your online facilitation capability up a notch. You may be familiar with the basics of facilitation but are now ready to try some advanced techniques. You will learn how to make the invisible audible and increase learner agency. Skilled facilitators also need to place learners at the center as they guide them to be co-creators of their own learning.

Chapter 5 provides in-depth professional tips on how to develop on-camera competency as a live online facilitator (the facilitator presence capability). You'll learn, for example, how to use the three-finger rule for framing. Although facilitators do not need to always be on camera, they should still know how to professionally polish their on-camera presence during purposeful connection moments.

Chapter 6 focuses on what you can do to further enhance your facilitator presence by improving audio quality and vocal delivery. Techniques include speaking with an informal, conversational style, using personal pronouns, and tips on how to slow your speaking rate. Learn how to improve facilitator presence by taking small actions to adjust audio quality and your voice.

Chapter 7 discusses how to refine your technical fluency. Facilitators need to strategically leverage tools in today's virtual training platforms to help achieve their desired learning outcomes. For example, just using a poll for the sake of using a poll can be a missed opportunity for building curiosity, checking knowledge, encouraging reflection, or providing immediate corrective feedback. This chapter explores the tools available in a facilitator's modern tool box and how to use them at the right time for the right reason with the right activity.

Chapter 8 details new ways to leverage movement to your advantage when training online with the sixth capability: dynamic engagement. For example, you will learn how to employ strategies to avoid learner habituation as well as how to draw attention rather than lose it. Facilitators will learn to leverage the power of movement in multiple ways to engage learners throughout virtual sessions.

Chapter 9 offers a framework for agile troubleshooting by addressing the technological challenges that can often occur. You will learn what you can do to minimize or alleviate the risk of things going wrong, manage the expected and unexpected, and keep training moving forward. For example, if you encounter a complex technical issue, have a ready-made, topic-relevant assignment in your back pocket to assign learners. This gives participants a related learning activity they can do independently, as a group on a whiteboard, or via paired chat while you or your producer troubleshoot.

Chapter 10 discusses the importance of evaluating impact and whether your live online sessions met their goals. This involves collecting data on the effectiveness of your virtual training program, so you can examine its effect from the learners' reactions to the training all the way to the broader impact on the organization. You'll want to measure the value of virtual training based on initial learning objectives, as well as what matters most to the learners, their managers, and your stakeholders. This chapter also explores the possibilities for future innovation in the industry.

Chapter 11 explores how to craft effective blended learning solutions. This chapter does not focus exclusively on one capability; instead it includes them all. It addresses how to successfully pair synchronous online training with asynchronous components to maximize learning's effectiveness. For example, you might offload independent activities like podcasts, reading articles, videos, infographics, on-demand tutorials, or reflection exercises as asynchronous elements to supplement virtual training classes as part of the overall training program. You'll also find evidence-based research supporting blended learning's superiority when it comes to improving learning outcomes.

Chapter 12 explores the unique challenge of hybrid or live mixed learning where virtual facilitators train learners concurrently who are both online and on-site in real time. To succeed in this environment, you'll need to tap into all the capabilities covered in the book. We will explore considerations like using a lead facilitator in one location and a co-facilitator in another, keeping class size small, and adapting learning activities for both locations. Whether live mixed learning is appropriate for your organization depends on the technology you must have to support it, your ability to source multiple facilitators, and your design flexibility, ability to keep total class size small, and access to additional IT support.

As you advance through the book, each chapter also begins by high-lighting "The Big Idea." Scan them to quickly identify which chapters are most relevant to you and your work. In addition to the big ideas and capability model, there are also 101 next level tips scattered throughout the book. These are actionable, and you can immediately begin practicing and applying them. A convenient summary of all prescriptive tips discussed can be found at the end of each chapter.

Become the Best Virtual Trainer You Can Be

As is true with everything in the professional training space, the end goal is learning transfer. We want to ensure virtual training participants apply what they've learned to their jobs and, ultimately, their workplaces and organizations. To that end, this book serves as a train-the-trainer resource for those who design and facilitate virtual training. Elevating virtual training design and delivery capabilities can have a ripple effect on virtual participants' learning and application and the impact of learning on their organizations.

Online facilitators and learning designers are essential to upskilling the global workforce. My goal is to challenge you to upskill yourself first and to raise the bar in both quality and skill. Hopefully, you will find this book to be a gem you can reference for novel ideas, practical tips, inspiration, helpful frameworks, evidence-based research, and professional development.

Because virtual training is here to stay, let's learn from evidence-based research, best practices, recommended strategies and techniques, and modern technology tools so we can make a difference for our learners, our organizations, and our global community. I welcome your feedback on this book and would love to hear from you. I consider it a privilege to invest in your professional success and thank you for reading. The challenge is to move from just getting by to doing your best work. So together, let's make the learning and development (L&D) world a better place. May the journey begin!

To your virtual success,
Diana L. Howles
linkedin.com/in/dianahowles
@DianaHowles

"The learning field is still struggling to create true and meaningful engagement activities that enhance learners' outcomes. We know how to use the various sub-tools in these platforms, ranging from polls to whiteboards to chat to breakout sessions. . . . I want to get smarter about how, when, why, duration, style, and options for engagement activities."

—Elliott Masie, Chair of the Learning COLLABORATIVE
and CEO of The MASIE Center (2021)

CHAPTER 1

Introducing the Virtual Trainer Capability Model

Virtual training has become ubiquitous. "Online education is here to stay . . . and can make an organization more future-proof" (ul Haq 2021). Its use also continues to grow exponentially. "A May 2020 forecast from Global Market Insights predicts that virtual classroom technology will grow at a compound annual growth rate of 11 percent between 2020 and 2026, faster than the overall learning category average of 8 percent" (Bersin 2020).

Trends also show the traditional in-person classroom in a diminishing role compared with virtual training. ATD's *2020 State of the Industry* reported that the use of traditional instructor-led classrooms for training declined to 40 percent in 2019 after averaging around 50 percent in prior years (ATD 2020). Virtual training in 2019 already showed rapid growth accounting for 19 percent of total learning, a 100 percent increase from 2012–2018 (ATD 2020). This use then skyrocketed during the COVID-19 pandemic beginning in 2020 with widespread virtual training adoption due to the shift to remote work for many organizations. In early 2021, for example, 98 percent of organizations surveyed reported using some virtual training, and 88 percent predicted their virtual training budgets would either remain as is or even increase in 2022 (ATD 2021). This is yet another strong indicator that virtual training is likely to continue well into the foreseeable future as a top training venue. Because of its popularity and widespread use, more skilled online facilitators and virtual trainers are needed.

Upskilling (building skills for a current role) and *reskilling* (building skills for a new role) are top priorities now for organizations across a variety of industries. As organizations shifted from mostly working on-site to mostly working from home and then transitioned back to hybrid work models, the tremendous need to upskill and reskill grew. According to LinkedIn Learning's *2020 Workplace Learning Report*, "digital transformation is catalyzing an upskilling and reskilling revolution" (Van Nuys 2020). In 2021, LinkedIn Learning reported upskilling and reskilling as the number-one area of focus for L&D programs according to more than 1,200 learning professionals from over 25 countries. For example, Amazon was investing more than $700 million to train and upskill employees, and PwC was spending $3 billion to upskill employees over the next several years with the mantra "New World, New Skills" (Van Nuys 2021).

Employees are also being tasked with doing more with less because of the Great Resignation, a term attributed to Professor Anthony Klotz from Texas A&M University (Kane 2021). The Great Resignation describes the mass exodus of employees from their previous employers that ensued in the US and in some European countries in 2021 in the wake of the COVID-19 pandemic. According to the US Department of Labor, 11.5 million employees in the US voluntarily left their jobs in the spring and early summer of 2021 (Kane 2021). This mass workforce departure has been linked to employees rethinking priorities during the pandemic and choosing to leave jobs due to burnout, stress, exhaustion, family demands, the desire to try something new, or to actively pursue a professional or personal dream.

Replacing these departing workers requires reskilling. Equipping current employees to close gaps left behind requires reskilling. And promoting individual contributors into leadership positions requires reskilling. So, who and how will these reskilling and upskilling efforts be delivered? Much of it relies heavily on learning and development departments, and virtual training will most likely be the top training delivery method. Because much of the workforce continues to work from anywhere, virtual training is more conducive to hybrid and remote work.

With its rapid growth and widespread adoption, virtual training is now a core business skill for learning and development professionals. However, for virtual training professionals to best support employee skill development, facilitators, designers, developers, and producers must also hone their own skills. Due to rapidly changing technologies, multiple platforms, widespread global adoption of vILT, and popular hybrid workplace models, the role of a virtual trainer has become even more challenging. Couple this with 24/7 distractions and temptations to multitask, and the challenges multiply.

To rise and face these challenges, learning leaders, virtual trainers, designers, developers, and producers must operate at higher levels of excellence. Whether or not they do will either support or hinder their ability to improve employee proficiencies, close gaps in workplace performance, and equip staff for new or current roles. Regardless of your experience with traditional in-person training, virtual training requires new and expanded skills to be successful. Now is the time to upskill and grow your capabilities as a virtual training professional.

But where should you start? What skills or abilities are most important beyond knowing how to use the tools a platform offers? How can you become an expert who knows how and why certain engagement activities should or should not be used? What if you have been delivering online training for a year or two but now desire to move past just getting by to doing your best work? This book is here to help you by outlining all the core capabilities essential to upskilling yourself, along with multiple strategies and tips to take your virtual training to the next level.

 THE BIG IDEA
Use the Virtual Trainer Capability Model to professionally upskill in eight core areas of development.

The Virtual Trainer Capability Model

In my 20 years as a virtual trainer, I sought out best practices by experimenting, observing, researching, and tweaking strategies used in my own virtual classes and from what I observed in other classes. I tried to learn from my mistakes. If there were techniques that didn't work well, I analyzed why and modified them. If strategies worked well, I replicated them in other classes and tried to expand on them. For example, I observed that participants seemed more willing to participate in whiteboards than in chat with earlier technology platforms because writing on whiteboards back then was always anonymous. Contrast this with chat where their colleagues could see their names and who said what.

So, I realized I needed to use the whiteboards to get everyone to think more deeply about core concepts when responding to thoughtful questions because they'd be more willing to participate if I emphasized that their typing was anonymous. I also studied media like radio to learn what lessons might transfer well to virtual training. I remember advocating for virtual trainers to partner with a co-facilitator because two voices working together (like what you might hear in radio interviews or podcasts) creates greater vocal variety and interest.

This observation, analysis, and experience helped me hone my own virtual training skill set. But what really helped me transition to the next level was my development across multiple areas of expertise. For example, it was essential I become technically literate with each platform I used. To train effectively, not only did I need to know every tool at my disposal but also discern which learning activities would work best with each. Paired with this technology know-how, I also needed to troubleshoot technical issues when they emerged. Over the years, I witnessed a variety of platforms come and go with common features and some variations, but generally there were only slight changes to these tools and platforms. However, the more universal adoption of virtual training throughout the COVID-19 pandemic prompted rapid, frequent, and substantive updates to several virtual training platforms across the industry. It was important to stay fluent in my knowledge of these improvements.

Another development area of expertise for me was verbal communication skills. In the early days of using web conferencing software for training, we relied heavily on audio, not video. Video was available, but it was usually a tiny window in the corner of the screen and, because of limited bandwidth, the quality was not very good. So, many of us displayed a still picture of ourselves in that corner instead and relied mostly on our voices. As video technology began to improve, I started heavily researching the on-camera medium. This led to me to establish a sense of presence vocally and visually, recognizing how important that was for learners. I was very aware also that developing a professional on-camera presence was a new literacy for many. Around 2015, I began researching and training professionals on how to best use multimedia to support learning.

Also integral to my own professional development was learning how to facilitate in a virtual environment. There were clearly some differences in the online medium, although we could leverage some in-person facilitation skills. And, of course, cultivating an online environment for learners that was supportive and inclusive became a top priority as well. Finally, because I used to teach public speaking at the university level, I knew there were strategic techniques for designing and displaying visual aids, and that this was especially important in virtual training with its multimedia options.

More recently, it occurred to me that a comprehensive framework to guide virtual trainers' professional development was missing. We develop others, but we sometimes forget to develop ourselves. And so, I created the Virtual Trainer Capability Model. As I embarked on this journey, the foundational question I used to guide framework development was, "What is most important for live online practitioners to know and be able to do?"

I based the model on my own virtual training experience, research studies in the field, the existing body of published work on the subject, and input and reaction from trusted colleagues. The intent was to create a comprehensive development path toward full competence in essential areas of expertise. Initially, the model began as a list of 16 capabilities. As I ran these categories by respected colleagues in the field, measured them against research, and weighed them against my own experience, I eventually narrowed the list down. To be honest, it was with great struggle and much iterative work that the current model emerged. In sum, the Virtual Trainer Capability Model identifies eight major areas that address the most important knowledge and skills virtual trainers and online facilitators need to be successful. These capabilities will guide your professional development and prepare your current and future readiness.

The target users of the model are those who design and facilitate live online classes. This may include virtual training facilitators and trainers, learning designers and developers, producers, online instructors, adult educators, and professors who teach online classes. By growing your knowledge and skills in these eight core capabilities, you will elevate yourself from novice to expert.

Just as puzzle pieces play a role contributing to the whole, the eight capability areas also comprise a whole. This is why the model is visually depicted as puzzle pieces (Figure 1-1). The model's circular shape communicates how connected each component is and how they overlap with one another. The core eight areas of professional development for virtual trainers are:

- Experience design
- Environment shaping
- Online facilitation
- Facilitator presence
- Technical fluency
- Dynamic engagement
- Agile troubleshooting
- Evaluating impact

Let's take a closer look at each.

Figure 1-1. Virtual Trainer Capability Model

Experience Design Capability

As a virtual trainer, you may not always be involved in designing the instruction that underlies the training you deliver; however, you should be knowledgeable and skilled in how you design the experience for the learner. Design determines scope, sequence, strategy, learning activities, skill practices, and more. Approaching instructional design solely from your own "design cave" without input from others misses an opportunity to improve quality. Contrast this with designers who ask for input from representative learners very early in the process. When I initiate focus groups or run designs by a few learners one-on-one in the beginning stages of the design process, their input has always proved to be immensely valuable.

Going beyond what we know as traditional instructional design, there are other important elements to learn about creating experiences that extend beyond the virtual session. This capability will challenge you to think differently about how you currently design while helping you understand that every learner touchpoint (from A to Z) is part of the learner experience. For example, creating an experience map to envision your learners' overarching journey can be a helpful way to visualize and identify opportunities for reinforcing and enhancing participants' learning experiences.

Environment Shaping Capability

Virtual trainers are also responsible for leading and creating positive learning climates. Cultivating psychological safety, inclusivity, personalization, and global cultural competence go a long way to creating virtual spaces where learners are comfortable engaging with others. This capability includes being respectful of all cultures as part of global cultural competence. For example, in international and cross-cultural classes, use broader examples from other countries, research and avoid offensive on-camera hand gestures from participating cultures, and thoughtfully weigh the best start times for sessions to accommodate learners.

Developing this capability also helps facilitators be mindful of the cumulative small things they can do to build environments that welcome the unique contributions of every learner. For example, a virtual facilitator who begins a session acting impatient or frustrated can unintentionally poison the energy of what could have otherwise been a productive virtual environment. Energy is contagious, and negative energy trickles down easily to others. Contrast this with facilitators who begin a virtual session with enthusiasm and passion. They affirm participants' contributions and cultivate a safe space in which learners are comfortable participating, sharing, and learning.

Online Facilitation Capability

Virtual facilitators also need to communicate clearly and in a compelling manner. This includes prompting learners to participate, posing thoughtful open-ended questions, keeping a watchful eye on who is contributing and who isn't, and checking in with those who have not yet shared. Online facilitation is an expanded skill set from traditional facilitation. For example, facilitators need to learn how to verbalize what is unseen for participants, be flexible with format, and guide participants to be co-creators of their own learning. Because of the differences between online facilitation and in-person facilitation, this capability is critical to developing beyond the basics.

Facilitator Presence Capability

Another key core business skill in which virtual trainers need to develop literacy is on-camera competency. This is the online facilitator's ability to project themselves professionally on camera. In addition to framing themselves, adjusting movement, and lighting themselves well on camera, virtual trainers must also demonstrate superb verbal communication skills. They need to express ideas and concepts with concise language, clarity, expression, and eloquence in a way learners can logically follow and understand. In addition, they need the know-how to optimize their own technical equipment to create the best possible audio quality for learners.

How facilitators leverage their on-camera skills, voice, and audio equipment all contribute to how they come across online. I call this facilitator presence. Ultimately, when done well, it conveys a sense of the facilitator "being there," regardless of time and distance. An example of establishing poor facilitator presence is when a facilitator speaks in a monotone voice with minimum inflection, uses their device's built-in microphone (which makes it sound like they're in a cave), and shares a poorly lit camera angle of themselves looking oddly truncated at the chin. Contrast this with an effective facilitator, who leverages a variety of vocal inflections, uses a high-quality external USB microphone, lights themselves well from the front, and centers themselves in the frame with a small margin of headroom.

Technical Fluency Capability

Although technology should not be the primary driver of the learning experience, virtual trainers must possess the knowledge and skills to strategically use tools to support learning goals and outcomes. Reaching technical fluency means you are digitally literate. You have developed your capability to full competency because you can now effectively leverage common tools and onscreen interactions, are comfortable with the ins and outs of platforms, and can successfully pair apps and other digital learning tools with training. This capability also includes the all-around know-how when it comes to the software and hardware needed to support virtual training. Knowing when to partner with a producer who is technically fluent and developing a positive working relationship with them is also a skill.

A facilitator might reveal their technical deficiency by not knowing when or how to leverage platform tools. For example, assigning 10 participants into a breakout with six tasks for them to complete within a five-minute time limit, and then struggling to successfully divide them into breakouts demonstrates a lack of technical fluency. In this instance, the breakouts have too many people, too much to do, and too little time in which to do it. In contrast, technically fluent facilitators and producers know the value of creating breakouts with only three or four participants and a focused challenge, task, or activity, all while allowing sufficient time for brief introductions and for groups to complete the activity without rushing. Proficient facilitators seamlessly know what buttons to click to successfully divide participants, open and start breakouts, pop into some to check on group progress, send a broadcast message to prepare participants to return, and close breakouts to bring them back for a debrief.

Dynamic Engagement Capability

Virtual trainers can successfully capture learners' attention with a variety of strategies. Some strategies are designed to prevent learners from habituating to certain stimuli or to prevent participants from disengaging. This capability requires a wide variety of movement visually and vocally to help direct, focus, and captivate learners throughout virtual training programs. An example of poor performance in this capability is when a facilitator only displays nine static slides to anchor a 90-minute virtual training session. In this example, there is little visual change, variety, or dynamic momentum to keep attention, especially if participants are left looking at the same static slide for 10 minutes.

At its core, virtual training as an online medium is highly visual and verbal. Think of all the visual content these technology platforms feature, such as slides, on-camera participants, digital whiteboards, polls, chat text, and even some facilitators holding placards when they turn on video. Movement within these visual pieces should involve frequent changes or dynamic focusing elements like annotation. Even cumulatively building elements on a whiteboard can stimulate dynamic engagement. Because extremes of too much and no movement at all are both undesirable, there still needs to be a semblance of balance. One exemplar of this capability is scaffolding content visually by progressively building slide content to direct focus and add emphasis and variety. It is one of the best strategies at our disposal for engaging learners.

Agile Troubleshooting Capability

Because online facilitators frequently work with virtual technologies, the odds that something technical can or will go wrong are high. The agile troubleshooting capability helps you develop the skill, confidence, and expertise to effectively resolve technical issues like a pro. Agility means you develop skills that enable you to think and act quickly, as well as adapt and pivot when needed. Ideally, partnering with a producer who can manage the technical side for you is extremely helpful, but facilitators should still be prepared to troubleshoot as a backup, or in the event you are unable to be paired with a producer.

Part of this capability also includes preventive action. For example, a facilitator ideally sends a welcome email to participants well before class day, encouraging them to test their connections with the link provided, and inviting them to log in five to 10 minutes early on class day. Both actions create space for early troubleshooting and resolution, if needed. Overall, this capability encompasses skills for diagnosing, troubleshooting solutions or workarounds, and recovery from the adrenaline rush when things go wrong.

Recovery is resilience. It's the ability to move forward constructively as soon as possible after a glitch, all the while leading learners to do the same. A poor example of this is a facilitator who panics and get stuck emotionally in the turmoil of a technical disruption. As a result, they are unable to think clearly, which also makes them less likely to find a solution. A proficient, agile troubleshooter, however, has thought of solutions to the most common technical issues ahead of time. Because of their preparation, they know what to try first. Additionally, agile troubleshooters do their best to maintain a calm, attentive mindset regardless of what emerges, and they can pivot to a different activity if needed. They don't get stuck lamenting about what could have been, and instead accept what is. This way, they become more open to opportunities to course correct. Lastly, they must know their platform inside and out to be prepared to resolve any surprises.

Evaluating Impact Capability

Virtual professionals, like all providers of learning solutions, should measure the value of their training programs. This is how you know whether your investment of time, money, and resources has met its goal and was worth the effort. Developing in this capability means identifying what you will measure and how from the very outset. Ideally, your metrics begin by aligning with your knowledge and performance objectives.

An example of poor performance in this capability is the absence of any evaluation whatsoever. In this situation, you wouldn't know the value-add of your program except by anecdote. If leaders asked whether the program's goals were achieved, you wouldn't be able to answer. Most importantly, you wouldn't be able to improve the course without knowing your baseline. Contrast this with a virtual training professional who objectively measures and collects data on the effectiveness of their programs beyond attendance. Because whether learners attend virtual training does not prove they have learned anything or can apply the information in their functional work. To be honest, it only documents that they logged in. As you develop in this capability, it is important to identify metrics to track the different levels of evaluation that are most appropriate to the needs of your organization, leadership, stakeholders, and learners. And because evaluation and innovation go together, you also need to be an innovator, experimenting with the technology for continuous ways to improve live online learning.

Capabilities by Chapter

Most chapters in this book focus primarily on a key capability. This is not to say that chapter discussions exclude other capabilities; however, most chapters align with one. As the puzzle metaphor of the visual model communicates though, all eight capabilities are tightly interconnected. As you achieve competence in all capability areas, you will discover for yourself their interdependent reliance on one another. Table 1-1 identifies which capability is the focus of each chapter.

Table 1-1. Primary Capabilities by Chapter

Chapter	Chapter Title	Primary Capability
2	Designing Virtual Learning Experiences	Experience Design
3	Shaping a Successful Virtual Learning Environment	Environment Shaping
4	Applying the Secrets of Effective Online Facilitation	Online Facilitation
5	Developing Your Professional On-Camera Competence	Facilitator Presence
6	Enhancing Facilitator Presence Through Audio and Vocal Delivery	Facilitator Presence
7	Leveraging Your Platform's Technical Tools	Technical Fluency
8	Following the Dynamic Principle of Engagement	Dynamic Engagement
9	Troubleshooting and Recovery With Agility	Agile Troubleshooting
10	Evaluating and Innovating in the Virtual Space	Evaluating Impact
11	Flipping Virtual Training With Blended Learning	All
12	Combining On-Site and Online Learners in Live Mixed Learning	All

101 Professional Tips

To support your skill and knowledge development in the virtual training capabilities, you will also find a treasure trove of actionable professional tips scattered throughout this book. These tips are categorized under each capability and serve as prescriptive principles you and your teams can apply to help you design and facilitate successful live online learning. You'll find a summary of the pro tips discussed at the end of each chapter.

Applying the Virtual Trainer Capability Model in Your Organization

As you continue to produce and facilitate live online learning, use the Virtual Trainer Capability Model as a professional development benchmark for you and your virtual training teams. Use it as a gauge to elevate virtual training standards. To gain a broader perspective of how professional development fits into the business, consider examining your organization's vision, mission, and strategic goals. From there, align your training initiatives and professional development efforts with the higher-level initiatives of the organization.

Virtual trainers should also consider having conversations with their managers to review the capability model together. This provides a mutual opportunity to discuss a facilitator's areas of strengths as well as opportunities for improvement. Work with your manager to create a specific development plan for growing your skills in design or virtual facilitation. You can attach your development plan to your performance goals for the year. Write out specific goals to help you adopt the practical tips most relevant to you.

In addition to the capabilities, you might even identify which professional tips in the book resonate most with you. Set target goals for yourself after examining your current skills to gauge which ones you'd like to work on improving over time. For example, one of your goals might be to "consistently apply three specific tips from the on-camera competency chapter to my upcoming virtual training events over the next two months." Once you identify targets, set a timeline for application, practice, and feedback, and commit to your own professional development. Set check-ins to create accountability and discuss challenges and how things are progressing. Begin with the capabilities where you have the most opportunity for improvement, in addition to sharpening your strengths. The end goal is full proficiency and competence in each of the eight areas.

Finally, you might also consider sharing the model with leadership to use as a reference for assessing current skill levels of your virtual facilitators, and as a hiring rubric for adding new staff. The model can set a comparison trajectory of professional development for you or your professional virtual training team. Allow the model to help you discern the skills of candidates you're considering for virtual facilitation and design positions in your organization. Ask final candidates to deliver a mini virtual training session online where you can assess their knowledge and skill in each of the capability areas during the interview process. This will guarantee that the new employees you hire are the most qualified candidates to advance your organization through effective live online learning.

Summary

Virtual training has clearly exploded in recent years. Throughout the COVID-19 pandemic, the world's widespread adoption of this training delivery method was essential to move a remote workforce forward. As the world continues to embrace virtual training and hybrid models for virtual learning, the aim of this book is to help improve quality by equipping you with the needed skills and knowledge to be a more advanced designer and facilitator.

In today's remote work environment, skilled virtual facilitation is essential for trainers and educators. You may be skilled as an in-person classroom trainer, yet in the virtual space you need more specific skills to facilitate online interactivity, skillfully manage multitasking, be technically fluent, oversee logistics and troubleshooting, master being on camera in a professional and powerful way, leverage your voice, and engage virtual learners.

Because of this necessity, learning experience design and live online facilitation in today's world are essential core business skills. By sharpening your skills and constructing new knowledge, you are better equipped to meet the needs of the modern-day hybrid work environment with innovation and impact. Use the Virtual Trainer Capability Model to professionally upskill your expertise in these eight key development areas, so you can take it to the next level!

"At its best, e-learning is as good as the best classroom learning. And at its worst, it is as bad as the worst classroom learning. The difference is design . . . design is the 1,001 decisions, big and small, that affect the outcome."

—William Horton, author, *E-Learning by Design*

CHAPTER 2

Designing Virtual Learning Experiences

When developing her first few virtual training sessions, Emma spent a lot of planning time writing precise learning objectives, organizing content, creating supporting graphics, and coming up with learning activities. But when each session ended, she realized that something was missing. Participants were passive, asked few questions, and didn't really seem to engage. From a learner's perspective, the training experiences were mediocre at best and didn't seem to have much impact after they ended. What could Emma do differently with virtual training design to improve the learning experience?

When you design a virtual training session, how do you envision participants responding? Are they motivated right from the start? Are they interacting with others? Are they practicing challenging tasks related to their work? My colleagues and I have a list of descriptors we'd like learners to say and feel about their online experience. These include terms like *practical, relevant, engaging, meaningful, interactive,* and *in depth.* When learners log out of your online sessions, what do you want them to feel, think, and say about it? In short, what kind of learning experience do you want them to have?

Chapter 1 introduced the Virtual Trainer Capability Model and the eight core capabilities for professionally developing virtual trainers, learning designers, and instructors of online professional development and training programs. In this chapter, we'll focus on the first capability, experience design. As virtual trainers, our goal is to approach the craft of designing instruction as a learning experience. Our design task is somewhat analogous to what an architect does. Skilled architects start with a vision of what to build, for whom, and the purposes it will serve. Then this translates into a design blueprint for building and delivering a first-rate experience. We, too, need to invest time and effort to develop impactful learning designs that will help us deliver exceptional virtual learning experiences.

Your job title may be instructional designer, e-learning developer, or learning and development specialist because you design live online learning programs. Or perhaps you are a virtual facilitator who also designs the online training programs you facilitate. Regardless of your formal title, if you assist with virtual learning design in any way, this chapter will challenge you to think differently, more holistically, and more intentionally about learning design. You will become familiar with learning experience design (LXD) principles and practices to apply to live online learning. You'll also gain insight into how skilled learning experience designers are learner-centered and how they integrate cognitive, emotional, social, and behavioral dimensions of learning into impactful training experiences. And you'll learn how to apply design thinking strategies that unleash creative thinking, as well as ways to enhance the learner's journey throughout a virtual training program. All this is aimed at making the virtual learning experience more engaging, meaningful, and impactful.

THE BIG IDEA
Design virtual training as learning experiences that integrate the cognitive, emotional, social, and behavioral learning dimensions.

Learning Experience Design (LXD) for Virtual Training

In your role within learning and development, and as a user of various products and services, you have likely heard the terms *user experience, customer experience, patient experience, employee experience,* and more recently *learner experience.* These concepts reflect a rising importance placed on an end user's overall experience with a product or service. This fundamental shift that centers on the end user when making design decisions is often the difference in better product quality, increased sales, greater customer loyalty, better patient choice, and, for us, improved learning outcomes and learner satisfaction.

What Is Learning Experience Design?

For me and others, the concept of learning experience design (LXD) is more than just a surface rebranding of conventional instructional design practices. Most traditional instructional design models, which originated during World War II, are not well matched to today's digital learning environments. One helpful way to understand LXD is to think of it as an evolution of conventional instructional design—like instructional design 2.0. LXD builds on many of the core principles of traditional instructional design (ID 1.0) but provides a broader and more modern-day set of tools, strategies, and terms to approach learning design. Today's online learning environments are more technology enabled, more learner-driven, and more learner-centered. LXD is about rejuvenating and enriching conventional instructional design practices to achieve learning and performance goals and meet the needs of modern learners in today's digital work environment.

Experience is a key word here. Significant learning outcomes are a by-product of rich experiences. Einstein has been quoted as saying "Learning is an experience. Everything else is just information" (Immersive Learning News 2020). Authors Sharon Boller and Laura Fletcher (2020) in their book, *Design Thinking for Training and Development,* summarize the role of today's instructional designers as follows: "We don't create learning. Instead, people have an experience as they learn." Throughout this book, I will encourage you to adopt an LXD mindset for virtual training and leverage the capabilities of evolving technology tools and new learning spaces.

Influences on LXD

LXD has evolved by adopting practices and principles from several other disciplines. Building on its instructional design foundation, it has been heavily influenced by at least three other professional disciplines that I integrate into our learning design approach. These include user experience design, design thinking, and evidence-based practice. First, LXD borrows heavily from the field of user experience design (UXD). The term UXD was first coined by cognitive psychologist Donald Norman in the 1990s when working at Apple. Norman and others recognized that computer hardware and software needed to be more human-friendly and user-centered.

UXD has evolved into a broad field of professional practice. Commonly used in developing websites, software applications, and interfaces for computers and other technology devices, UXD applies human-centered design principles to improve people's interactions with technology. UXD professionals use empirical methods such as user observation, interviews, evidence-based research, and user testing and feedback in various branches of psychology to gain insight into the needs and behaviors of users. This then helps to create better interactive experiences. UX is to the user what LX is to the learner. Learning experience design incorporates many of the practices and strategies of UXD and applies them to improve the online learner experience.

Another influence that has become integral to both LXD and UXD is design thinking. Design thinking is a flexible human-centered, problem-solving approach used in a variety of disciplines. According to the Interaction Design Foundation (2021), "The design thinking process is iterative, flexible, and focused on collaboration between designers and users, with an emphasis on bringing ideas to life based on how real users think, feel and behave." Made popular in the US in the early 1990s by the global design firm IDEO, design thinking has roots going back to the 1970s and Scandinavian participatory design approaches. The main emphasis is on designing human-centered and experienced-centered products and services. It is as much a mindset as it is a process and set of practices.

Design thinking invites multiple stakeholders, including users and learners, into the design process. It includes stages of empathy for learners by defining design challenges and performance gaps from multiple perspectives, followed by ideating and brainstorming. Rapidly testing out ideas coupled with learner feedback and iteration of potential solutions are a few of its main strategies. The design thinking process is iterative, collaborative, and almost always results in creative and impactful new ideas and solutions. Michael Allen's Successive Approximation

Method (SAM) heavily integrates design thinking practices (Allen 2012). Boller and Fletcher's 2020 book, *Design Thinking for Training and Development*, provides a framework and principles for adapting design thinking for training design projects. A full implementation of design thinking is most effective for generating solutions to high-stakes instructional challenges. However, to create virtual training experiences, we can adapt and integrate many design thinking practices into our learning design process, which we cover later in this chapter.

A third major influence for LXD can be broadly framed as evidence-based practice. This concept was first used in the healthcare industry but has spread to other professional disciplines including education and training. Compared to conventional instructional design, LXD places a greater emphasis on making learning design decisions based on empirical evidence and learning science research. LXD draws upon cognitive neuroscience, psychology, social science, computer-based learning, media and communications, and other human-centered disciplines. Leaders in this area include Ruth Clark, Clark Quinn, Will Thalheimer, Julie Dirksen, and others who study and explain this research for learning design professionals. Evidence-based practice in LXD also entails being more empirically grounded. It involves testing out new design ideas; closely observing learners; collecting data about learner behaviors, feelings, and reactions; and evaluation as integral elements throughout the learning design process.

There are other streams of influence that have shaped the growth of LXD. Worth mentioning are immersive learning strategies emerging from new technologies. These range from interactive case scenarios, digital games, and simulations to virtual and augmented realities. They emphasize contextualizing learning; individuals are given challenges, make decisions, and get feedback all aimed at making learning more active, relevant, and engaging. Cognitive psychologist Clark Quinn's learning experience framework draws on game design principles supported by cognitive science as a foundation for increasing meaningfulness and learner engagement (Quinn 2021). Gamification expert Karl Kapp also presents compelling evidence to inspire instructional designers to think more like game designers (Kapp, Blair, and Mesch 2014). It's difficult not to use the words "experience" and "engaging" when describing any of the types of learning designs mentioned earlier.

LXD is a holistic, learner-centered approach that incorporates principles and practices from multiple disciplines to rejuvenate traditional instructional design for modern learning environments. As a learning experience designer, we lead with the experience we want learners to have, not the content we want them to consume. So, how might all this apply to virtual training and live online learning?

PRO TIP 1
Apply LXD by leading with experience, not content.

Applying LXD to Virtual Training

To apply LXD in a virtual context, think of it as the sum of a learner's interactions with content, people, and technology. It can begin with the very first email a learner receives after registering for a virtual training event, all the way to the completion of any post-session work, follow-up action plans, and evaluation. According to The Learning Guild's director of research, Jane Bozarth (2020), "LXD recognizes that learning often happens in a context larger than a single course and may be comprised of many different elements."

Designing learning experiences in live online training is not about presenting content with a few learning activities or delivering mini lectures interspersed with a few polls. LXD is about experience. Admittedly, it's difficult to break free from the entrenched content-centric tendencies reflected in the design of many training programs. LXD's more holistic orientation encompasses all the touchpoints in the learning process from A to Z. Previously, the learning and development community did not have a well-articulated language and framework to implement LXD. To help you apply this to your virtual training designs, we'll reference the 4 Dimensions of Learning model described in the next section. We'll be threading the elements of this framework throughout the book.

4 Dimensions of Learning: An LXD Model

In their book *Designing the Online Learning Experience*, Simone Conceição and Les Howles (2021) from the University of Wisconsin identify four constituent elements underlying the design of engaging and impactful learning experiences (Figure 2-1). Their framework is based on research on learner engagement in formal environments including adult online education and training programs. Because of the formal structure of most virtual training, I've found designing learning around these four dimensions to be particularly useful. The four dimensions are cognitive, emotional, social, and behavioral (Conceição and Howles 2021). The key is to tightly integrate these dimensions into the design of learning activities, lessons, and other kinds of events that take place in a virtual instructor-led training (vILT) environment. Let's take a look at each dimension and how it can be integrated into the design.

Figure 2-1. Four Dimensions of Learning

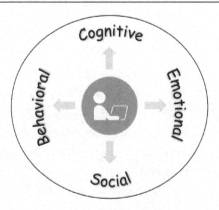

Reprinted with permission from Stylus Publishing (Conceição and Howles 2021).

Cognitive Dimension

The cognitive dimension of learning pertains to the mental processes supporting how individuals acquire, assimilate, store, and recall knowledge for application. It is the bedrock of all formal learning where verbal and visual language are used to convey and shape ideas. One doesn't need to look much further than Benjamin Bloom's (1956) longstanding and still widely used levels of cognitive learning to get an idea of the scope of this domain. The cognitive dimension of learning has received the most attention in education and training as well as in learning science research. Many professional training programs focus on learners acquiring and understanding facts, concepts, principles, procedures, and processes. Acquiring such knowledge enables individuals to form mental models that support job-related problem solving, decision making, and performance.

Learning science research provides numerous principles for enhancing cognitive learning and how to chunk and present information. You can apply these principles through multimedia message design based on cognitive load theory, which I reference throughout this book (Mayer 2014), and through practice strategies such as spaced repetition, retrieval practice, and feedback. Much of what we do in virtual training on the cognitive level focuses on learning concepts and information. The ultimate goal of learning is for newly acquired knowledge to be transferred and applied to the work context.

In many virtual training sessions, instructors tend to focus heavily on cognitive learning through presentation segments supplemented with PowerPoint visual media. To facilitate cognitive learning, one virtual training strategy includes pausing to ask questions, which is covered in much greater depth in chapter 4. This also provides opportunities for individuals to connect new knowledge to prior knowledge so it can be solidified in long-term memory. Another strategy for augmenting cognitive learning in virtual training is to design mentally challenging learning activities where participants are asked to recall, apply what they just learned, and solve hypothetical problems.

One of the most powerful ways to solidify newly acquired knowledge is to follow up with learning activities in short periods where individuals reflect on an activity, their decision-making process, and the results obtained. This is also explored in greater depth in chapter 4. When ending virtual training sessions, facilitators can prompt individuals to identify one or two ways they can apply their new knowledge outside training.

These strategies and a host of others can be designed to support the cognitive dimension of learning in virtual training contexts. From a cognitive learning perspective, all the various learning activities require learners to draw upon their mental resources to assimilate the new information. The idea is to prevent rote and surface-level learning and promote deeper learning so that learners' new knowledge is stored in long-term memory for recall beyond class. In my virtual training sessions, when I want learners to understand and deeply process certain concepts and principles, I make sure to include multimedia and illustrations to clarify and then lead discussions to digest it further. I also share stories from my own experience and sometimes use mnemonics to help them remember the steps we practice.

The cognitive dimension of learning runs deep and interconnects with the other three dimensions. For example, it's hard to imagine learning how to perform complex tasks (behavioral dimension) and engaging with others in collaborative problem solving (social dimension) without cognitive processes coming into play. Focusing on the cognitive dimension is only part of achieving engaging, meaningful, and impactful learning experiences. In recent years, cognitive neuroscience has clarified that the cognitive dimension is inextricably linked with affect or emotions, which is where we focus next.

Emotional Dimension

As humans, we are clearly more than just cognitive beings. Learning science research is now making it abundantly clear that emotions and cognition are deeply intertwined. As educational neuroscientist Janet Zadina (2014) states, "emotions and learning cannot be separate." The emotional dimension permeates a person's entire learning experience, and skilled facilitators intentionally weave emotional elements into their teaching from start to finish.

As trainers, what we are mainly focusing on here is learner motivation, which is deeply rooted in individual emotional states. Learner motivation drives invested mental effort, which supports cognitive learning (Paas et al. 2005). Learners need to be willing to start a learning experience and sustain interest and effort throughout. If not, learning outcomes will, at best, be mediocre. Several simple strategies I like to use to increase learner motivation throughout a live virtual session include baiting curiosity and introducing challenges, problems, and even puzzling situations to solve. I especially like to assign these as breakout activities for small groups.

Beginning training by stating a dry list of objectives can sometimes do extraordinarily little to stimulate motivation, especially in a virtual setting when participants might be looking for any excuse to check text messages or email. Instead, you can reframe those designer-centered objectives into more interesting learner-centered statements highlighting how participants will benefit from the live online session. Keep your original objectives to drive your design but modify them into more motivating statements when you share them with learners. I sometimes rephrase my objectives into questions to which participants would likely want the answers. Ideally, this would stimulate their curiosity and motivation, so they think, "Yeah, I want to learn that" or "I need to know how to do that."

PRO TIP 2
Use traditional learning objectives to drive design, but reframe the objectives shared with learners to be more motivational for them.

It is also important to recognize that both positive and negative emotions contribute to performance outcomes and a learner's overall experience. We all know that enjoyable learning activities can make learners more engaged and motivated. However, it's easy to forget that challenging learning activities with episodes of confusion and struggle—if managed well by a facilitator—can potentially yield some of the deepest and most memorable learning outcomes (D'Mello et al. 2014). Think back to when you have heard a learner who was initially struggling then exclaim "Aha! I got it!" You can almost hear the pride in their voice, and you feel the positivity of their emotions because of this accomplishment. This then can fuel more motivation.

In my designs for virtual training, I try to incorporate emotional and motivational elements by reminding learners they can do it and that I believe in them. I prepare them by sharing right before an assignment that a task may be challenging, and our producer and I will be right there to support them. For example, when I train novice trainers virtually on how to write learning objectives, I always warn them that it's hard thinking work but they can do it. After I demonstrate how to do it, writing examples (both legitimate and funny) on a digital whiteboard, I have learners practice in small breakout groups and then write some independently. Sometimes they tell me later it was "hard thinking work" but they got it with plenty of practice and feedback! I also try to explain the rationale for a learning activity before we do it to help trigger motivation.

Virtual trainers also have additional emotional concerns for their learners. Because virtual environments are technology mediated, learners may be confronted with user interfaces and tools that are not user-friendly. Usability issues can be frustrating for learners. The virtual facilitator must anticipate these types of negative technology interactions, which can sour any learning experience. For example, in my sessions if learners are new to a platform, experience limited bandwidth, or have connection issues, I do my best to reframe whatever is happening with a "cup half-full" mindset instead of a "half-empty" one. Conducting tech checks beforehand and providing ways for them to acclimate to the environment can help alleviate these too. (We discuss preventive measures and how to troubleshoot to avoid souring learning experiences in greater depth in chapter 9.) When I teach virtual classes for universities, I request learners log into the course management system or LMS a week before to acclimate so they can feel more comfortable in the class environment. All this helps to support a positive emotional learning experience.

As part of the learning design process, it is the trainer's responsibility to have a mapped-out plan that incorporates various kinds of motivational strategies for the flow of instructional events. Learners' emotional and motivational states are often difficult to discern in virtual environments. But as we move into the next two dimensions of learning, we can often get a better read of the learning experience in terms of how learners socially interact and what they are doing.

Social Dimension

A virtual training learning experience should be interspersed with social interactions. The social dimension involves two main types of interactions: learner-to-instructor and learner-to-learner (Moore 2013). Live virtual sessions where participants can hear and see each other fosters a sense of heightened social presence. The virtual instructor capitalizes on this by conveying enthusiasm for the topic through voice and physical gestures, by providing immediate constructive feedback, and by creating a personable, warm, caring climate of psychological safety, which we'll explore more in chapter 3.

These live interactions and a sense of social presence influence the cognitive and emotional dimensions of learning. A person's level of motivation and mental effort can be enhanced due to the presence of others who are also involved in the same task. A good analogy is the energy and effort boost that often occur when exercising alongside others at a fitness club. On the learner and student side, "Multiple studies published in the *Harvard Business Review, Science, Nature,* and *Proceedings of the National Academy of Sciences* have found that students learn best in active, social learning environments" (Bersin 2020). According to 2,000 learners surveyed in LinkedIn's *2020 Workplace Learning Report,* approximately half of millennials and boomers surveyed, and more than half of Gen X and Gen Z learners who participated, feel more motivated to learn in social environments. "Learners across all generations also want to learn with their colleagues to exchange ideas, share insights, and ask questions" (Van Nuys 2020).

So, live online learning is and should be a social experience. But the challenge with designing these learning experiences is creating engaging learning activities that promote participation and dialogue. The facilitator's task in designing such activities is to encourage individuals to share their experience and knowledge, ask questions without feeling embarrassed, and welcome dialogue. At the same time, conversations need to stay on target and focused on learning goals. These productive interactions occur by making space for learners to collaborate and learn from one another, such as placing them in breakouts to solve problems and complete tasks. In my training sessions on how to facilitate virtually, I give learners a hypothetical scenario where they experience a major technology glitch, and they must discuss as a team how they would address it productively.

Part of being learner-centered in a virtual space also involves sensitivity to learner differences. For example, introverted individuals may not contribute as much within a group learning situation and because of this should not feel forced to participate. I let my learners know that if they prefer to work independently on some assignments to let me know privately through chat, and I am happy to place them in an independent breakout room or ask that they remain muted in the main room. Some introverts find they learn the material better this way.

Another aspect of social learning involves learners observing experts performing a complex procedure or task and being able to engage with these experts. For example, if managers need to learn how to approve or decline staff requests to take courses in the LMS, you may bring in an LMS administrator to model it for them and field their questions so they can interact directly with the expert.

A skilled virtual trainer as a learning designer needs to take all these social learning factors into consideration. The trick is discerning when, what kind, and how much social interaction will add the most value to the learner experience. And, of course, the interaction always needs to support the learning goals. Just as emotional and motivational elements must be strategically and intentionally interspersed throughout a virtual training session, so must social interactions be carefully planned, designed, and implemented by virtual facilitators.

It's also important not to force social interactions into the virtual training session without a clear instructional rationale. Social interaction can be a time killer if not managed well. There are many contextual factors at play here, such as the type of content, learning objectives, timeframe, number of learners, platform constraints, and learner characteristics. For example, topics that have a lot of ambiguity might require more discussion as opposed to highly defined tasks and technical content. The trick is getting the right balance depending on the training context.

It's quite easy to see the crossover value of social interactions with the cognitive and emotional dimensions. In sum, the social dimension can play a significant supportive role. As some people might argue, all learning is social.

Next let's explore the final learning dimension for virtual training, behavioral.

Behavioral Dimension

As many L&D professionals likely agree, much of our training includes too much telling and not enough doing. This tendency is often accentuated in the live online training context where everyone is connected remotely. It's important to reiterate, however, that although LXD emphasizes being learner-centered, it is equally centered on improving performance and acquiring job-related knowledge. We need to also view the behavioral dimension of learning as encompassing more than performing psycho-motor operations. Just as behavioral and performance objectives are not all about physical skills, we use the concept of behavior here in a broad sense where there is considerable crossover with the other three dimensions. This is because learner behavior is shaped by how one thinks (cognitive), how one feels (emotional), and by what one hears and sees from others (social).

The behavioral dimension of learning involves action, practice, application, and performance. It's often associated with active learning, a key ingredient for creating engaging and impactful learning experiences. In many of my virtual training sessions, I try to include a variety of what e-learning expert William Horton (2012) refers to as "do type learning activities." Learners can work alone or in small groups for these activities. In this way, they can try out and practice applying what they're learning on the cognitive level. They do this through decision-making scenarios, practice exercises with feedback, role plays, mini games, and other kinds of active learning exercises linked to performance goals. For example, in breakouts you might include skill practices with role plays where learners practice giving constructive feedback, so they are better equipped to do so on the job. A good design strategy recommended by Clark Quinn (2021) to prioritize the behavioral dimension of learning is to use a backward design approach. The design sequence begins first by establishing clear performance objectives. The next step is to design practice-oriented learning activities based on the objectives. Focus on supporting content comes later. These "do type" practice activities can also be used as informal assessments to evaluate how learners are translating new knowledge into action. Too often the tendency with virtual training is to convey content during a virtual learning session. When this happens, the "do type" activities take a backstage when they warrant more attention.

The emotional-motivational connection can sometimes be subtle but is nonetheless a powerful driver behind the behavioral dimension. David Merrill's First Principles and John Keller's ARCS model (attention, relevance, confidence, and satisfaction) remind us that practice and doing activities play a dual role in learning (Merrill 2017; Keller 2009).

Not only can learners reinforce competencies through practice, but they can also become motivated to learn and practice more when they experience success accomplishing even small tasks during training. This is also where learning design should build in buffers of time for facilitators to provide guided feedback and reflection following key activities. In this way, the social and cognitive dimensions work synergistically along with the behavioral dimension to promote deeper and more memorable learning experiences.

Finally, the behavioral dimension also encompasses learners interacting with the functions, features, and tools in virtual training platforms. Users contributing in meaningful ways on whiteboards, posting chat responses, completing independent assignments, giving virtual presentations, or role playing in breakouts are all examples of doing.

Integrating All Four Dimensions

In their book *Designing the Online Learning Experience*, Conceição and Howles (2021) state that "learning experience design focuses on the structure and psychodynamics of individual and group experiences that take place in the context of a particular learning environment." For us, this context is a virtual class environment where the psychodynamics play out with learner interactions among facilitators and learning colleagues. Structuring virtual learning experiences means synergistically interweaving the four dimensions. This is where some of the biggest learning design challenges can occur.

There is no single formula for integrating the four dimensions because each learning situation is different, and the emphasis given to a particular learning dimension can vary depending on the instructional context. A learning designer must therefore take into consideration at least three major factors:

- The type of learning objectives (performance skill or knowledge)
- The nature of the content (well-defined or ill-defined)
- Learner characteristics (motivation and prior knowledge)

For example, in virtual training sessions for developing technical skills or standard procedures, the learning goals and content often involve concepts and behaviors that are well-defined with little ambiguity. This is often best taught through expert demonstrations, Q&A, and practice exercises. In this context, the behavioral and cognitive dimension should be weighted more heavily in learning design with less prominent social interaction.

If, however, a training situation involves learners who lack motivation for the learning content, the learning design should incorporate more motivational and emotional elements throughout the session, beginning the moment individuals enter the virtual learning space and preferably even before. If the learning goals focus on complex decision-making skills or certain kinds of people business skills, social interactions and group problem solving activities can considerably enrich the learning experience.

Including elements of all four dimensions into training design is almost always a good idea and makes for more well-rounded and engaging learning experiences. However, the relative weight you award to each will depend on the circumstances. Although the four dimensions of learning may appear simple, it is the intentional and balanced integration of them into your virtual training where the LXD skill lies.

PRO TIP 3
Integrate the four learning dimensions throughout the virtual learning experiences you design.

Learner and Task-Centered Design

As we practice using the experience design capability, it's important to recognize it's not just about pleasing learners. The bottom line of LXD must also be about improving workplace performance. Yet we strive to do this in a way that is meaningful and satisfying for learners, which is also a measurement of how we evaluate the training, as discussed further in chapter 10. So, as we practice LXD, we need to strike a balance between learner and task centeredness. Let's start by focusing on the learner-centered aspect, what it means, and how to apply it to your designs.

Learner-Centered Empathic Design

A foundational principle of LXD, based on design thinking, is empathy for the learner. Empathy is often a misconstrued concept and can be interpreted in different ways. When applied to live online learning, empathy is approaching the design and delivery of a live online learning experience from a virtual learner's perspective. What this means in essence is envisioning how a learner might think, feel, socially interact, and behave throughout their live online journey. This concept of empathy applies to all LXD work and can be referred to as empathic design (Conceição and Howles 2021).

Holding this learner perspective throughout the design process naturally leads to better learning experiences. This is because it establishes a closer alignment with learners for learning designers and facilitators. However, one of the biggest barriers to doing this is a pervasive and well-known psychological tendency called the "false consensus effect" (Ross, Greene, and House 1977). This is where we tend to project our beliefs, behaviors, and preferences onto other people, assuming they will respond the way we do. One of the most-often heard mantras in the field of user experience design when developing software applications is "You are not the user!" For LXD professionals, this translates to: "You are not the learner!" Acknowledging one's own vulnerability to the false consensus bias and a tendency to confidently assume you know what learners need and how they should be trained is the first step to practicing empathic learning design.

When we fully apply learner-centered empathic design, we realize learning experiences are more than just what happens in a live online class. The experience begins before learners even log into a virtual course and extends after learners exit the platform. For example, a learner's initial impression of your virtual training might occur via a pre-session communication from their LMS notifying them they are registered for a virtual class. This leads us to ask ourselves, what might it be like to be on the receiving end of this message? Does the communication convey emotional excitement for the course, or does it feel sterile and distant? Does the message help establish a social connection with learners? Is it personable? In all of this, we want to place ourselves in the shoes of the virtual learner and incorporate strategies from the cognitive, emotional, social, and behavioral dimensions of learning.

Practicing empathy in a live class was best illustrated by one of the most talented math teachers I've had the privilege of meeting. He had the remarkable ability to temporarily set aside what he knew about solving difficult mathematics problems, and instead look at them from a learner's perspective, posing the same kinds of questions they might be asking. He would enact and articulate their confusion, struggle, and misconceptions and guide them to a deeper understanding. As you can imagine, he was a remarkable teacher. This is a good example of empathy that skilled facilitators can put into practice. You begin where your learners are.

When you work with subject matter experts (SMEs) to design learning, it's also important to keep in mind that their understanding of a topic or skill is often skewed toward content and performance accuracy, and not as much on the learner and learning experience. Studies by Richard Clark have revealed that when teaching complex tasks, experts tend to omit well over 50 percent of necessary information that would be helpful to novice learners (Clark and Elen 2006). This is because a majority of experts' skill has become automated and is not as easily accessible to conscious awareness. Also, accomplished experts, when designing and delivering instruction, tend to focus more on describing their actions rather than the thought process underlying what they are doing. This is key. Learners need to also understand how an expert is thinking about the problem. So, when working with SMEs, it's important to continue emphasizing the learner perspective when designing instruction. Encourage SMEs to be more explicit about their underlying thought processes and help them uncover the seemingly simple but essential assumptions they unknowingly take for granted. This helps facilitate empathic design.

As virtual facilitators, we can look for opportunities to practice developing empathy in various aspects of our lives. For example, when I acted in stage plays, I always tried to find at least one opportunity during a rehearsal before opening night to sit in a seat in the last row of the auditorium. I imagined the perspective of a potential audience member as I sat in this seat. I then remembered that view from the last row when I was on stage. In my mind's eye, I still recalled what it looked and felt like. I discovered this to be transformative because I noticed a shift inside that helped me to fill space on stage more fully. For example, I was more conscious of "cheating toward the audience" (turning my face toward the audience) when I delivered my lines, as well as gesturing bigger so they could be more easily seen from far away.

Empathic design strategies expand our perspectives in ways we may not have previously realized. This is how we keep learners' needs and desires in the foreground. When we do this, we prioritize the learner's perspective over our own design ideas, decisions, and preferences. The result is an enhanced and more effective learning solution. This is the empathic mindset of the learning experience designer and facilitator.

PRO TIP 4
Be empathic by prioritizing your learners' perspective over your own design ideas, decisions, and preferences.

Task-Centered Design Thinking

Empathy also goes along with workplace performance improvement. Many training programs place an emphasis on knowing about a topic or discipline, as opposed to knowing how to perform it or apply knowledge. Deliberately integrating the behavior dimension into training attempts to bridge what Pfeffer and Sutton (2000) describe in the title of their book as *The Knowing-Doing Gap*. The tendency of training programs to overemphasize content and inert knowledge has been one of the greatest laments in the field of learning design as reflected in the *eLearning Manifesto* (Allen et al. 2014). In virtual training, we want to shift from a content- and instructor-centered focus to a performance- and task-centered perspective. This involves helping learners transfer the knowledge they've acquired at the cognitive level and apply it in real-world contexts such as making decisions, performing tasks, and having an impact on the organization.

As we have established, LXD incorporates design thinking, a holistic and human-centered way to solve problems. As we examine most training programs, their purpose often focuses on solving workplace performance problems and challenges. Because of this, LXD also must have a greater impact on individual workplace performance as employees upskill, reskill, and practice applying job-related tasks. This, of course, places a greater emphasis on the behavioral dimension of learning when designing virtual training.

After the green light has been given to proceed with a training solution, and virtual training has been selected as the appropriate delivery approach, here are some of the design thinking strategies I include in my initial exploratory phase of learning design:

- I rewrite learning objectives as performance objectives (what learners need to do). This serves as a basis for identifying what the focus of each learning activity should be. I then meet with stakeholders to collect their input on objectives and get final approval.

- I try to focus on the design of practice activities associated with a few of the most important learning objectives before thinking about content design. I create a rough outline or sketch for a practice activity and how it might flow. I regard these initial ideas as starting points that are OK to throw away. The first idea, no matter how good it might seem, is seldom the best idea.

- Next, I spend a little time validating some of the initial assumptions made by stakeholders and SMEs regarding learner needs and learning outcomes. I get out of my designer cave and hold video calls or brief informal conversations with people. If possible, I talk first with a few prospective learners and a stakeholder or two to get their reactions to the direction.

- If I'm working with a colleague or SME, I share this information with them and begin ideation and very rapid prototype outline sketches of a few of the learning practice activities. I'm not thinking about content at this point, but the performance tasks I want to simulate in each learning activity. The content comes later and gets wrapped around them.

This task-centered aspect of creating virtual training programs is an iterative process. It involves clarifying performance problems, ideating creative solutions, testing instructional strategies, and receiving feedback. We need to strike the right balance between learner engagement, meaningfulness, and performance impact. Sharon Boller and Laura Fletcher (2020) refer to this as hitting the sweet spot when incorporating design thinking into their training approach. In a work context, virtual training and learning have a bottom line. Therefore, prioritize the needs of stakeholders and learners.

Strategies for Applying LXD to Virtual Training

Let's build on what we've learned about LXD thus far by looking at several core strategies for designing virtual training. You'll find that these strategies can be applied broadly in almost any training design context, but our focus naturally is to enhance the learner experience in live virtual training environments.

Include Learners and Stakeholders in the Design Process

The instructional design for many training programs usually involves input from a limited number of individuals. In most organizations, an instructor or learning designer works with a SME to craft the design. As they create a training program, they make dozens of assumptions and decisions about what information learners need, how they will use it in their work context, what kinds of learning activities to include, and how they think learners will respond to the various design elements of the training. Input and ideas from other stakeholders, particularly those destined to be recipients of the instruction, are often seen as unnecessary and time consuming, especially when training is converted from in-person to virtual.

However, skilled designers adopt principles of design thinking in developing products, services, and professional development programs, and recognize the value of collaboration and feedback starting early in the design process. Many use a strategy often referred to as "participatory design," which had been used successfully for decades in northern Europe before design thinking became popularized in the mid-1990s (DiSalvo et al. 2017). This design strategy, with its emphasis on user centeredness, has become a core practice in design thinking and UXD. It involves obtaining ideas and feedback from various stakeholders in making design decisions. Its most central principle is that the users or recipients of any product or service should have input into the design from the very beginning. This strategy is most useful for larger high-stakes training projects where live virtual training sessions may be part of a blend of instructional components such as coaching, on-demand microlearning modules, and performance support. However, it can also be useful in designing performance-focused learning activities that are part of live virtual or traditional in-person training sessions.

For example, one of my colleagues once worked for a major corporation as a program designer for a traditional classroom-based leadership development course with some online components. His colleagues offered conflicting opinions about what instructional methods to use in designing this course, as well as conflicting assumptions regarding target learner characteristics, needs, and learning preferences. Deciding to hear directly from learners themselves, he invited about 10 managers who were to be candidates to take the course to a one-hour lunch where he provided complimentary pizza and beverages. During this informal meeting, he shared the course goals, assumptions he and other training colleagues had about the prospective participants, and some initial course design ideas. The insights and design ideas obtained from participants were so fruitful, they significantly changed the trajectory of the initial course design. Furthermore, session participants expressed gratitude for being asked to provide input and ideas for a course they and their colleagues would likely be required to attend. In the end, that leadership training course became the most highly praised and most requested offering within all the company's management development curriculum.

From a conventional instructional design perspective, actively soliciting learner feedback about design ideas may be viewed as a weakness professionally. In the last example, the course designer's manager, after hearing about the ideation session with prospective learners, light-heartedly exclaimed "That's cheating!" However, for myself and others who have used participatory design, we have observed that some of our best learning design ideas have come from collaboration with learners as well as other colleagues. Most individuals frequently express gratitude for being consulted and enjoy participating in the learning design process. Although some instructors and designers may see it as "cheating" or unnecessary, this LXD strategy usually improves the learning experience and also does not require a lot of time.

For designers of live virtual training and other instructional programs, this LXD strategy helps you adopt a more open, collaborative design mindset. The trick is to use participatory design in an efficient way that involves the least amount of time for all stakeholders involved, yet yields the most useful input. Incorporating collaboration into learning design can be done through brief informal conversations with stakeholders where you share initial design plans and challenges and invite ideas and feedback. Asking good questions and listening is key. Arranging one-on-one informal conversations or small group meetings, either face-to-face or via web conferencing, works best to avoid consensus bias. A 20-minute conversation with a single individual or an hour-long small group session is often adequate depending on the complexity of the training project and the number of key stakeholders who are involved.

Feedforward

This strategy is a natural extension of including learners in design decisions. As you assemble your content and learning activities for a virtual training program, open your door to collaboration. It is critical you start these conversations as early as possible. Any design feedback you receive from others after a virtual training program has been nearly finalized or after implementation comes too late. People rarely want to go back and perform major surgery on something that has already been developed, even if the initial assumptions and design ideas were off base. Gathering feedforward from stakeholders at the conceptualization phase prevents this from happening. For example, when I was just beginning to think about creating a new virtual training program for clients, I ran the early concept of my vision for this course by three colleagues in the field. I met with each of them separately to get their input and reactions. At this early stage, I wasn't as invested as I otherwise might have been in my own ideas. They confirmed the concept and even fine-tuned and expanded my initial vision.

I have never regretted investing the time to have conversations with target users, colleagues, managers, stakeholders, or the time spent conducting short user interviews or doing dry run walk-throughs of virtual sessions with a few colleagues. I always learn many things from them to make them better, and they are always things I didn't see myself or previously overlooked.

It's true, the effort to understand your virtual learners and listen to them may take a bit more time, especially on the front end. Just remember that participatory and design thinking strategies may go slower initially so you can go faster later, and the quality of your final virtual training designs will be better because of it.

PRO TIP 5
Include target virtual learners in the early design process to solicit their feedback and gain their perspective on course design.

Develop Learner Personas

The conventional ADDIE instructional design process typically includes a target audience analysis. Most of the time, if performed at all, this analysis is done rapidly, focusing on the demographics and surface level characteristics of learners. The mental picture designers have of their learners often lacks depth and can be distorted by the designer's own self-projections and biases. This is because we tend to assume our virtual learners are like us, falling prey to the false consensus effect mentioned earlier. Furthermore, when we create disembodied lists of learner characteristics and needs, designers can lose a sense of real people and how they think, feel, socially interact, and behave in a work context. Those involved in making learning design decisions need to be on the same page and keep a similar mental image of their learners in the forefront of their minds. One LXD technique adapted from design thinking that helps in developing a shared vision of target learners is creating learner personas.

Personas are fictional character profiles who are given first names and attributes that reflect a major segment of the actual learners participating in your virtual training program. These personas should be based on your interviews, conversations, and interactions with them, along with any information provided by their supervisors and managers who are familiar with target learners. Creating two or three personas can provide an adequate composite representation of a target learner group for design purposes. You can even use animated or cartoon-like representations of your personas and describe their backgrounds, what motivates them, what turns them off, and how much prior knowledge they have about the training topic. This human-centered and creative approach to portraying your target virtual learners as real people can be invaluable. As you plan and design a training session, you now have a mental picture of, for example, Karra, Meredith, and Travis in the forefront of your mind. As you design, you think about how they might react to what you envision happening in your live online class—what they might think, feel, say, and do. Personas are especially helpful when working with SMEs or a design team. Continually referencing personas as real people reminds everyone to think beyond their own personal learning design preferences and adopt a more empathic learner-centered frame of reference instead.

When I designed an online virtual training program for new hires, I interviewed three separate new employees in the organization who had only been there a few weeks. I asked probing questions related to the topic I would be training for new hires. I quickly constructed two personas named Hank and Lindsey to share with my co-designer. Not only did this make the design process more fun, but we were better able to pattern the design of the virtual sessions around authentic perceptions and real new-hire questions. Persona character sketches don't have to be elaborate or detailed to remind yourself of who your real learners are. Figure 2-2 shows simple persona example from my design process.

Figure 2-2. Persona Example

"As a new hire, show me what all the business areas do, their services, and examples of top priority initiatives."	Worked as a Project Manager for 10 years. Is 45 yrs. old and has a business degree. Mother of 2 teenagers. Personal interests are traveling, biking, and hiking. Has been trained in facilitation skills, project management software, and is an MS Teams expert.	Tends to be quiet in social situations with new people. Learning preferences: Prefers a challenge and likes to solve problems. Motivated by helping others. Current knowledge of company is limited as new hire. Biggest challenge is technical skills. Stronger in people skills.

Recall the four dimensions of learning as you create your personas. Imagine their thoughts, feelings, and behavioral tendencies, and how they might engage socially and participate in virtual collaborative group activities. Experiment with this for the design of your next virtual training class. The best designers in any field always have a clear mental picture of the people for whom they are creating a product, service, or learning experience. As I have discovered, taking the time to construct a few simple personas to refer to while designing virtual training sessions has not only been fun, but has helped shift my own and my colleagues' instructional design thinking to be more learner centered. Please note that creating personas may not always be necessary for small, lower stakes, one-off virtual training sessions. But when working with colleagues where live virtual sessions might be a part of a much larger or highly visible training initiative, having a few personas to share with design colleagues can help everyone become more unified and learner-task centered in making design decisions.

PRO TIP 6
Create fictional virtual learner personas to guide your designs for larger-scale virtual training programs.

Map the Learner Experience

Another design thinking tool increasingly used by learning experience designers in developing online and blended courses is called experience mapping, sometimes also referred to as journey mapping. The purpose of an experience map is to provide a more holistic "big picture" sense of the experience from a learner's point of view. It is often used in conjunction with learner personas to help designers move beyond an instructor- or content-centered bias to a more learner-centered design mindset. An experience map traces learner interactions and the major touch points, instructional events, and moments that matter most to learners as they progress through an entire learning experience from start to finish. In practicing LXD, Jane Bozarth (2020) sums it up by saying that applying such strategies "involves creating and working from user personas rather than demographics and mapping out the journeys learners will take as they move to proficiency." A learner experience map is part of empathic design. Like personas, you have flexibility in how you structure experience maps and the amount of detail needed for your learning context.

An experience map can take the form of a sequential list, a flow diagram, a table, or even a storyboard. It identifies and briefly describes the major phases and key interactions learners may have with content, learning activities, people, software tools, and other digital artifacts in the planned learning design. Based on personas, you take note of what a virtual learner might be thinking, feeling, and doing at various key junctures throughout the learning experience. The map is typically organized around major structural components and instructor–learner touch points of the live session. This can include pre-session announcements, pre-work, and logging into the virtual environment. It then progresses into learner interactions within the virtual session including introductions, discussions, breakout activities, instructor presentation segments, reflection exercises, and scenario-based challenges, all the way to the session close and any post-work or follow-up activities. The template example in Table 2-1 illustrates one way an experience may be constructed.

Table 2-1. Experience Map Example

Phases	Pre-Class	Live Class	Post-Class
What Learner **DOES** (Independent and Social)	• Receives facilitator email with link to welcome video • LMS sends auto-email with session logistics and article to read beforehand	• Present challenging scenario at outset • Introduce guiding principles • Show exemplars and non-examples of guiding principles • Breakout activity to apply principles on own in small groups • Reflection activity • Create action plan	• Share action plan with manager • Incorporate a goal into performance appraisal • Present key learning points to peer team members
What Learner **THINKS FEELS**	• Am I at the right skill level for this class? • Will everyone know more than me?	• What's expected of me in this course? • How will I remember all the principles? • These good and bad examples make a lot of sense. • I can do this!	• My manager seems to care about what I've learned. • I'm excited to apply this to my next project.
Challenges	• Ensure learners read pre-work article • Learners' system compatibility with platform	• Different time zones for attendees • Having all the resources learners need to be successful in the small group breakout exercises • Performance support aid needed to reinforce application after class	• Manager follow-through • Participants held accountable for application

For example, in one of my online virtual events, the first touch point in my learning experience map consisted of an email with a link to a brief facilitator welcome video. The video addressed the cognitive and emotional dimensions of the learning experience, emphasizing how the class could benefit participants, and included motivational elements to get them excited and interested. A few days prior to the session, learners received another email with logistic and technical reminders and a link to a brief article related to the topic. The map continues, documenting each touch point.

There are several benefits to mapping out the learner's journey. First, you can begin to anticipate the types of questions learners might have and notice gaps and design changes that may need to be addressed. Second, you can also share the map with a colleague or even a prospective learner to walk through the experience and get feedback and ideas for tweaking it. Third, the experience map can also help you identify where and how you are interweaving the four learning dimensions throughout the entire virtual learning experience. Are there enough practice activities to cover all the objectives? Are social interactions included at the right times to reinforce cognitive learning? Finally, it's important to keep in mind that this is not a content outline or list of instructor actions. Rather, it's all about the learner and their anticipated journey through the learning experience. You can think of it almost like a scenario or story that includes a series of interconnected episodes comprising a learning journey that spotlights the learner.

PRO TIP 7
Create an experience map to envision your participants' virtual learning journey from start to finish.

Leverage the Peak-End Rule to End on a High Note

Earlier in this chapter, we discussed beginning a virtual training session in an emotionally motivating way. We also discussed how the four learning dimensions can be interwoven throughout an entire virtual session. Now we ask, how should a virtual learning experience end? Can we do this in a way that leaves learners feeling more positive and satisfied about their learning experience? This is where the peak-end rule comes into play. The peak-end rule refers to a cognitive bias that was first revealed by

Daniel Kahneman and Barbara Frederickson and has been applied widely to studying how individuals mentally process and recall all kinds of life experiences, including learning experiences (Kahneman et al. 1993; Finn 2010). Keep in mind that all learning experiences are highly subjective. When individuals recall and evaluate a learning experience, what happens toward the end of the experience is often remembered and weighted more heavily. Therefore, it is important for trainers to end their virtual training sessions on a high note.

The other aspect of this principle relies on the fact that when individuals reflect on and evaluate a learning experience, they tend to focus on the most intense emotional moments, which are referred to as peaks. Their evaluation of an entire learning experience can become colored, either positively or negatively, around these peak moments that matter to them regardless of how minor they may seem to a designer and facilitator. So, it pays to spend time discussing what is most important for them. Also, when constructing an experience map for your training sessions, it is a good idea to identify and anticipate critical points where potential bumps in the road might occur and where learners may experience a heightened sense of accomplishment and pleasure. Build into your learning design plan periods where learners reflect on significant learning moments to give them prominence in memory. On the flip side, anticipate and plan for how to respond to and manage potential learner frustrations and negative experiences.

In my virtual training sessions, I try to apply this principle in several different ways. First, my lesson designs typically include a variety of brief explanatory sections, group discussion, decision-based scenarios, practice exercises, and breakout activities. Following significant learning moments, we pause to reflect and discuss how everyone might apply what they have learned to their jobs. I also have backup plans for critical junctures where technology glitches might occur. Often, I conclude a session with a fun, interactive review game or other kind of activity that helps reinforce the most important content from the class.

It is important not to rush these types of activities. Give participants the time and space they need to do the deep thinking. I also let them know I will be silent while they do this reflective work. In other sessions, I include a whiteboard exercise as a final activity, where I give time to reflect and complete action plans first. Before learners start writing their action plans, I prepare them by letting them know I will ask everyone to share a take-away from class that they will apply right away. After the action plans are complete, I ask them to share this application idea on the virtual whiteboard. This gives the session a strong close and motivates learners for any subsequent training.

PRO TIP 8
Apply the peak-end rule by triggering learners' memories of what has mattered most to them in the learning experience.

Making the Shift From Designing Instruction to Designing Learning Experiences

If our goal is to create engaging, meaningful, and impactful learning experiences for live virtual training, we may need to make some fundamental shifts in how we think about and approach learning design. This involves both breaking from and upgrading many conventional instructional practices, which necessitates rethinking old mental models of how learning and instruction take place in synchronous learning environments infused with new technology affordances.

It is all too easy to approach the virtual training environment like a conventional classroom and try to design learning experiences that conform to a closed classroom model. Seasoned online facilitators are very aware that what works well in-person does not always translate to best virtual training practice. As virtual training expert Jennifer Hofmann (2004) explains, "The most common error for newcomers to the synchronous training arena is assuming that the same rules that apply in a traditional classroom apply in a synchronous classroom."

PRO TIP 9
Revamp your paradigm of a traditional four-walled classroom to an open, shared virtual learning space instead.

With new digital tools in virtual learning spaces, we move away from the traditional, conceptual model of a four-walled classroom. For example, facilitators can leverage polling tools, extend the voice of learners through chat boards, and provide multiple shared whiteboards with annotation tools for all participants. We can also include live experts from anywhere in the world to join our classes. In chapter 11, we talk more about adopting a blended approach where we can selectively combine and mix live virtual learning with other asynchronous components to add the greatest value. In short, virtual training technologies create new spaces for learning that enable new kinds of interactions and learning experiences.

Summary

As we apply LXD to virtual training, we expand and rejuvenate our conventional notions of traditional instructional design. Although the core concepts and practices used by many instructional designers and trainers may include LXD elements, our approach to LXD gives us a language and broader set of learning design strategies that are more holistic and learner-task centered.

The four learning dimensions framework serves as a foundation for designing learning experiences that skillfully integrate the cognitive, emotional. How we blend these elements can vary depending on the instructional context shaped by learning goals, type of content, and learner characteristics as well as the affordances of technology tools available within the virtual class environment. These elements work together to make learning experiences more engaging, meaningful, and impactful.

In LXD, we borrow practices from other fields, such as design thinking and user experience design (UXD), and incorporate evidence-based practices drawing from learning science research and our own data to make design decisions. LXD is more inclusive and people-centered, always keeping the learners' perspectives in the foreground and initiating collaboration with colleagues and learners throughout the design process. Learners can participate in the learning design process, providing feedforward and feedback as well as sharing ideas through brief interviews and conversations. With LXD, we learn about our learners to create personas that inform our learner experience maps and designs.

Good design always has and will continue to be the foundation for successful virtual learning. Not only is it important to thoughtfully design learner experiences that integrate all four dimensions, but we also need to create learning environments where virtual participants are engaged and supported. Moving forward, I encourage you to continue developing and practicing your knowledge and skills in LXD and the experience design capability.

In the next chapter, we focus on how to optimize learner engagement and performance outcomes. Specifically, we'll look at how to help learners thrive by shaping successful virtual learning environments.

Pro Tips for Practicing Your Experience Design Skills

TIP 1	Apply LXD by leading with experience, not content.
TIP 2	Use traditional learning objectives to drive design, but reframe the objectives shared with learners to be more motivational for them.
TIP 3	Integrate the four learning dimensions throughout the virtual learning experiences you design.
TIP 4	Be empathic by prioritizing your learners' perspective over your own design ideas, decisions, and preferences.
TIP 5	Include target virtual learners in the early design process to solicit their feedback and gain their perspective on course design.
TIP 6	Create fictional virtual learner personas to guide your designs for larger-scale virtual training programs.
TIP 7	Create an experience map to envision your participants' virtual learning journey from start to finish.
TIP 8	Apply the peak-end rule by triggering learners' memories of what has mattered most to them in the learning experience.
TIP 9	Revamp your paradigm of a traditional four-walled classroom to an open, shared virtual learning space instead.

"In order for online learning to be successful, developers need to create environments in which people can effectively learn."

—Jennifer Hofmann, Founder and CEO of InSync Training

CHAPTER 3

Shaping a Successful Virtual Learning Environment

The key to cultivating a successful learning environment is the virtual facilitator. This is because the synchronous facilitator—in partnership with the producer—is responsible for nurturing the environment that enables learners to blossom. Through their actions, tone, and words—whether they realize it or not—they can shape a positive, inclusive, and productive environment for virtual learning. The opposite is also true. Virtual facilitators and producers can inadvertently create environments that feel content-centric, sterile, apathetic, routine, intimidating, non-supportive, or even critical. Not only can this be a toxic environment, but it could create disengagement and hinder learning.

Although we tend to focus more on what happens inside an environment, we should realize that what happens within is influenced by the wrapper around it. In the context of virtual training, how learners and facilitators interact is shaped by the environment. For example, the degree to which learners choose to participate, whether they feel unwelcomed or undervalued, how safe they feel about speaking up even when they disagree, and how they are treated when they make mistakes during skill practices are all influenced by their surrounding environment.

Functional and healthy environments can be the foundation for building positive working relationships, learner-to-learner and instructor-to-learner, as established in chapter 2. "Participants need to feel like they have developed personal rapport with the instructor. It is even more important in an online environment than the traditional approach" (Hofmann 2004). When we successfully connect with learners and they connect with us, it can make all the difference for learning.

Virtual training technology platforms also play a role. The technology influences design decisions and facilitator behavior. Facilitators, in turn, shape the learning environment based on their decisions and actions. Then this learning environment shapes learners and their overall experience. So, technological platforms kickstart a domino effect of sorts by influencing a string of elements. According to the *2021 Educause Horizon Report, Teaching and Learning Edition*, "As the adoption of blended or hybrid learning models has accelerated, so too has the adoption of new learning technologies and tools that support and even shape the implementation of those models" (Pelletier et al. 2021).

This leads us to the next capability, environment shaping. Virtual trainers need to know how to skillfully create positive, productive environments. But how should a virtual facilitator do this? Ideally, learning environments support all four dimensions of learning (cognitive, emotional, social, and behavioral) to combat learner disengagement and reduce the temptation to multitask. Overall, this chapter answers the question: What can facilitators do to ensure virtual learners are comfortable and connected in their learning environment so they can actively contribute in meaningful ways?

THE BIG IDEA
Just as facilitators shape learning environments, learning environments shape learners and their overall experience.

What Is a Learning Environment?

The live online learning environment is a living ecosystem. It projects a feel, tone, and energy where cultural norms dictate acceptable and unacceptable behavior. These surroundings also dictate whether the space will be collaborative or competitive, welcoming or distant, conversational or rote, led with credible professionalism or fraught with technical chaos.

Environment shaping, then, includes everything a virtual trainer or online educator does to influence this ecosystem. Shaping an environment encompasses all the little and big things facilitators, as leaders of the environment, say or don't say, do or don't do, react to or don't react to. These are the established norms that lay the foundation for how the virtual training session will go and how all the interdependent parts will interact within it.

In this chapter, we specifically look at ways facilitators can develop their capability in environment shaping. We explore the 5 Cs Pyramid to understand the learner experience, lay out the welcome mat with activities before class, lead live sessions with enthusiasm and personalization, and foster psychological safety for learners. Regardless of how shiny the training technology's bells and whistles might be, at the end of the day, it's always still about people and learning.

The 5 Cs Pyramid: Staged Progression for Virtual Learners

The heart of this book is learner-centered experiences, as discussed in chapter 2. After 20 years of training online, I've noticed that many virtual learners experience a progression of mental stages when they join a virtual training session. Sometimes, they appear to fully progress through all these stages in only seconds, while for others, it may be much slower. I call these different stages the 5 Cs Pyramid (Figure 3-1). The usefulness of this pyramid is that it reminds you to be empathic toward the learner experience.

Figure 3-1. The Virtual Learner's 5 Cs Pyramid

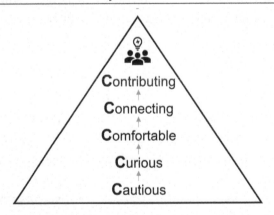

The goal, of course, is to move learners through all the stages as soon as possible without getting stuck in any one phase. It is important to note that much of this movement usually remains subconscious. For example, a learner may not actively think, "Is it safe for me to say something here?" Instead, they might think "I don't want to look stupid" or "I don't want to embarrass myself" without articulating those feelings aloud. Let's examine each of the 5 Cs more closely.

1. Cautious

This is the first stage, when learners log into a platform and internally ask themselves any number of questions reflecting early caution. For example, they may ask themselves, "Did I click the right link?" "Am I in the right class?" "Is my tech working?" "Can everyone hear me and see me?" "Can I hear and see others?" "Should I be on camera because everyone else is?" "If I click this, will I lose my chat?"

Being cautious about entering a new space makes sense. This might be analogous to your first day at a new job where you need to report to a building to pick up your computer and meet your manager. "Is this the right building?" "Did I find the right reception area?" "What do I need to show for security?" "Am I parked in the right lot?" You remain cautious until you collect more information. Once you ascertain answers to these pressing questions, you begin to settle in. The same is true for virtual learners. Being cautious as they log into virtual training is natural because it's a new class. In this chapter, we'll explore several strategies to move learners from caution to higher levels in the pyramid.

2. Curious

After moving past caution, learners realize they can be seen and heard and are in the right place. Next, they're curious. Their subconscious thoughts might be "Who else is here?" "Have my colleagues joined yet?" "Anyone I know?" "What do I think of them?" "Which one is the trainer?" Keep in mind these thoughts may remain subconscious and may not even be articulated.

Human beings are naturally curious. It's normal and perfectly acceptable. Again, our goal is not to force learners to skip this stage, but instead help them move through it. This stage might be analogous to a graduate attending a graduation ceremony. Because you're curious as a graduate first walking into the ceremony, you might be looking around to check who's there. You might scan the crowd for people you know because you're more comfortable around those people. Additionally, you might be curious about who's going to hand you your diploma, who's speaking at the lectern, and the path you'll take to get to the stage.

Notice how the emotional dimension is the underpinning of this stage as well. And likeability—whether we like it or not—also comes into play. In this stage, learners may ask "Do I like my facilitator?" "Is my facilitator credible?" "Are they professional?" "Will they just cover stuff I already know?" "Who else is on camera?" "Does my hair really look like that?"

As learners are looking for answers to their curious questions, they may miss things you are saying when you begin your virtual training class. Curious thoughts take priority and capture initial attention. So, rather than diving in immediately when you begin your virtual training session, you might just reference the kinds of questions they're already thinking and acknowledge them aloud. For example, you might say, "It's great to have 15 of us here today from 10 different companies across Europe." Or you can make sure that if you have critical opening comments, you signal their importance by slowing down your delivery for emphasis, and repeating them: "This is so important I'll say it again," or leading with a verbal signpost like "One of the most important things you'll hear today is . . ." We'll explore techniques like these more in chapters 4 and 6. These are ways to ensure you can redirect learners' curiosity back to what you're saying.

3. Comfortable

Imagine you were invited to attend a dinner party at someone else's house for the first time. As you arrive and they invite you inside, the space is new to you, and they direct you where to place your shoes and offer to take your coat. They may ask you if you would like a drink, and perhaps show you to the living room. They may even offer you a tour of their home. How welcomed and safe you feel in the space dictates your comfort. This comfort level then influences whether and how you participate and share in the space that is not yours. You are very aware that you are the guest in this scenario.

In virtual training, learners may feel like guests in a virtual space because they are not hosting. They did not invite others, they were invited.

Initially, learners understand that they surrender some amount of power to the host or leader of the event when they enter a space. However, throughout the course of the session you can and should give learners more voice, more challenge, and more power. This means they do more, and you do less. For them to spread their wings, take initiative, and speak up more, you need to ensure they feel comfortable in the space and eventually transition from comfortable guest to empowered contributor in the final stage.

4. Connecting

Let's say you were recently hired for a new job and will be working on-site two days a week and then remote for the remainder. There are likely some questions you have that are more pressing than others. For example, on day one, you may care more about where your office or workspace is when you work on-site, how close you are to the restroom, where the cafeteria is and how to get there, what computer, monitors, and equipment you'll be using, where to go to get your security badge, and how to locate your manager if they also work on-site a few days per week. Getting answers to these questions can take priority as you settle in. However, after you have found the answers, you will feel ready to meet people, learn their names and what they do at the company, and form relationships.

In a similar way, once learners acclimate to the virtual learning environment and have moved through the stages of caution and curiosity and become more comfortable, they are ready to start testing the waters and connecting with others. Connecting is about finding commonality, building positive work relationships, developing give and take, interacting socially, and learning about each other. This C clearly ties into the social dimension of learning discussed in chapter 2.

We know that connecting with people in productive ways is an important part of acclimating. Even brief introductions or sharing where you're connecting from in chat can inspire receptiveness and a willingness to broaden one's connections. As the facilitator, you can provide brief opportunities to spark interpersonal connection by leading exercises on whiteboards where learners can select an image or identify a word that most describes them.

One of the best ways to conduct introductions is through small breakouts near the beginning of class. People will feel more comfortable sharing and connecting in small groups at first, which warms them up for large group discussion later. (We'll talk more about this in chapter 7.) You can provide brief instructions like "Share your name, organization, role, and favorite type of pet." This way, in small groups of three to four people, participants can each take approximately a minute to introduce themselves, so it takes less time collectively. The pet prompt also sparks some fun and is an inroad to help people form bonds as they perhaps discover with delight that they both like dogs best, or hamsters, or perhaps, on a rare occasion, a pot-bellied pig. They may respond in kind by saying "Hey, horses are my favorite too!" Social connection has begun.

PRO TIP 10
Build community with connecting activities (even brief ones) to foster social learning and help learners discover commonality with one another.

5. Contributing

The final stage is a learner's interest and readiness to actively contribute in meaningful ways. Once a learner knows they are in the right place, have figured out who else is there and who they know, are beginning to feel more ease and comfort and likewise have let their guard down a bit, and have begun connecting with others, they are now more likely to contribute. We discussed how the social dimension of learning was linked to connecting. Ideally, contributing actively builds on all four dimensions of learning (cognitive, emotional, social, and behavioral). Evidence-based research suggests psychological engagement is essential for learning, and the cognitive and emotional dimensions together comprise this psychological engagement that can then lead to more social interaction and related activities (Clark 2020).

Overall, the 5 Cs Pyramid reminds us to support learners as they progress through the stages from cautious all the way to contributing as soon as possible. And we do not want them to remain stuck in one along the way. Our end goal is for them to be ready to actively give and receive. By contributing, I don't mean clicking an animated thumbs-up reaction or voting in a poll, as these are more surface-level contributions, although they can lead to more. Rather, I mean that the small opening of their contribution ideally grows throughout to the point where they share a professional experience or story that connects with the training material, build on their prior knowledge and share likewise in chat or in a breakout, talk about insights they're having from the training content, ask thoughtful questions, fully practice skills learned in class, take part in the role plays, actively listen and share in breakout groups, or offer feedback to others during a skill practice. These are just a few of the many ways learners can engage and contribute to the overall learning experience.

PRO TIP 11
Reference the 5 Cs Pyramid to guide your empathic responses to virtual learners as they first acclimate.

Virtual facilitators need to shape virtual learning environments so they are conducive to learners progressing up the pyramid from cautious to contributing. Using the 5 Cs as our guide, let's look next at strategies to help facilitators do this. These strategies include laying out the welcome mat, opening live sessions with enthusiasm and personalization, and cultivating psychological safety with learners. All these strategies support the environment shaping capability. The skills needed for this capability include communication skills, clarifying expectations, proactively minimizing interruptions, rapport building, facilitating learners discovering their commonality, and, ultimately, building community.

Laying Out the Welcome Mat

Nurturing a positive and welcoming virtual learning environment is the natural outcome of a learner-centric approach. When virtual trainers are empathic to the learner experience, they recognize the importance of first impressions and how the communications and lead-up to a session can set the tone for class. To be learner-centric, facilitators should greet their class in such a way that learners immediately feel welcomed, seen, and heard. In other words, you want to lay out the welcome mat.

Laying out the welcome mat is everything we do beforehand to set the right tone for class. Notably, it reminds us to set expectations for productive and positive learning. Participants should also immediately feel they have entered a supportive space with positive energy. It only takes minutes to create a favorable or unfavorable impression, and sometimes even less.

As we've established, our goal is to help learners move from cautious to contributing. Of course, you would also welcome them in real time on class day. In this section, we'll focus specifically on three things you can do to welcome them through multiple touchpoints before they come to a live online session. First, you can send learners a pre-session communication to set expectations above and beyond the one they may receive automatically from their LMS. Second, you can send a welcome video for participants to view ahead of time. And third, you can meet for a brief tech check before class if the platform is new to them or if they are new to the venue.

PRO TIP 12
Welcome participants via multiple touchpoints in multiple ways.

Establish Expectations in Pre-Session Communication

When you plot out a learner experience map as we discussed in chapter 2, you will be able to view and improve on all the touchpoints a learner will receive, and this will help you make decisions about timing and which messaging should come when. Many learning management systems allow you to customize automatic messages as reminders sent to learners about upcoming virtual training. These automated messages communicate to learners that they're registered, when the class or program will take place, and the technology required. This is certainly an opportunity to customize the LMS messaging by including rewritten learning objectives that are more motivational for learners (as discussed in chapter 2) along with the expectations for the training program. For example, one expectation might be that the training is interactive, and they should come ready to participate.

It's also helpful to incorporate an email welcome communication from the trainer. LMS emails are rarely brimming with personality. So, in addition to the automated invite that comes from the LMS with necessary links, dates, and times, send a welcome email just from you to share your excitement about the class and that you are looking forward to working with them. This allows you to personalize pre-session messaging and is also an opportunity for learners to hear directly from you beforehand. When you level-set expectations in any pre-session messaging, it can be a great way to alleviate the learners' first and second Cs of the 5 Cs pyramid. Learners may have some level of anxiety and feel cautious as well as curious about the class. Use pre-session emails to help address those questions ahead of time and showcase your excitement, which helps them look forward to it. Then when they join the live virtual training session, they'll be able to move quicker through the 5 Cs, so you can get them to the contributing stage earlier.

It is also important in pre-session messaging to remind learners to find an area free from distractions for virtual training. You should still remind participants of this at the outset of the session, but finding a quiet area is best accomplished well before the training begins. Advise them to find a space where they can close a door if possible, and to inform those they live with or who work nearby that they're in a training session and should not be disturbed. I sometimes post a sign on my door that reminds people to be quiet as they walk by.

 PRO TIP 13
Continuously incentivize and reward active participation from learners.

Send a Welcome Video

One of the best ways to ensure your virtual training session gets off to a great start is to create an instructor welcome video (Figure 3-2). This video can help set the tone for a productive live online class and set expectations for the class. More importantly, it can also alleviate some of the caution and curiosity learners might have when they first join a virtual training session, jumpstart the relationship building between the learner and facilitator, and prepare participants to contribute sooner. If they've already had a chance to see you in a video, they know what you look like, which helps address their curiosity about you. Ideally, you want them to find you friendly and approachable. As a client of mine put it, "Adding a video introduction of yourself will also allow the learner to connect with you right away so once the course has started, they feel they already know you and have built some form of relationship with you. I believe this will also give the learner some form of comfort upon arrival and it's a great way to break the ice."

Make your video available for learners to view one week before your live online class, and require this as part of their pre-work. When I teach a program that will meet multiple times, I always include a welcome video for participants to view a week before we begin. This is not so far in advance that they will forget what I said in the video, and it's not last-minute either. I usually include a link to my welcome video in my welcoming instructor communication; other times, my client will send out my welcome communication with the link to the video, or I'll post the video in the LMS as pre-work for them. (A sample script of a welcome video is included in chapter 11.)

Figure 3-2. Still Image of Trainer Welcome Video

What Are the Elements of a Successful Welcome Video?

Begin with the end in mind. Identify the result or final effect you want the welcome video to have on your learners. For example, you want them to come away from the video excited about and looking forward to the course. This ties into the emotional factor of motivation that we'll talk more about in chapter 4. As author Clark Quinn (2021) articulates, "Motivation starts before the experience really begins. We want to have learners eager for the experience." Your pre-session welcome video message can sow the seeds of enthusiasm for learners. The video can also showcase you and your presence.

Your welcome video can be shot on a mobile device depending on the quality of your camera. Alternatively, you can record yourself speaking from your desktop or laptop computer using its camera. Be sure to follow the guidelines in chapter 5 for how to come across effectively on camera when you record. To strengthen the impact of your welcome video, consider the following best practices:

- Convey enthusiasm for the topic by genuinely being excited yourself. Smile as you talk (when appropriate to what you're saying). You want to convey that you are approachable, likable, and friendly to develop rapport.
- Build your professional credibility by sharing a few things about yourself, such as how long you've been training and your years of experience with the training topic.
- Set expectations for course work. For example, if it will be a blended learning program (see chapter 11), let them know the different course components. Share that there will be both asynchronous and synchronous work. Clarify that they will need to complete pre-work assignments before each live session. If they will be expected do a final presentation or final teach-back, give them this head's up in the welcome video as well.
- Avoid referencing specific information that would outdate your welcome video so you can re-use it for repeat runs of this program or training class. For example, say the title of the course but avoid mentioning any dates.
- Keep it brief—between one and two minutes. Video messages should be to-the-point and serve to introduce you and course expectations, enough to satisfy participants' caution and curiosity, and also start building connections. Anything more than three minutes is too long for a welcome video.
- Consider adding text overlays to show a few words onscreen next to you while you talk about them; for example, display "Action Plans" when you talk about how everyone will complete an action plan at the end of the virtual training program to be shared with their manager. You can use products like Camtasia or other video editors to add the text overlays.

- For a nuanced professional touch, add instrumental music to the background of your welcome video. Obviously, your words and image are the feature of the video, and the music underneath should support the video's function. Ensure the volume of the music is very low. Music should never call attention to itself, be distracting, make it difficult to understand what you're saying, or compete with your messaging. Alternatively, you could add music to the intro and the outro to infuse energy into the opening and close. Video editing software makes it easy for you to select royalty-free music assets and sound effects that you're free to use without copyright clearance. For example, several musical selections are available to choose from right within the Camtasia Studio Library during your video editing. To prevent an abrupt stop to the music when your video ends, use the program's audio features to fade it out for a smoother close.
- Require learners to view the video by a deadline (like the day before the first class begins), and create a worksheet to ensure they check it off and let you know it's complete. Or set up the training program in the LMS so that it will track completion of items; then you can run reports to track whether learners have viewed the video. One technique that works effectively is generating an automatic reminder email to follow up individually with those who have not yet completed it a day before the deadline.

Conduct a Tech Check

To mitigate and alleviate initial caution when learners are new to a platform, you might consider scheduling a tech check a few days or a week before the session. I conduct these one-on-ones with learners if I know I'm teaching employees who are new to a specific platform. They leave the tech check knowing how to do it and have the confidence they can do it again (for example, they have confirmed their platform access, functioning audio, functioning camera, and their ability to successfully view and interact with the interface). I usually plan 10-minute slots during a drop-in window of time. The benefit of a one-on-one tech check is that it not only alleviates stress about the technology issues and allows you time to resolve issues well before class begins, but also you are afforded the opportunity to get to know your learners more intimately.

Minimize Distractions

Just as you can create a welcoming in-person environment conducive to the type of interaction you hope to have, you can also create a welcoming online environment by reducing distractions and handling interruptions well. Intermediate and advanced facilitators do what they can to minimize interruptions and distractions for their learners throughout virtual training. Some preventive measures you can take with learners include pre-class messages encouraging them to find an area free from distraction or noise, and reminders when you go over netiquette at the outset of virtual training to close applications, turn off phone notifications, and find a quiet space.

But what about when interruptions occur during virtual training? If there's feedback in the audio or you hear people talking in the background or dogs barking, you want to address that right away. If it's allowed to continue, your learners will be distracted by it. You can ask your producer through private chat to find the person with their mic on and have them muted; if you have a seasoned producer, they may be on top of that already without you asking. As the facilitator, you could also calmly and politely say, "We're getting some audio background noise. Again, we appreciate you muting your line as a courtesy to colleagues when you're not speaking. Thanks, everyone."

Learners can also be inwardly distracted. You can address this by acknowledging where they've been and then refocus them to be present. For example, you might say, "You may have just come from a meeting where your deadline was moved up or you just got off a video call that added items to your to-do list. But let's set that all aside for now, and you can pick it up again after this class. Right now, let's turn our attention to this moment and be present here for the next 90 minutes together. I encourage you to make the most of it. This professional development time is for you."

PRO TIP 14
Proactively minimize potential distractions and interruptions to promote learning.

Opening Live Sessions With Enthusiasm and Personalization

The opening of a virtual training session is where the tone is set and the environment begins to take shape. Therefore, it's important to take several steps on the front-end to do this well. For example, to effectively shape a learning environment, you should open and lead with upbeat, positive enthusiasm. This effervescence can create a communal space that learners want to be a part of, instead of run from.

Additionally, when you open a virtual training session, remember to always explain why the training is needed. As cognitive psychologist Clark Quinn (2021) notes, "We should introduce the audience to what they'll learn, touching on why they should care, and what it will provide for them. Opening up learners emotionally is an investment in the retention of learning." By touching on the WIIFM (what's in it for me?), we trigger intrinsic motivation for learners to be more present in the experience. Once they know why they should care and how a training program might benefit them, this influences their motivation to be attentive. It also serves us well to remember to engage learners with all four core dimensions of learning (in addition to emotion as part of learner motivation).

Moreover, our goal is to move learners from the cautious stage to the contributing stage as soon as possible. To do this, there are different techniques we can use when we greet participants, provide a brief platform tour, clarify netiquette, include to-the-point introductions, and elicit learner participation from the outset. Let's explore these next.

Greet Participants With Enthusiasm

Developing capability in environment shaping helps you be mindful of the little things you can do to create a positive environment. One of those little things is projecting the energy that you want your learners to also demonstrate. Enthusiasm has always been a hallmark of great teachers, educators, and trainers. Energy is contagious, and whether it's negative or positive, it can trickle down easily to learners.

For example, a virtual facilitator who begins a session frustrated and upset about a technical issue that just happened can unintentionally poison the energy of what could have otherwise been a positive environment. Contrast this with a facilitator who begins virtual sessions with passion and enthusiasm for the topic. Best-in-class online facilitators are genuinely excited about the training topic (for some topics, we need to dig deep and find the "nugget"), as this also helps with the emotional dimension of learning to spark the same feelings in virtual learners.

Remember, too, that energy takes a hit online. Work to project twice the level of passion, energy, and enthusiasm you would normally have because of what can be lost through the electronic transmission. As one of my colleagues in the field put it best, if the trainer is not excited, why should the learners be?

Use Learners' Names Often

One of the best ways to engage learners with enthusiasm is to greet them by name as they first log in. Although it's generally not feasible to do this for every learner entry, you can still do it intermittently or by greeting them in batches. Your producer may also do this for you while you attend to last-minute review of your notes or prep. For example, every few minutes you could greet different individuals you see joining, saying "Good morning, Krister, Claudia, and Ji-Ho. Great to have you with us! We'll get started here in just a few minutes." Or "Welcome everyone! I see Naomi and Ahmed just joined us, good morning, good afternoon, and good evening wherever you are in the world. We'll begin in just about five minutes."

Speaking learners' first names aloud is effective because most people have been responding to their names since birth, and it becomes a deeply ingrained response. So, when we hear our first name called, we immediately sit up a little straighter and give the speaker our full attention. This personalization is a level of customization that is easy to do and makes it feel like you're talking directly to participants—a personal and memorable touch!

Incorporate Learners' Names Into Examples

You can also offer customized examples in your training topics and insert some of your participants' names into these examples for added focus. So if you were training on negotiation skills, you might say "One of our key concepts is to recognize that when the person with whom I'm negotiating says no, it is not the end of the conversation, it is only the beginning. For example, let's assume Austin and Travis are having this discussion, and Travis says no. So, Austin digs deeper by asking probing questions to uncover what the core premise is underneath Travis's no response. Once Austin understands Travis's objection, he can figure out a way to address the concern, and from there, work toward a compromise." In this example, Austin and Travis are listening intently because they have been woven into the content, as are the other participants because they're listening to see if their names will be used too.

 PRO TIP 15
Build connection with personalization, calling learners by their first names throughout and weaving their names into customized examples to grab learner attention.

Display Welcoming Messages

Welcoming learners while you're on camera is an effective way to convey enthusiasm. By being on camera, you'll find that others are more likely to turn on their cameras too. This means you would not project any slides but greet participants on camera to establish relationships instead. At the close of your session, you can come back on camera as you bid farewell to all. This serves as a nice bookend for kickoff and closing out the virtual training.

Another technique is to include a welcoming title slide. This slide, with correct title of program, again helps assure learners they are in the right place and accelerates them out of the cautious zone.

Additionally, you can post a welcome message in chat before learners arrive. This way, they'll see it when they first log in. At SkillPath, when we trained in virtual sessions, we always posted a welcoming message to participants in chat on the various platforms. We were also trained to change the color of our text in chat, so the facilitator text would pop out for learners, which is something we used a lot in Adobe Connect. However, depending on your platform this could have adverse effects. In Adobe Connect, Zoom, and other platforms, I'm used to typing in my welcome in chat 30 minutes beforehand as I get set up. One time when I used Microsoft Teams, however, I typed a welcome in the chat so it would be ready to go when learners arrived. But, connected through Teams' chat, my learners received the message in real time, and I received several messages back along the lines of, "I thought we were starting at 10 a.m." or, "Did the training get moved up to 9:30?" Oops! I learned to not send my message early in some platforms. I chatted back letting them know they could disregard the message I was prepping for setup, and that they were correct about the start time.

Acknowledge International Attendees

If you know you have attendees from several countries or a mix of time zones, acknowledge this to all. Remember, learners want to be seen. If they're joining in the middle of the night, they also often wish to share this extra effort with everyone. For example, you might hear them say "Very early morning here in XXX" or "Joining after hours from XXX." So, when you begin, you might say something like, "Good morning, good afternoon, and good evening wherever you are in the world."

Novice virtual trainers often focus solely on their own location. For example, they might say, "It's raining and cloudy where I am." But the training session is not about us. Better to say, "Let me know in chat what the weather is doing where you are. It's raining here. Ahh, warm and sunny in Florida, but rainy and cold in Seattle, and dark, cold, and the middle of the night for . . ." You can briefly acknowledge what the weather is where you are as an example, but then shine the spotlight back on your participants. This is a way to strategically break the ice and can be used as another tactic to help learners move from *cautious* to *contribute* on the 5 Cs Pyramid.

The environment shaping capability also includes being respectful of all cultures. For international, cross-cultural classes, you should thoughtfully weigh the start times of the sessions to best accommodate learners, varying the start time if it's a recurring class or finding the best alternate times to hold live class by collecting input from some of the actual learners.

When I've taught international sessions, I've sometimes taken a night shift if it meant the class would take place during daytime for the attendees.

Take Learners on a Brief Platform Tour

Establishing where everything is located on a platform and how to find it is important to always include at the start of a virtual training session. Once learners establish where everything is, and it becomes more automated for them, their working memory is freed up to focus on the content instead of where that button is. To incorporate the doing aspect of the behavioral dimension of learning, it's great to have them do a fun, easy warm-up using that feature or tool while you talk about it. For example, the brief tour might remind them where chat is and ask them to type what time they woke up that morning as a fun warm-up. Then show them where the hand-raising feature is and have them practice lowering and raising their hands. You can also remind them how to mute themselves and turn on their cameras, and where to locate their annotation toolbar.

Although I always recommend a brief platform tour at the outset, I also recommend reminding learners again right before you ask them to use a feature or tool (if it's more complicated to find). Repetition, repetition, repetition. For example, when you ask them to use their annotation toolbar while you're presenting slides or bring up a whiteboard, remind them where they can locate that feature.

Note that part of this task is to acknowledge that tools may be in a different location than other platforms they've used before, or they may even appear different than yours because you are logged in as host or organizer. Thus, it's always helpful to have a separate monitor where you are also logged in as a participant, in addition to your host login. For example, in Zoom, for participants to annotate a slide while the facilitator is screen sharing, participants need to click View Options in the menu at the top of the Zoom window to see the Annotate option. However, for facilitators, when you're screen sharing, you can click Annotate in the Floating Controls Toolbar, which then opens the annotation toolbar for you. In addition, a second monitor can help you observe firsthand any delays for learners as you advance slides. I remember using a platform years ago where there was a two-second delay after I switched my slides before learners saw what I was seeing. So, back then I had to remind myself to count "one-one thousand, two-one thousand" in my head before I started talking about the slide after I advanced it.

Establish Netiquette Guidelines

Some call them ground rules; others call them housekeeping items. I prefer to call them *netiquette*, a portmanteau of *internet* and *etiquette*. We use these to establish expectations for respectful interactions and how we agree to be together in the shared, virtual space. Although some guidelines should also be communicated in the pre-session messaging, you can reinforce them as you open the virtual training session.

Setting expectations like clarifying netiquette, how to minimize distractions, and how to communicate with learners and the trainer also have ties to improved performance outcomes. According to a 2021 ATD research report on virtual training, "Nearly all expectation-setting practices for learners identified for the research had significant connections to better organizational performance." For example, muting is important unless speaking if you have a larger group of learners who are in noisy environments. However, if you have eight or fewer learners and they are in relatively quiet locations, you might want to ask them to not mute. The reason for this is because muting can kill conversation since the need to unmute creates a tiny bit of friction before participating. Removing that friction can aid in fostering richer, more fluid, and deeper discussions.

Some items to include on a netiquette slide are:
- "We want to hear from everyone. This is your class. Be prepared to fully participate."
- "Please mute if there is distracting noise in your background."
- "Be respectful of each other's comments, suggestions, insights, and questions. We value inclusivity."
- "Make sure you are in an environment free of distraction. Close your door, minimize any applications on your device, set your phone to vibrate, close your email, and so on."
- "Ask lots of questions—there are no right or wrong questions today."

- "Chat will be available during most of our virtual training session. We will be turning it off during focus sections. Please keep your typed responses to a few phrases or words in chat instead of multiple sentences to ensure scannable viewing for all."
- "Let our producer know in the technical chat pod if you have any technical issues."

In your netiquette guidelines, you might also recommend learners hide their self-view on camera after they've appropriately adjusted themselves in the camera frame, and offer the steps to do so. I recommend people learn how to hide their self-view because it can become a distraction. According to Harvard Business School professor Amy Edmondson and leadership consultant Gene Daley, "Seeing oneself on the screen can heighten self-consciousness, inhibiting psychological safety. Selecting 'hide self-view' can help" (Edmondson and Daley 2020). Since people are generally drawn to looking at themselves when they talk, like they're looking in a mirror, they won't be focusing on the other learners or the facilitator. You'll even notice some people adjusting their hair as they look at their reflected image. Because of this popular tendency, Microsoft Teams has even moved the live camera of oneself on the platform away from the images of everyone else. This is one way to direct more attention to everyone else's photos and live video.

You want to establish netiquette boundaries in three ways: visually, verbally, and behaviorally. These parameters guide how learners agree to meet in this space going forward. It's also helpful to display a slide that has pictorial representations with some reminder text to illustrate what the guidelines are. These reminders are also reinforced by the facilitator and producer as leaders of the live event.

Clarifying netiquette behaviorally means that learners must be called out right away if any of the rules are not upheld. For example, if you have a group of 20 and have asked them to mute, but you hear background noise that continues for several seconds, you can look at the participant panel to see who has their mic on, ask if there's anything they would like to contribute, and then ask them politely to mute in accordance with the agreed-upon netiquette. When there is immediate follow-up, learners quickly grasp that these guidelines are being enforced, which encourages greater cooperation.

You might also direct them to close their email, turn off email notifications, close applications they won't be using, silence their mobile devices, or even remove their mobile devices from the immediate area unless you'll be using them during class. And as is the case with all adult learners, always explain why. Adults need the rationale. Let them know research has found that processing takes a hit when we are task switching, and we are unable to process as deeply. Additionally, closing applications that are not needed for class conserves their bandwidth. Another important and often forgotten piece of behavior reinforcement is expert modeling. Facilitators should model good netiquette by ensuring there is no distracting audio in the background, making sure your live video is professional and you are on camera for important interactions, being respectful in words and actions when others offer comments, and welcoming all training-related questions whether they be major or minor.

 PRO TIP 16
Communicate netiquette expectations at the outset and reinforce them throughout if needed.

Use Get-to-the-Point Introductions

Another common error for virtual trainers is the temptation to provide a lengthy introduction about themselves. Bottom line: Learners don't care about these details. Yes, it's important to establish credibility as a trainer and to combat distractions and multitasking. However, when a facilitator introduction turns into extensive background information, related degrees, the history of whatever, and the why behind the why, it can quickly escalate to a snooze fest.

As a best practice, keep your on-camera intro brief and to-the-point. Brevity is always better. Your producer may even introduce you or your customer or the manager of the employees with whom you're training. If not, go ahead and introduce yourself.

Regarding participant introductions, keep these brief as well, so you don't spend half an hour on introductions when the class is only 90 minutes.

That's a third of live class time! Instead try intros in small group breakouts or via chat by having learners share their name, their role in their organization, and another item related to the training topic. You might also address this through whiteboard activities.

Elicit Learner Participation From the Outset

When learners first log in to a virtual training, they arrive from a variety of different states and activities (some just finished a meeting, others just presented to a board, others were working independently on some writing, and so on). As we will explore further in the next chapter, to make the most out of the learning experience, participants need to move from their current resting, passive state to an active, engaged state. They need help fighting the inertia of sitting back and not getting involved.

The key is to never allow learners to remain in this passive sit-and-get state, because it becomes increasingly difficult to transition them out of it. Instead, we want to involve them from the very beginning. For example, when learners first join you might give them something to do, such as introduce themselves in the chat. Alternatively, you might display a looping slideshow that includes information about the facilitator, expectations for the course, some of the platform tools you'll be using, and an assignment like answering a trivia question. It's always more impactful if your trivia question can tie into your training topic as well.

When there is not a lot of change or movement, learners can also habituate to the environment and begin to pay less attention, which we will discuss further in chapter 8. In this state of lowered attentiveness, they are not giving their full attention to the information. For this reason, we want to be talking with them, calling on them, using their names in examples, demonstrating things, and actively having them do something.

However, there is a fine line; be careful not to include too many actions for learners when they first log in and as they are waiting for class to begin, which can overload learners. Remember they're acclimating through the 5 Cs, and having to take on multiple tasks right away might cause them to remain in the cautious stage. Assigning one clear task is acceptable, but a class of novice virtual learners, for example, should not be tasked with six things to do when they first log in.

Up to this point in the chapter we've covered strategies for laying out the welcome mat and opening with enthusiasm. To ensure learners feel comfortable with the environment you're shaping and with you the facilitator and their fellow learners, we can draw on findings for what makes teams click. Google set out to find what makes the most effective teams in an experiment called Project Aristotle. Over several years, after analyzing more than 180 teams, researchers determined five key characteristics of effective teams, and top of the list was psychological safety (Burnison 2019). Let's examine this now.

 PRO TIP 17
Include brief, to-the-point introductions for initial connection through chat, breakouts, whiteboard activities, or even verbal introductions when class size is small.

Cultivating Psychological Safety

In 1999, organizational behavioral scientist and professor Amy Edmondson coined the term *psychological safety*. According to Edmondson (2019), "Psychological safety describes a climate where people feel safe enough to take interpersonal risks by speaking up and sharing concerns, questions, or ideas." A psychologically safe environment is one where everyone believes they won't be punished or embarrassed for taking risks around others. In other words, they feel safe to admit a mistake, entertain productive disagreement, ask for help, generate ideas, or share a critical comment for the sake of improvement and productivity. I have high standards for virtual trainers, and one of them is digging deep and caring. The popular axiom is true: People don't care what you know until they know that you care.

Edmondson is also quick to point out that psychological safety does not necessarily mean squelching conflict. Learners need to know they are in a safe space to share. The opposite of psychological safety would be a learning environment where there was fear about looking bad, anxiety about perfection, fear of admitting mistakes, blame-setting when things go wrong, conformity in viewpoints, and even group-think because respectful dissident voices are not expressed.

Cultivating psychological safety could start with establishing very clear expectations for how people will behave in the virtual training environment. For example, at the outset of training, you might say something like,

> I realize most people strive to look good in front of other people, including our managers and colleagues. But in this learning space, the biggest growth comes from making mistakes. We learn the most when we make them, and they help us improve. You are not here to impress me. You're here to learn. So, for the sake of your own professional development, speak up when you have an insight, speak up when you need help, and speak up when you have an idea to share. It's up to all of us to embrace everyone's contributions with interest and respect. We are all here for the same purpose—to learn. So let's share this journey together and make it a safe space for everyone.

This could also mean weighing leadership's attendance in the virtual training carefully. If a senior leader, director, or manager wishes to join, it might be better for them to share how the training ties into their strategic objectives at the opening but then leave as the training moves on. Sometimes people are uncomfortable speaking and sharing freely if their supervisors are present. You can always circle back to leadership after the virtual training has ended.

Cultivating an environment where learners are not afraid of being embarrassed, judged, criticized, or singled out is an important component of establishing a productive virtual learning environment. And it is an ongoing process. As Britt Andreatta (2018) explains, "Be aware that your words and actions have an impact on others. Think about how you create psychological safety for others and how you earn their trust. These moments are easily harmed by unintentional insensitivity that does more damage than many people realize."

Encourage Different Perspectives

How can we cultivate psychological safety in virtual training? Through our words, tone, and behavior. We want to lead the effort to create a space where we explicitly set the expectation that we want to hear from all voices and that all voices matter. We set the stage for this in writing, with our netiquette slide at the beginning; we reinforce this by saying it verbally; and when learners contribute comments, we always affirm and appreciate their efforts, demonstrating this principle with our behavior. We must not ignore comments or cut people off or dismiss a comment as irrelevant. Instead, we must listen intently to what they say and follow-up or even dig deeper into their comments to learn more and recognize their contributions. Edmonson (2020) even recommends using open-ended questions like "What are we missing?" "Who has a different perspective?" or "What might happen if . . . ?" These questions positively encourage different perspectives in a healthy way. This is because "disagreement and dissent are signs of healthy conflict" (Edmondson 2020). Other questions I've used in virtual training classes include "What might be an example of this?" "Tell me more," and "Help me understand why . . . "

Leverage Virtual Tools to Foster Psychological Safety

There are specific virtual training platform tools you can use to support psychological safety, which we'll explore in greater depth in chapter 7. For now, you can strategically use features like small breakout groups or anonymous tools to break the ice and provide a safer space to open up at first.

Learners feel more comfortable sharing in a smaller group and are more likely to voice ideas that can later be raised to the group at large during the debriefing. These ideas otherwise might go unspoken in the large group dynamic because in a larger the group, there is a smaller percentage of active participants. With smaller groups, we are more likely to hear from everyone. Working on specific assignments in small groups provides a psychologically safe space to build relationships and test out ideas first, which makes it easier for participants to share later with a large group (Edmondson and Daley 2020).

You can also leverage anonymous tools to support psychological safety. For example, I have observed that my learners participate more when we use the whiteboard if it is anonymous. I remind them of this out loud as well. Contrast this with chat and raising your virtual hand or talking out loud, where everyone can see who said and did what. (Note that many platforms, like Zoom, now reveal your names when you use the whiteboard, so turn off this feature is you want to leverage anonymity.)

Other anonymous tools include polling. Polling can be leveraged to read the room or take the temperature on a topic among learners. Afterward, people are more likely to speak up to support why they voted the way they did once they see where they range in terms of the majority and minority. There are fewer unknown variables once the poll results are broadcast, so it feels like a safer space to share why you voted how you did depending on how the group at-large voted and whether you were an outlier. As Amy Edmondson and Gene Daley (2020) report, "Anonymous polls make it easy to express an opinion without fear of being singled out."

Model Vulnerability

Mistakes and failures are how we learn. Yet we have been conditioned by some of our cultures to always look good in front of others and especially those in higher positions of authority, such as an instructor. As virtual facilitators we are leaders and we need to set the tone that vulnerability is OK. As Britt Andreatta (2018) articulates, we need to model the characteristics that help shape psychological safety by "proactively inviting input through questions that broaden and deepen the discussion . . . Celebrate failures as learning."

One way is to use vulnerable phrases that you then hope learners will reciprocate. A facilitator might say, "I need your help," or "I've listed some that I could think of on this slide, but what other ones can you think of? I'd love to hear your input," or "I want to hear about your biggest challenges when you . . ." This way, virtual facilitators model the tough topics and demonstrate they can be talked about. Learners, in turn, mirror that behavior.

Whether a virtual training session feels rewarding or punitive ultimately influences whether learners participate and how they interact with each other and with their facilitator. Think about a meeting where a dictatorial boss openly chastises or threatens to fire anyone who disagrees with their ideas. This hostile work environment inspires dysfunction because it creates a punitive environment for employees who share real ideas, and they are only rewarded for compliance. Although this example is harsh, it also illustrates the power of the leader. As leaders in virtual training, the facilitator and producer must own and share the responsibility of ensuring participants feel welcomed, at ease, psychologically safe, and valued in virtual training sessions.

PRO TIP 18
Cultivate psychological safety during virtual training by creating a safe space for learners to take interpersonal risks and make mistakes without fear of criticism, shame, or embarrassment from the facilitator or other learners.

Affirm and Reward Learners: "I See You—I Want to Hear From You"

In addition to asking probing, open-ended questions, we also want to affirm learners' contributions. Media mogul Oprah Winfrey has shared many times through various media that after 25 years of interviewing thousands of people on the *Oprah Winfrey Show*, there was one important takeaway that stood out from everything else: Everyone has a need to be seen and heard; in essence, we all matter because we do. This principle resonates deeply with me as a virtual trainer and facilitator. Our learners want to be seen and heard too. We have discussed welcoming learners, calling out their responses when they are on target, seeing them as individuals, and facilitating learner-to-learner and learner-to-facilitator connections, but we also want to recognize their contributions—the last C in the 5 Cs Pyramid.

How do we recognize learners' contributions? By what we pay attention to and what we say and do. If learners say something out loud and we say nothing afterward, they will likely not speak again. Even a "Yeah," "That's right," "You're on the right track," or "Couldn't have said it better myself" are verbal confirmations for affirmation and reward. Learners look to you as the authority in the virtual space and on the subject matter. It is rewarding when you authentically compliment them. As facilitators, we can elevate learners' self-esteem and confidence to become their best selves (Biech 2017). Nonverbal communication can also go a long way to show affirmation. For example, when learners see their facilitator smiling (or other people smiling at them), it is rewarding to the brain. As you engage in discussions with them, make sure you genuinely provide a compliment when warranted (such as "That's a really great point," "Well said," or "Excellent work").

You can also work to build on learners' contributions as a way of affirming them verbally. This demonstrates that their comment was insightful enough to spend a bit more time on it; for example, "Let's see if we can build on that; Joe what do you think," "Where could we take that from here?" or "That's a really interesting point. Tell me more about how you think that might work?" Ensuring your verbal tone demonstrates how pleased you are when learners demonstrate a new skill or knowledge in what you're training is rewarding too.

If you provide affirmation and rewards as learners begin to contribute, you will see their participation grow. However, it might not always be prudent to call out every single contribution, such as in the chat. A novice facilitator might say, "The chat is blowing up. People seem to have lots of questions about this," and then proceed to read every comment aloud verbatim. Intermediate facilitators, on the other hand, can be mindful of how to leverage these contributions in a way that doesn't overload participants or take too long. Remember, chat responses are visible for all to read in the session. You can sort through the chat strategically and highlight a few that are on target or that you wish to comment on later. You will experience some cognitive overload as a facilitator at some point because you are advancing slides, speaking, watching chat, reading chat, and deciding to highlight a few—all at the same time. If this becomes too much for you, enlist the help of your producer. For example, you might say "Cheryl, what are some of the posts we're seeing in chat so far?"

It's always helpful to learners when you affirm their contributions and participation aloud, but don't overdo it. What gets rewarded, gets repeated.

Summary

Overall, our goal is to cultivate a welcoming environment where all learners feel seen, heard, supported, valued, and respected. As author Elaine Biech (2017) writes, "Create a learning environment of trust and respect." To build a trusting environment, it is up to the facilitator to be authentic, genuine, and a present listener; to be respectful in comments, have your learners' best interest at heart, and care about their journeys; and to model mutual respect. Ultimately, you shape the environment that influences the virtual learners' experiences.

As we have explored, there are many strategies you can use to create a respectful online environment. These environments become the wrapper that influences everything that happens within. By laying out a welcome mat in a variety of ways pre-session, leading the sessions with enthusiasm and personalization, and nurturing psychological safety, you can cultivate a successful learning environment. This way learners are comfortable sharing and contributing without fear of being judged or embarrassed.

Not only is it important to build a supportive learning environment, you also need to be expertly skilled in virtual facilitation. This is because virtual learning environments require an expanded skill set from traditional classroom facilitation. In the next chapter, we'll uncover the secrets to successful online facilitation!

Pro Tips for Practicing Your Environment Shaping Skills

TIP 10	Build community with connecting activities (even brief ones) to foster social learning and help learners discover commonality with one another.
TIP 11	Reference the 5 Cs Pyramid to guide your empathic responses to virtual learners as they first acclimate.
TIP 12	Welcome participants via multiple touchpoints in multiple ways.
TIP 13	Continually incentivize and reward active participation from learners.
TIP 14	Proactively minimize potential distractions and interruptions to promote learning.
TIP 15	Build connection with personalization, calling learners by their first names throughout and weaving their names into customized examples to grab learner attention.
TIP 16	Communicate netiquette expectations at the outset and reinforce them throughout if needed.
TIP 17	Include brief, to-the-point introductions for initial connection through chat, breakouts, whiteboard activities, or even verbal introductions when class size is small.
TIP 18	Cultivate psychological safety during virtual training by creating a safe space for learners to take interpersonal risks and make mistakes without fear of criticism, shame, or embarrassment from the facilitator or other learners.

"Eventually, an experienced virtual facilitator can gather feedback from an audience and get a sense of the 'pulse' of the room with as much accuracy as most classroom facilitators."

—Darlene Christopher, author, *The Successful Virtual Classroom*

CHAPTER 4

Applying the Secrets of Effective Online Facilitation

A seasoned technical trainer in the medical field was participating in one of my Train-the-Virtual-Trainer classes to further develop her facilitation skills. Although a very experienced in-person trainer, she was new to virtual training. As one of the assignments for this class, participants were required to select a training topic from their profession and facilitate a teach-back via a virtual training platform. Participants were also required to incorporate a few virtual tools into their learning activity, and be prepared to explain their rationale for why those tools supported their learning objectives. After finishing her teach-back to a small group of mock learners, I asked, "How did that go for you?" Her reply was telling. She let out an exhausted sigh and said, "There's a lot going on."

Indeed, virtual facilitation has many moving parts, and perhaps one of the biggest challenges to doing it well is managing everything all at once. Her honest assessment highlights the inherent complexity, even for the seasoned practitioner. Online facilitation can be a perfect storm of managing technical surprises, virtual tools, learner participation, instructional content, and more. The online format has a different feel, interpersonal dynamic, less available sensory input, and many more distractions. There is no denying that to keep things running smoothly, facilitators in online synchronous environments require a high level of knowledge and skill—and, ideally, a producer to assist you, which we will discuss later in this chapter.

The good news is virtual facilitation is a skill. Because of this, you can improve both your proficiency and comfort level through rehearsal and repetition. Even time spent shadowing a seasoned facilitator as a mentor or coach can be invaluable. Over time, you can become adept at managing the moving parts. The more experience you gain, the more automated some of the facilitation and engagement tasks become. And the more automated some tasks become, the easier it is to manage the different elements.

When I was helping teach a teenager in our family how to drive, I thought I was being helpful by pointing out things while they drove. For example, I suggested when to apply the brakes, where to come to a full stop at an intersection, and how to pass cars parked along the roadside. By the time we fully stopped at an intersection, the learning driver's comment to me was "I didn't hear a word you said." In that moment, I was reminded that new skills as demanding as driving require a novice's complete mental attention. Here the pupil became my teacher. Going forward, I offered verbal comments only when we were pulled over or parked. Eventually, as their driving proficiency improved, I observed some of those tasks becoming more automated. This allowed for more verbal conversation and processing while driving, which only continued to grow with experience.

This story offers valuable lessons for virtual facilitation as well. For novice facilitators, this role can require all your energy and full attention. You can easily experience cognitive overload and be overwhelmed by the sheer number of concurrent activities to manage. However, the more familiar you become with managing the platform, tools, and tasks through preparation, repetition, and experience, some of these tasks— like remembering to frequently scan chat throughout the session—will become more automated.

Fortunately, you can carry over some of your in-person facilitation skills too. For example, online facilitators still need to ask good questions to gauge where a group is, dig deeper with follow-up prompts when learners share, ensure everyone has the opportunity to contribute, and provide clear transitions between sub-topics. However, there are also skills unique to virtual facilitation. As virtual training expert Jennifer Hofmann (2019) affirms, "Even seasoned traditional classroom facilitators need to build their skills to be successful in the virtual classroom. Your new skill set will include new tricks that build upon your existing facilitation toolset." These special skills are the focus of this chapter.

When I ask clients what they most want to learn about live online learning, the most common response is, "How can I engage virtual participants?" Naturally, this is very important, but we also need to remember that there is a marketable difference between *learners clicking for the sake of clicking* and *engagement*. It is not physical busyness like learners voting in frequent polls. Engagement means learners are actively investing themselves both emotionally and mentally in what they are doing. Ruth Clark (2020) notes that "engagement is essential, but it is psychological engagement rather than physical engagement that counts." To aid learning, we want learners deeply invested emotionally and cognitively. To expand this concept further, we strive to engage learners with all four learning dimensions as discussed in chapter 2; that is, cognitively, emotionally, socially, and behaviorally. And because we design learning experiences, we also lead them as learning experience facilitators.

One of the best ways to deeply engage participants throughout virtual training is to guide them to be co-creators of their own learning. To do this, we need to fully develop our capability in the area of online facilitation. Let's explore the secrets to effective online facilitation now, so you can facilitate your virtual sessions with aplomb.

THE BIG IDEA
Skilled virtual facilitators guide learners to be co-creators of their own learning.

Navigating the Black Hole

When the telephone was first patented in 1876, the technology was so new that when the phone rang and people answered, nobody said anything. There was only silence on both ends. With all visual cues removed, it is possible they just didn't know what to say, or, more importantly, when to say it. Hard to imagine, right? This seems humorous now, because answering a phone and saying hello is so automatic. And, of course, we now have advanced technology that lets us know exactly who is calling. Back then, however, it must have felt a bit like being in a black hole.

It was Thomas Edison who eventually urged people to say "hello" when answering a telephone, which was the first time this word became equivalent to "hi" (Krulwich 2011). This way both parties knew when the conversation should begin. Scottish-born inventor Alexander Graham Bell—Edison's rival—patented the first working telephone and thought people should say "ahoy" when answering instead (Krulwich 2011). Ironically, Bell refused telephone installation in his own study because he felt it was an intrusion from the outside world and would distract him from his professional work (MacLeod 1999). Flash forward to our modern era where telephony and electronic voice transmission are integral to professional work. If only Edison and Bell could observe the world at work today!

If we apply this black hole metaphor to live online training, there are certainly times when learners might feel like they are in a bit of a black hole. This is especially true when facilitators and co-participants are not on camera. With only audio cues and a visible onscreen platform, learners lack sensory cues to which we are normally accustomed. In physical environments, we rely on these cues to help us fully interpret our surroundings. So, there are specific techniques you can apply to help learners adjust to the virtual classroom. In this chapter we'll look at five techniques to aid learning:

1. Verbalize the unseen.
2. Leverage announced silence.
3. Wait before filling uncomfortable silences.
4. Apply the pausing principle.
5. Employ the testing effect.

Verbalize the Unseen
In traditional classroom training, longer periods of unexpected silence are acceptable because they can still be visually understood and interpreted by physically present learners. For example, in-room participants see for themselves what is happening as a facilitator searches for supplies in the front of the room, switches from slides to video, troubleshoots a laser pointer, or pauses to connect to a SMART Board. However, in virtual training facilitators may not realize when they inadvertently create periods of unannounced, extended silence when no one can see what they're doing.

Without access to visual cues online, learners do not know what is happening. If there are unannounced pregnant pauses, they may wonder if they lost audio, the facilitator's audio dropped, the facilitator accidentally muted themselves, something is wrong with the connection, or the platform is experiencing technical issues. The reality is the facilitator may simply be performing an unseen task. For example, they might be glancing at the LMS roster to compare names with everyone listed in the participant panel, or trying to locate a second PowerPoint deck that wasn't where they thought it was, or relocating chat because it was undocked and disappeared when they closed something else.

Not knowing what is happening or why it is taking so long not only interrupts the flow and cadence but calls attention away from content. In some cases, it can even create learner anxiety. As facilitators, we need to minimize anxiety to support learning. According to educational neuroscientist Janet Zadina (2014), "Anxiety has a negative impact on thinking and higher-order executive functions . . . we must take measures to reduce anxiety." When individuals become anxious or their fight-or-flight response is triggered, blood and resources are diverted away from the brain to extremities like hands and feet. This equips people to fight (hands) and run away from danger (feet). So, the ability to think well, make decisions, and acquire new knowledge takes a hit for a higher purpose—survival. Clearly, virtual classes are not dangerous or life threatening, but our body's physiological reaction to stress is the same and can trigger panic and anxiety. The bottom line is that anxiety and learning do not mix, and feeling like you're in a black hole does not help. So, what can facilitators do?

One technique is to verbalize what learners cannot see. I call this "talking your task." This means commenting aloud during pregnant pauses to briefly explain the reason. Do this when you need to attend to something that takes longer than it should. Here are a few examples of talking your task:

- "OK, I'm bringing up the PDF here."
- "Just one moment please, while I open the whiteboard for us. You'll see it shortly."
- "I'm switching over to my next slide deck. Please go ahead and read the scenario on page 12 of your digital participant guide and then we'll take a look at the slides for this next section."

- "I just had a window close on me. It'll be just one moment here while I bring this back. Appreciate your patience."
- "Let's clear these annotations before we move on . . . there we are."

Making the invisible audible with professionalism and brevity keeps learners connected and informed. These auditory cues replace lost visual cues. Most importantly, when you talk your task learners are not left in the lurch wondering whether something went wrong. You can liken this to when you schedule a medical appointment via phone that is not a video call. If you call and request a preferred date for a medical appointment with a receptionist, but only hear silence, you wonder if the scheduler even heard you. If, however, the receptionist says, "I really appreciate your patience. Our system is running a bit slower today . . . after all, it's Monday! It'll be just another minute please," you'll settle in knowing all is well. The reason is because now you are informed. You received verbal confirmation as a replacement for the absence of visual confirmation. As facilitators, we want to do the same for our learners at key junctures.

We may not think to narrate through the silence, because we know what is happening. It's easy to get locked into our own insular perspective. However, in these unseen moments, learners may not understand what is happening, what just happened, or what is about to happen. They are left to wait and wonder, and perhaps even become anxious or think something went wrong. It's important to note this absolutely does not mean to share everything ad nauseam. Some things are best kept behind the curtain. However, you can provide just enough to give the rationale for the current silence and to assure them all is well. Intermediate and advanced-level facilitators lead the effort to professionally verbalize what participants cannot see. As part of our job, we bring them along every step of the way.

 PRO TIP 19
Make the invisible audible by talking your task.

Let's examine another technique that is part of verbalizing the unseen. This strategic practice can be used to influence learners when we need to persuade them to do something different or take new action in their workplace. In this technique, facilitators speculate what learners' objections might be, acknowledge those objections aloud, and then address them. The key is to bring up those potential objections at the time you think learners might be thinking them. From there, you address the concern. An example of this might be if you said, "Some of you are probably wondering how this new project management system we're learning to use today is going to make the process more efficient." Although you cannot hear learners' thoughts—except for what they share in chat—you can still guess what their objections, reactions, or questions might be.

Say, for example, you are training leaders virtually on different types of behavioral styles. You explain that they will be assessing the behavioral styles of their direct reports, so they can adapt their own styles to their employees' preferred styles when they work with them. In this context, let's look at an example where you might explore potential objections. You might say something like, "Now some of you are thinking why should I have to change my preferred style when I work with my direct reports? Isn't that the point of having a variety of styles?" When a facilitator speaks aloud what a learner was just thinking, it can immediately grab their attention. Next, you move ahead to address their concern. You might say, "Those are legitimate questions. As leaders, it's our job to inspire and bring out the best in our employees. We adapt our style to theirs so we can lead them more effectively."

I use this technique when internal managers or an external client contact lets me know before a virtual training that there may be resistance with a few participants about moving to a new process or embracing change in the workplace. If you acknowledge aloud some potential objections they're thinking, it can be very powerful. This is also an attention-getting technique. There's an element of surprise at play as they wonder how you knew what they were thinking. Guaranteed, they're listening to the next thing you say.

 PRO TIP 20
Acknowledge and address potential learner objections aloud at the time they might be thinking them.

Leverage "Announced Silence" to Aid Learning

If you are familiar with radio broadcasting, you know that silence during a broadcast is called dead air. In the radio industry, dead air is never good.

Some professionals suggest the same is true for virtual training. They advocate virtual facilitators avoid silence at all costs. However, I see this quite differently.

I believe silence can be used to aid learning. In the previous section, we explored how unannounced extended silence is problematic unless we make the invisible audible. Otherwise, learners will be left in the lurch and often automatically assume something is wrong. Let's now look at how announced silence can be leveraged to aid live online learning.

Silence can be used strategically if certain boundaries are in place. For example, participants need to know it's coming, what their task is during the silence, and how long it will last. By providing advance warning about silence, learners are assured everything is OK. Most importantly, you give learners time to think without a competing voice in the background. This way, they can complete reflections or other thinking tasks in quiet. This is what I call "announced silence." It allows space for cognitive processing and can promote deeper learning. You simply need to provide fair warning.

According to cognitive load theory and evidence-based design, it's more effective for trainers to initially reveal a complex visual, pause, and let participants process it. This helps learners create a mental framework that your verbal commentary will fill in later. If you show learners a complex visual, it is important to pause and allow them to briefly digest the visual first before you explain it (Schnotz 2014). Otherwise, it can be too challenging for them to listen to your commentary and study a complicated visual at the same time. It also helps reduce cogitative load. Once you start explaining it, focus first on the visual's structural elements. From there, gradually delve into its more detailed aspects. In this way, you create space for learners to process, focus, and think without the distraction of a facilitator's voice in the background. For example, you might say aloud, "I'll be quiet for the next few minute while you study this diagram. When we come back together, let me know how you think it could be improved by applying the principles we've discussed."

When you ask thoughtful questions for participants to respond to in chat, you also might say, "I'll be silent for a bit here while you think and respond to that question." As the axiom goes, silence can be golden. Intermediate and advanced-level facilitators leverage announced silence with parameters. It's a powerful tool. Use announced silence to promote deeper learning when participants are:

- Actively engaged in thinking about a response (this can be individual prep time before entering a breakout activity)
- Reviewing an assignment's instructions in the participant guide
- Looking at a complex visual for the first time
- Viewing a slide that is more text-heavy that they can read on their own
- Reflecting on something they've learned by typing responses in a digital participant workbook
- Filling out an action plan
- Thinking about a rhetorical or open-ended question you've posed
- Working independently on a task or exercise
- Completing their digital evaluation in class

One of the virtual training programs my company offers is how to design effective visuals for deeper learning. In this class, we explore the pillars of good visual design. When some virtual platforms did not yet support shared whiteboards, we used to show learners an example slide with bulleted content and ask them to complete a real-time drawing assignment to find a more effective way to illustrate the content. By either using a digital pen and tablet or a pen and paper in their remote locations, they drew visuals that more appropriately depicted the sample content. This was an opportunity for learners to individually practice and apply the visual design principles we had just discussed. I asked them to email their drawings using their smartphones or tablets and to let me know whether I had their permission to share a few of them with the rest of the class. During a break, I reviewed them and pulled a few examples to share when the class at large reconvened. This way, we could discuss them and use their work to reinforce key learning points.

To set up this independent drawing exercise, I told them: "I will be silent for several minutes while you work on this. Then we'll come together again and talk about your design process and your rationale for depicting this content differently." It's also important to communicate that if participants have questions while they work, they can privately let you know in chat. The point here is to give them quiet space to think. By giving learners silence to think, reflect, and work, you enhance their ability to practice and apply what they're learning.

Here are some things facilitators can do during silence while participants work independently:

- Keep an eye on chat in case participants have individual questions that come up while they're working.
- Mute yourself to remove any background noise from your environment.
- Review the roster names to pre-select a few participants I've seen demonstrate leadership so far who I think would be a strong facilitator for an upcoming breakout. Before the breakout, I always ask those individuals if they would be willing to lead, and they almost always respond "yes."
- Review notes made on the roster about who made some "golden nugget" comments or insights. I like to do this so it's fresh in my mind and I can tie back to their contributions again later when it makes sense in the content.
- Scroll up and review chat comments from the virtual training session so far.
- Chat privately with your producer about how it's going, if they need anything or if there's anything they need you to know (like they need to leave for a bit and be right back, or if there were any critical questions you missed in the chat).
- Check the time estimates on your facilitator guide to determine if you're behind, ahead, or on schedule. This helps me determine whether I need to take out a section, speed up a little bit, or slow down and take more time.
- Review speaking notes to see if you left out anything critical so far that you could bring in later, and if there's an opportunity to do so with impact.
- Get a drink of water.
- Take a standing break and move around to increase circulation and keep energy levels heightened.

Note, too, that silence should be used judiciously. This is not a technique to overuse as it can weaken its effect. Overall, strategically leverage announced silence for deep-thinking work and be sure to always prepare learners for it ahead of time.

PRO TIP 21
Use announced silence to give learners brief spaces to complete activities or study complex visuals, and communicate beforehand when, why, and how long you'll be silent.

Wait Before Filling Uncomfortable Silences

It's fine to admit feeling uncomfortable during prolonged silences, announced or not. However, when you pose questions and nobody speaks at first, remember it always takes longer for the first person to share. If you wait long enough, someone will usually step up to fill the void. Do your best to hold your tongue (yes, it's a trainer's occupational hazard to fill silence with talking). Or consider placing yourself on mute for the moment.

In the late 1960s, Mary Budd Rowe (1986) discovered an instructional variable referred to as "wait-time." She found that while teachers tended to wait only one second after posing a question to learners, waiting up to five seconds was optimal instead. When educators and virtual trainers apply this wait-time principle, it can transform virtual class discussions because it gives learners increased thinking time and reflection for active learning. Although this study was conducted in-person and with younger learners, it still has application for online adult learners. By simply waiting longer (five to six seconds instead of one to two seconds), we afford learners the opportunity to think, reflect, process, and then respond. Hold your tongue before quickly moving on or answering your own questions aloud. Give learners a bit more time to think and respond.

Apply the Pausing Principle

We've discussed announced silence and the wait-time principle, but what about using pausing in general as an active learning strategy? Strategic pausing is also deep seeded in evidence-based research. It is referred to as the "pausing principle," and has been well documented in educational research since the 1980s (Di Vesta and Smith 1979). What is most important about this active learning strategy is that pressing pause, opens space for learners to think, reflect, and refocus their attention. If you use the right type of pausing activities, you can increase learner engagement and retention. Gail Taylor Rice recommends regularly asking learners to look back at what they've learned and apply it to their specific contexts. For example, a closing pause activity gives learners time to process what they've learned and decide how they will use the content (Rice 2018). At the end of my virtual training classes, I ask learners to pause and identify one takeaway they can apply as a next step based on their role, and then type it anonymously on the whiteboard. This way, they're thinking about it and sharing it with others.

There are a variety of activities and techniques you can use during pauses to enhance learning. One technique is to ask questions during the pause. For example, you can pause to ask learners a difficult, probing question, which allows you to check for understanding. You can also pause to ask learners to think about how they might apply what they just learned or discuss content. Pausing occasionally to ask a question triggers learners to actively think, not tune out. For example, you might say, "Let me know in chat or feel free to come off mute to let us know how you can apply these negotiation skills in your internal customer meetings." Strategically weave in questions where it makes sense to stop and pause to reflect or interject curiosity. This not only creates a space for learners to find ways to relate to the content, but it's also an opportunity to practice recalling the information. Of course, if learners have questions at any time during the session, you want to stop and at least briefly address them, even if you elaborate on it more later, because when they ask the question is when they care most about the answer.

When I train virtually, I prefer to plan for multiple pause points throughout. This is an opportunity to welcome questions, insights, and additional comments. A powerful tool at your disposal here is the open-ended question. As we've discussed, it's far better to lead with open-ended questions than closed-ended questions. For example, you might ask "What questions do you have at this point?" This opens up the field more broadly and keeps the conversation on topic versus asking "Do you have any questions?" A closed-end prompt is limiting and can simply be answered with a yes or no.

In virtual training, you can also build in pauses to do more than just open the floor for questions. Another way to look at the pausing principle is that it can facilitate reflection time for learners to think back about what was discussed. Amusingly, I once attended a virtual session focused on the topic of reflection. The speakers talked about how important it was and how instructors should incorporate reflections into their online training sessions. The irony was that the instructors never initiated an opportunity for all of us to stop and reflect on reflection during the virtual training session on reflection. Easier said than done!

Watch for opportunities after meatier content sections or breakouts to pause and reflect by giving learners writing, thinking, discussion, or debriefing activities. Ideally, these exercises can help wire their neural networks. If learners don't find course content naturally exciting, their body may not signal their brain to be alert and devote their full attention to it. However, as educational neuroscientist Janet Zadina (2014) explains, learners can also wire their brain's neural networks by doing something with the content, such as when learners "think about it, talk about it, read about it, or use it."

Employ the Testing Effect

Another facilitation technique you can use to aid learning is to pause and quiz learners with polling questions. Interestingly, the beneficial effects of incorporating polling questions have more to do with the pausing principle than with the polls. By actively pausing, you create a buffer space for learners to process, review, and recall. It is this underlying method of pausing or stopping that is responsible for aiding learning because learners are thinking deeply.

This active recall to aid learning is called the testing effect. "A wealth of empirical research has found that the retention of studied material can be enhanced by testing" (Kang, McDermott, and Roediger 2007). Simply, the testing effect shows that when learners are asked questions about the material covered and then receive immediate corrective feedback, it can make a significant difference in learning and memory. The point here is that learners are practicing recall in their neural networks and solidifying those paths in their brain. This is analogous to pioneering a hiking trail. The more often you hike on the trail, the more trodden the trail becomes. The more you practice recalling something in your brain, the more you wire that recall path.

One of my learners in a virtual training class on virtual training conducted a teach-back where she taught mock learners how to read sonograms. Afterward, she used polls to quiz us on the content. If our answers were not correct, she immediately provided corrective feedback in the moment. As a result, we learned more during the polling because it employed recall and we received immediate, corrective feedback. The more learners practice recall, the better able they'll be able to recall in the future.

By using natural or planned pauses to test for knowledge, you're turning what can be seen as dead time or the black hole of silence into deep learning opportunities.

Creating a Conversational Space

In chapter 3, we explored how virtual learners can feel like they're entering someone's home as a guest at the beginning of a session. Learners understand they were the invitee, not the inviter. But what if they knew they were more than guests? What if we invite them to become co-creators of their own learning? In part, this means we talk less and allow them to talk more. It means releasing some control to ask where they would like to go next. It means empowering them by reducing our spotlight. Creating a space where all in attendance are on equal footing, equally respected, and all invited to contribute begins with establishing a safe, co-owned conversational space. As virtual facilitators, we start where learners are and bring them along from there.

Make the Virtual Space Inclusive to All

Online, both public and private spaces exist. Private messaging in chat is an example of private space because a single message is intentionally directed to one person by selecting their name only. This can be useful when a learner wishes to direct a message to a facilitator in private, the facilitator wishes to return a message to a learner in private, or when a producer and facilitator need to send messages back and forth to each other. For example, some of my producers post me private messages about time checks, such as when we are 10 minutes away from ending time. This message is for my eyes only, so we don't distract learners. Another example of private space is when learners enter individual breakouts where they may be tasked with working on a small sub-project alone, or when two people are in a breakout together and able to share a private conversation.

Public space, then, exists any time the group at large is live together. It is when comments are shared that all can hear or see. For example, this could be through group chat, a whiteboard activity, or coming off mute and speaking aloud. And in this public space, ensuring everyone feels included and able to contribute to the conversation is a key virtual facilitation skill. Remember, any pre-discussions before class begins can set the tone for your virtual training class.

One context where public space can inadvertently turn into private space is during the pre-session welcome. If you engage in conversation with people when they first join and before class begins, be wary of the sole participant who may dominate the space and use it for private conversation. Novice facilitators might allow whatever conversation happens to unfold as-is. However, intermediate or advanced facilitators are strategically mindful of creating a space that welcomes all, and do not allow one learner to dominate the conversation, get too in the weeds about personal items, or speak exclusively to a producer or trainer without realizing the broader audience listening as well.

As session leader, you or your producer can intervene to keep the public space public. One way is by inviting others into the conversation. For example, if one person is talking about the virtual platform they use for training and not allowing anyone else to speak, you might ask, "Josie, Shameka, and Matthew, what platforms do each of your organizations use?" This way you direct targeted questions to other participants. What is the experience for other learners if one participant monopolizes the conversation before virtual training begins? As online facilitators, we need to intervene to create a conversational space conducive for all.

Another way of ensuring all feel respected and comfortable is inviting them to include their gender pronouns after their typed name. This can display near their live video feed if the platform allows the option to rename or edit—for example, "Seth Smith (he/him/his)." If they are comfortable sharing this information, it can be helpful for facilitators. In past years, I made the mistake of accidentally assuming a masculine-identifying learner's name was feminine (they were not on video and had not come off mute yet); thankfully, he came off mute to correct me, which I was grateful for and naturally apologized for, while making a careful note to myself. So, be respectful by noting participants' pronouns, calling learners by their first names if that's the convention for their culture and organization, and using a gender-neutral group greeting like "everyone" when addressing the crowd (rather than "ladies and gentlemen" or "guys").

Part of skilled facilitation also requires ensuring all participants are learning and have an opportunity to be included. If one learner begins to overrun a conversation, steer the conversation off point, or share comments that are too personal or irrelevant to the group at large, it is your responsibility as the facilitator to get the conversation back on track. This can be done with a paired response that includes a polite closing prompt and then a question to transition to the group. For example, you might say "Sounds like you'll be very busy. That's a great application example. Thanks, Leita. OK, let's hear from someone else. Qiang, how do you think you could apply this to your role?" In this example, the facilitator's response respectfully includes a reaction, summary, and appreciation. This closes the original conversation. Then the question prompt clears a path for participation from others to keep the momentum going forward.

You can also intentionally create a public conversational space when a learner posts a message in chat to which you respond aloud. As you scan the chat, you might laugh agreeingly and say, "You are so right, Pablo!" and then move on to discuss something else. However, remember this is a public space. Now there are 19 other learners who are wondering what was so funny about Pablo's comment and what was he so right about. Because of their natural curiosity, they may shift their focus to chat. Then you'll have participants trying to scroll up and down the chat queue, looking for Pablo's name, only to discover he posted lots of comments that day or there are multiple Pablos in the class. By now, your learners have missed everything you might have said for the last several minutes.

So, when you reference something in chat as facilitator, you certainly do not need to read a post in its entirety or verbatim unless it's short, but do briefly summarize for the group at large to bring everyone in on the comment. For example, a facilitator might say, "Pablo says he's used this attention getter in some past presentations, and it works every time. You are so right, Pablo!" Beginning with Pablo's name grabs his attention. It also grabs the attention of other learners because they're wondering if you'll say their comment out loud too. And it clarifies that the words coming next are not the facilitator's own words but from a learner. Treat public space as a forum where all can be included and find a place in the conversation.

Prime Learners for What Is Ahead With Verbal Signposts

Did you ever play the game as a child where you had a handkerchief around your eyes, and someone led you around a living space to find hidden treasures? You may have tripped over toys or stubbed your toes on furniture all because you were motivated to discover the prizes on the obstacle course. You likely performed better if you had a guide to navigate you, perhaps someone who said, "Watch out for the couch on your left" or "there's a dog toy in front of your right foot." These signposts are helpful when you can't rely on the sensory cues you pick up yourself.

In the online space, learners have fewer sensory cues and feel better if they receive guidance. This guidance might consist of letting them know where they are headed, what's coming next, or what you'll soon be asking them to do. Even providing a heads-up that a potential quiz is coming can incent some learners to pay closer attention. Verbal signposts can also be used to call out the most important points. Here are some examples:

- "In a few minutes, we're going to work on independent assignments."
- "I'm going to ask each of you to share one thing in just a bit."
- "If there's one thing you need to remember most, it's this . . ."
- "Later on, we'll take a brief quiz on these principles to check your knowledge."
- "In a little bit, you'll be asked to improve how this graph displays."
- "After we look at some non-examples, I'm going to call on a few people to hear your thoughts about how to make these more effective."
- "As you watch this video, notice two things Fredrik does that really make a difference in the conversation."
- "In a moment I'm going to ask you to share one of your takeaways from today."

In your virtual training classes, calling on learners by name is also a wonderful way to get their attention. Learners will immediately sit up a little straighter when they hear their name called. And guaranteed, you will have their undivided attention for the next five to 10 minutes as well, because they will be listening intently to see if you say their name again. If you are going to call on learners though, I recommend letting learners know up front you may call on them to provide advance warning. In your netiquette at the beginning of training, you can even warn learners you will be calling on them at times, so they can prepare accordingly.

I also believe it's helpful to give learners a heads-up that an activity is coming where they may be called upon to share. This allows them time to begin thinking about it. For example, I might say, "A few slides from now, I'm going to ask everyone to share one principle they will apply on their job tomorrow and why. All of us will be typing these on the digital whiteboard." Again, this buys them some advance time to think and prepare for what they might share, so you can appropriately set them up for success and their responses will be more thoughtful.

 PRO TIP 23
Give learners a heads-up when they may be called upon to share.

The Value of Instructional Clarity

Inevitably, once you place learners in breakouts, the first thing they will say in their small group is, "What are we supposed to do again?" This is not unique to online training. Even in traditional classroom training, you must make sure you are crystal clear about instructions and expectations for small-group work. I often ask for a volunteer among online learners to paraphrase back the instructions they heard before releasing everyone into their small groups. This is a check to ensure they are very clear on their group task.

Other ways you can clarify instructions include providing at least one example of what you're expecting and sometimes a non-example. These examples can head off any misunderstandings. I am continually surprised by people who teach online, give an assignment, and never include an example of what's expected from learners' work. Examples not only equip your learners for success but are also part of good communication and help to clarify the desired outcome.

One of my golden rules that has served me well in the virtual space is to give instructions for more complicated exercises three ways, three times. For example, with a breakout activity, I might provide a visual anchor where learners can read the assignment summary in text; second, I'll verbally explain it; and third, I'll post a brief reminder in chat or a post a link to their digital participant guide where the instructions are. This way access to instructions is readily available and there is plenty of opportunity to clarify instructions before and during the exercise.

PRO TIP 24
Provide instructions three ways, three times for more involved activities.

Empowering Learners

As skilled facilitators, we can use multiple techniques to encourage, prompt, and empower learners. For example, you might challenge them to lead discussion, identify and commit to their own application of the training, require them to submit and follow-through on an action plan, or give them difficult decisions to make in scenario-based learning. All of these activities can help empower learners.

As author and speaker Michael Bungay Stanier (2021) says, the more learners grow in power, the more your power is reduced. It's about releasing command and control at pivotal points for the benefit of learners within guided structure. However, if we allow them to do whatever they like, it can result in floundering. "We have a great deal of evidence showing that pure discovery learning is both inefficient and ineffective" (Clark 2020). According to evidence-based research, guided instruction is needed to improve both performance outcomes and learning outcomes. We can empower them to make decisions within a guided structure.

Where you can provide the most impact is by modeling how something should be done as well as providing feedback to learners (Clark 2020). When I train participants on how to give constructive feedback, I always ask for a volunteer to help me role play. First, we demonstrate how not to give constructive feedback. The participant has the easier role and usually goes along with it and has a lot of fun. Then I ask for another volunteer and together we model how to give constructive feedback while the other learners watch us demonstrate the principles we just discussed. Afterward, we debrief as a group and discuss feedback. This sets learners up for greater success because their next step is to practice it themselves in paired breakouts. This modeling is what many trainers tend to leave out before asking learners to practice something in small breakout groups. So, we can empower learners to practice what they're learning by providing expert modeling beforehand and feedback afterward.

What Gets Rewarded Gets Repeated: Spark Discussion, Don't Extinguish It

Another way to empower learners is to genuinely acknowledge and affirm their contributions and build on them when they engage with the content. This is because what gets rewarded gets repeated. When we say "Claudia, that's a really great point! Have you also thought about . . ." it can motivate participants to stay connected. As author Jennifer Hofmann (2019) notes, "It feels great to answer a question correctly and to receive positive feedback from facilitators and peers."

This positive reinforcement can be very motivating. However, praise must be genuine. When a comment is disingenuous, people can tell. If a learner shares and then, right afterward, the facilitator says, "Anyone else?" or "Thanks for that" or "Thanks for sharing," without any further input, is the participant really motivated to share again? These trite, generic phrases from the facilitator can come across as rote, sterile, and distant. Better to dig deeper, ask follow-up questions, offer a genuine compliment, or expand with an additional comment. So, you might say their first name, comment on what they said, and then expand on it a bit with a follow-up. For example, "Ahh, yes, Amalia, that's so insightful. It's those little things we do as leaders that really make a difference, isn't it? What do the rest of you think are important leadership traits?" If a participant answers incorrectly, provide correction in a non-punitive way. For example, you might say, "Tell me more about how you arrived at that," or "You're so close. Let's unpack this a bit more." Even empathy statements can demonstrate you're listening and spark deeper conversation, such as "That must have been so frustrating. How was it eventually resolved?"

In chat, for example, it can also be rewarding to call out the first names of some participants and summarize their posts briefly. However, be wary of being too deferential. You should not read every comment from the chat aloud. That gets old quickly. Learners can read too. Instead, choose three to five posts that hit the mark or serve as great transitions or steer the discussion in a fruitful direction. The point of reading a few names and their posts aloud is to affirm participation, check knowledge, reward effort, and allow space for participants to be co-creators of the learning experience. If participants feel rewarded, it encourages more of the same behavior.

PRO TIP 25
Genuinely affirm learners' contributions aloud, build on their responses, and where appropriate dig deeper.

Connect Back to Learners' Previous Comments

Beginning facilitators may see chat comments and say "I see the chat blowing up here," or "Many of you are commenting about XYZ." Although this is a good starting point, facilitators can expand on it even more. One advanced technique is to continually refer to previous learners' comments by drawing connections as you go. Link previous comments to discussions going forward where appropriate. By this, I don't mean just acknowledging the comment at the time it is shared by a learner, but later and throughout the session, referring back to something a learner said and referencing it again in context. For example, "As Finn mentioned earlier, positional intimidation can be an obstacle to communicating assertively. What else might be an obstacle?"

To help you effectively bring back a learner's comment, keep a physical notebook nearby. There is so much happening digitally in front of you, with many screens and many tools. So, keep an analog paper pad and pen nearby to jot down a running list of first names and what I call "gold nugget comments." Sometimes the quickest way to remember what someone said is to glance down and see it on paper. I like to keep a printed roster of all the names in my class, and when someone shares a gold nugget, I write it next to their name to remind me to reference it later. This way, you'll be able to quickly find it when your brain prompts you. These references show your attentiveness, which subtly invites theirs, communicates you care, builds rapport and trust, reinforces content, rewards participation, and invites learners to co-create and co-facilitate. They will feel proud that you highlighted and tied back to something they said earlier and this can motivate them to continue contributing in meaningful ways.

Allow for Learner Agency and Voice

Learner agency is when learners are given the space and responsibility to make choices in a learning experience. They have the freedom to take initiative and decide which of several activity options interests them most. Although training can sometimes feel like it's being levied on you, ultimately you have to choose whether you'll learn (Cross 2007). Choice can embolden learners by giving them confidence. Not only can it create a deeper level of engagement with the subject matter, but it can also fan the flame of intrinsic motivation. By increasing learners' choices and options, we increase intrinsic motivation (Zuckerman et al. 1978). Optimizing learner agency gives learners more investment, and when someone places a stake in the ground figuratively, they become naturally more vested.

In their book, *Let Them Choose: Cafeteria Learning Style for Adults*, authors Jillian Douglas and Shannon McKenzie propose a facilitation and design technique where trainers allow participants to choose from among various activities and options. Although there may be multiple learning activities available, in the end, learners attain the same learning objectives. "When learners are in charge of their own learning and have the freedom to make their own choices (that is, experiencing a greater sense of autonomy), it means that not only can they do their jobs better (gaining competency and moving toward mastery), but they also have the opportunity to discover the intimate connection between their everyday tasks and the company's larger sense of purpose, mission, and values (fostering a deeper sense of purpose)" (Douglas and McKenzie 2016).

Learner agency also ties into self-determination theory (SDT), which is one of the most influential frameworks for motivation and emerged from the work of psychologist Edward Deci (Miller 2014). According to professors Edward Deci and Richard Ryan (2000), self-determination theory posits three major areas of motivation for individuals: competence, relatedness, and autonomy. "We strive to be good at things, to develop bonds with other people, and to make our own choices. People are the most intrinsically motivated and experience the most growth in environments that support these three basic needs" (Miller 2014).

With SDT, it's also important to note that one of the best ways to boost intrinsic motivation for virtual training is to explain the rationale for why. For example, in chapter 3, we discussed the importance of including the why in your pre-communication messaging and at the beginning of training classes. As a skilled virtual facilitator, you must continue looking for ways to increase learner agency and build in motivation, which is the emotional dimension of learning. In addition to the emotional dimension, building competence ties into the cognitive and behavioral dimensions of learning, and relational bonds tie into the social dimension of learning.

This isn't to say learning is all freeform, because you still provide a structure in which participants make choices. One example is to let learners choose how to communicate with you. For example, after posing a thoughtful discussion question, you might say, "You can either let us know in chat or feel free to come off mute and share. Would love to hear from you either way." Most tend to respond in chat, but sometimes you'll get a few who prefer to speak aloud. The point is they get to choose. It may seem like a minor point, but the more ownership learners take, the more this can blossom for them. Making their own decisions within the context of guided structure can increase independence and co-ownership.

PRO TIP 27
Present multiple options to learners within a guided structure.

There are many ways you can incorporate more choice and learner agency into virtual training programs. For example, when your training requires learners to do a teach-back or a presentation, request they select the topic. As you explain concepts, you can also give them license to select which sub-topic they would like to discuss first. For example, you might say, "We'll be covering three key areas today, which you see on this visual. Let me know on the poll displaying now, which one would you like to address first?" Another way you can incorporate choice is to allow them to choose which review method you'll use. For example, you could say "We can either do an online bingo review game or a gameshow-like course review," and ask which they would prefer. Of course, both games need to be ready to go just in case. As you offer the choice, make it clear their voice matters and you want to hear from them. They could either respond in a poll, in chat, or raise their virtual hand for review game A and then review game B. You might say, "Everyone has a vote today in which review game we're going to play. I want to hear from you. Here we go, the poll is open."

For additional options outside the platform, you could also use online surveys such as Poll Everywhere, to display live learner responses. This way participants can vote on which subject area they want to learn about first, as long as a linear structure isn't required to learn certain information. To do this, facilitators must chunk their sections by topic so they can quickly pivot appropriately or have their producer ready to do so on their behalf. Let's look at a few more virtual training examples where you can incorporate more choice and learner agency.

You might offer learners more choice through breakout activities. For instance, virtual platforms like InSpace allow participants to move themselves into a breakout of their choice, Zoom has an option that lets participants choose a breakout, and Microsoft Teams and Zoom allow renaming breakouts. Additionally, instead of assigning one scenario for all breakouts to work on, you might include options from which they can choose. For example, list three different challenging scenarios in the digital workbooks for participants as a reference. Allow time for everyone to briefly review them all. Then place learners in breakouts by asking them to choose one of the three. All scenarios challenge their application of the content and accomplish the same objective, but they have a choice in which one they'll tackle. Be sure to allow extra time for the team to make their selection, in addition to the time needed to complete the activity and to decide how they'll address the scenario they chose.

Although it may be easy to assume all will benefit from working together in small breakout discussion groups, this is not always the case. Some introverts may feel more comfortable doing independent work. If you poll learners ahead of time or find out their preferences for working in small groups or working alone, you can plan appropriately for your live online learning. For example, if one of my learners lets me know ahead of time that they feel more comfortable working independently, then I might place them in their own breakout to work on an assignment. Don't make a big deal of it or call attention to it, just allow some to work independently because they feel less anxious on their own and may learn better than if grouped with others. As Jillian Douglas and Shannon McKenzie (2016) also observed, "Certain activities worked better for some learners and not for others—some thrived in group activities, while others preferred to be alone. If learners felt uncomfortable about speaking aloud in a group setting or competing against others, it ended up hindering their learning." By incorporating choice in how breakouts are used for small groups or independent work, allowing some introverts to work independently can also help support autonomous learning.

Giving virtual learners more space and freedom also encourages them to take more initiative, which will help them use their voice in assignments, on whiteboards, in chat, or verbally in the group at large or in breakouts. The variety of activities will also help foster engagement. As Jennifer Hofmann (2019) notes, "Facilitators need to spend a lot of energy to make sure that learners are consistently engaged. From my experience, well-designed virtual lessons encourage learner communication every three to five minutes." By encouraging communication, engagement should only grow with more comments, reflections, insights, and questions from learners. To ensure you're empowering learners and not reducing them to the role of passive recipient, welcome their thoughts and questions at the times in which they voice their question and not just during prescribed times at the end of a segment.

PRO TIP 28
Increase learner agency by creating more opportunity for their voice to be heard and guided choice.

Be the Force That Changes Learner Inertia

Inertia is the initial resistance to move from one state to another. It applies to all objects and all things. In other words, when you move from a state of rest to a state of action, the transition period will be difficult. It can feel like you are going against a river's current or climbing uphill. Think of the last time you went on holiday for one or two weeks. When you returned to work, what was the morning of your first day back like? Did you require more cups of coffee? Did you have a hard time getting into a productive flow? Your answer most likely is yes. Meet inertia. The transition from a vacation mindset and restful state to a workplace state was probably a bit rough at first.

This applies to virtual training too. Before logging into an online class, consider what learners may have been doing beforehand. They may have just logged off a meeting. They may have been working independently, writing, or scanning email. Remember, when they first join, their inertia resists moving from the state they're currently in—a state of inaction. To move into a participatory state requires an uphill shift for them. Therefore, the very first time they unmute and speak aloud, post a chat, or write on a whiteboard will require the most effort on their part. However, once they have successfully done this and find it emotionally rewarding, you will notice their participation increase and they will notice it becomes easier.

As a facilitator, you want to be the force that changes their inertia. Do this by encouraging them to use virtual tools right away when they join. One way to prompt this is to give learners a platform tour. When my producers give a brief platform tour at the beginning of every virtual training, we prompt participants to raise their virtual hands as we talk about the hand-raising feature and where it's located. When we highlight the chat, we ask them to post something easy like which city, province, territory, state, or country they're connecting from. When we first ask them to participate and invite them to move to action, we understand there may be a little resistance initially.

Light, fun, easy warm-ups are also important at the outset for this reason. Learners, like athletes, need warm-ups. You will find that once they unmute and talk aloud, they are also more likely to talk again. The ice has been broken, so to speak. Novice facilitators place a group discussion where it seems to fit with content overall. Intermediate and advanced facilitators strategically place group discussions after participants are warmed up, like shortly after a breakout and breakout debrief if they are well prepped for the discussion by then. Once you help learners transition from any initial resistance, you'll begin to see them feel more comfortable in the space. Observe how frequently they participate and the depth of their participation so you can keep a pulse on how to encourage them to open up even more.

Facilitators are the force that can help transition passive observers from a "sit and get" mentality to active participants. "Session interactivity is the single most important priority for success in the virtual classroom" (Clark and Kwinn 2007). We guide learners be co-creators of their own learning.

PRO TIP 29
Help participants get past inertia by getting them involved right away.

Partnering With a Producer

One of the most helpful best practices for live online facilitation is to partner with a producer. The producer manages the technical aspects like troubleshooting, monitoring the chat, and assisting as needed so the facilitator can better focus on learners and the instructional content. There are just so many duties with live online learning that it can be incredibly challenging and stressful to manage alone, can require more testing ahead of time, and can take more time to resolve and work through issues. I love working with a producer because I know the producer has my back. They support learners' use of the platform and resolve technical issues so I carry less stress load and, as a result, I can be a better facilitator.

While an official producer might seem like a luxury to those who are learning departments of one, this does not need to be a full-time role. There are creative solutions. For example, you can ask a summer intern, a trusted confidant, a colleague, or a succession planning candidate who is looking for an opportunity to step into an entry-level L&D role. Back before our field formally recommended producers, I occasionally asked my business partner to sit next to me to help with the technical aspects of virtual training or webinars. Sometimes, I asked a client contact to serve in this assistive role. Partnering with a producer helps virtual training be successful, whether it's managing time, assisting with multiple tasks, or even carrying out facilitative tasks.

Time Management

Carefully managing time throughout your virtual training session is a must. Virtual training pioneer Jennifer Hofmann identifies time management as a critical competency to becoming a masterful facilitator, noting how surprisingly difficult this can be for facilitators. As Hofmann (2019) explains, online time management is the "ability to manage a virtual event in such a way that learners are engaged and desired outcomes are met, and the event is kept to a strict timetable."

I find that if I thoughtfully prepare how long each section might take ahead of time in my facilitator guide (for example, the opening exercise, a breakout, or a whiteboard activity), I can always check time estimates as I go. This tells me quickly if I need to speed up or slow down without learners ever knowing. I have found it's helpful to include the actual time in the guide; for example, 10–10:10 a.m. The challenge with listing time by minutes (such as 5 minutes or 8 minutes) is that with a quick glance, you are not able to gain a sense of whether you're behind, ahead, or on schedule. In the moment, you do not want to spend the mental capacity to figure out if it's been 10 minutes since you began an activity. Additionally, always build in a buffer of at least 10 minutes overall to give yourself wiggle room as needed. Keeping the time visible on a device, nearby clock, or smartwatch is also essential.

Skilled facilitators can also adjust estimated time on the fly as needed. For example, if participants are engaged in rich group discussion, you might make the impromptu decision to give them more time for the discussion. A novice facilitator might prefer to stick to the planned, original time estimates and cut off a rich but extended discussion. However, an intermediate-to-advanced facilitator weighs learning as the higher priority. If you determine there is greater value in lengthening the discussion, you might decide to cut the next break shorter or remove an activity near the end.

Of course, you never want to say aloud "We really need to move on now, we've already spent too much time discussing this," or "We have a lot to cover, so we'll have to leave it there." This is the type of comment that kills conversation and would hinder future discussions with the group. Keep the juggling of time, content, and schedule behind the curtain. As Walt Disney World has taught their cast members, keep backstage items backstage. This helps make it a better experience for guests. Remember, we are creating positive experiences for learners.

Partnering with a producer makes this much easier to manage. Referencing a shared facilitator guide makes it easier to follow estimated times for each instructional segment. The pre-estimated timed segments help you adjust on the fly as needed. As mentioned previously, some of my producers even send me a private chat when we're getting close to the end in case I need to wrap up an activity quicker.

Task Switching and Multitasking

There is no doubt that synchronous training requires managing multiple activities concurrently. This can be taxing on the facilitator. The good news is that the more experience you gain facilitating online learning events, the more automated some of the rote tasks will become (such as scanning chat, saving a whiteboard, or quickly finding the annotation toolbar). The more experience you have doing these activities, the less cognitive thinking they require. This, then, frees up precious thinking resources for other tasks that require more mental processing such as explaining your visuals, reading particpants' responses, and listening to their questions. When facilitators try to manage all of this at once, they can experience cognitive overload, which is "the amount of mental work imposed on working memory" (Clark and Kwinn 2007). It can feel overwhelming and becomes too much to handle mentally. (Cognitive load, of course, also applies to learners, which will be addressed more in chapter 8.)

Another term that some reference is task switching. This is when the brain focuses heavily on a single task like writing a paper, but then a distraction comes up where they must switch to a different task and then come back to the original task. Concentration level and flow take a hit when returning to the original task. When we train online, we're not so much deeply focused on a single task, but rather scanning the dashboard and keeping abreast of all that is happening. For example, you might be monitoring chat, watching the hand raises in a participant panel, sharing your screen with visuals, talking aloud, and annotating your slides. How can a facilitator manage all this at once?

Well, when your hands are full, you hire more hands. This is the beauty of partnering with a producer. When you work with a producer, you offload many of these tasks. For example, you can ask your producer to pull up the polls and broadcast results, let you know when there are key questions in chat you missed, help learners with technical issues, and bring up the whiteboard. If they mainly assist with technical issues, virtual training expert Kassy LaBorie (2021) refers to them as a technical producer. They earn their worth in gold assisting you. At the end of all virtual training sessions, I always give a shout-out to our producer because it truly is a partnership. You might say something like, "And special thanks as always to Maria, our producer, for keeping everything running smoothly today."

Advanced Functions for Producers

Sometimes producers can even take on more advanced roles beyond the technical aspects. If they are a seasoned producer, this enables them to share more in the facilitation responsibilities. Kassy LaBorie (2021), in *Producing Virtual Training, Meetings, and Webinars: Master the Technology to Engage Participants*, calls this type of producer a facilitative producer. When I work with seasoned producers, for example, I ask them to pop into different breakouts to check on group progress if they're also familiar with the topic, because with the two of us, we can cover more ground and at least one of us can visit every breakout. I have also worked with a producer who had a high-end camera and a very professional, blurred backdrop so I asked her ahead of time if we could use her as an exemplar when we talked about professional backgrounds for an online presence class. So, a producer's level of involvement depends on their experience and familiarity with the training topic. Regardless, partnering with a producer is a recommended best practice.

Summary

When I referred to a client's experience at the beginning of this chapter, she had accurately assessed that online facilitators have "a lot going on." Facilitators truly do wear many hats. We play multiple roles: facilitator, observer, connector, communicator, and time manager to name a few. As you continue to grow in your facilitation skill set, you'll find many of the tasks become more automated, and therefore less taxing. Of course, partnering with a producer or co-facilitator can also help immensely with task sharing and overall execution.

There are many tips and techniques you can apply to keep learners engaged and elevate your facilitation skills. Overall, we want to help learners successfully navigate the black hole of sensory input, and we want to recognize, respect, and reward their participation. Skilled virtual facilitators guide learners to be co-creators of their own learning while deeply engaging them cognitively, emotionally, socially, and behaviorally.

Not only is it important to be a skilled facilitator, but it's also important to build your on-camera facilitator presence. In the next chapter, we'll look at what you can do to specifically build your on-camera competence.

As you apply these pro tips with continued practice, you will be on your way to becoming an expert in the online facilitation capability. Remember, you are the force that changes learners' inertia. As skilled facilitators we can help participants transition from initial resistance to meaningful contribution. We do not force learners, but we slowly reward, nurture, and encourage their involvement in multiple ways. So, as you go forward, may the virtual facilitation force be with you and come out of you!

Pro Tips for Practicing your Online Facilitation Skills

TIP 19	Make the invisible audible by talking your task.
TIP 20	Acknowledge and address potential learner objections aloud at the time they might be thinking them.
TIP 21	Use announced silence to give learners brief spaces to complete activities or study complex visuals, and communicate beforehand when, why, and how long you'll be silent.
TIP 22	Treat virtual public space as a conversational space for all.
TIP 23	Give learners a heads-up when they may be called upon to share.
TIP 24	Provide instructions three ways, three times for more involved activities.
TIP 25	Genuinely affirm learners' contributions aloud, build on their responses, and where appropriate dig deeper.
TIP 26	Draw connections to learners' previous comments by referring to them throughout.
TIP 27	Present multiple options to learners within a guided structure.
TIP 28	Increase learner agency by creating more opportunity for their voice to be heard and guided choice.
TIP 29	Help participants get past inertia by getting them involved right away.

"Understand that face-to-face interactions are hugely important to the brain. So, anything that you can do in a virtual classroom that approximates face-to-face interaction . . . do it."

—Janet Zadina, Educational Neuroscientist

CHAPTER 5

Developing Your Professional On-Camera Competence

Imagine you are the virtual learner in this scenario. You log in to attend virtual training only to be greeted by an empty video frame. A webcam is on, but the facilitator is nowhere to be seen. Eventually, you watch a figure take their place on a chair. A spinning ceiling fan hangs conveniently just above the facilitator's head, and they are silhouetted by a sunny window behind them. Your trainer's face is cropped at the chin and appears larger than life as it peers down at you. The room behind them has a bright overhead light that creates a halo-like glare on the screen. As the facilitator begins to talk, they move their hands rapidly in and out of view, calling your attention to the blurs as the camera tries to capture the rapid movement. Sometimes their hands block the camera view, and, at times, even their face. In the background, you detect several bicycles against the wall. You try to figure out what brand they are and how they compare to your own bike since there's that race coming up soon. . . .

Clearly, this is not the visual experience you want learners to have, especially as a first impression. So, what might an exemplar look like? Let's contrast this opening scenario with a different one. Imagine again that you are the learner. This time, you log in to find your facilitator easy to see, well-lit, and wearing a smile that makes them seem friendly and approachable. You can hear them very well and notice their virtual background, which makes them look professional and credible. As you look at them onscreen, it feels as though they are right across from you and looking right at you. You see some of their upper body and even a few hand gestures as they begin to greet and welcome you to class. You think to yourself, "I bet this is going to be a really good class."

As you can see, artfully weaving a facilitator's live video into virtual training requires more than just turning on a webcam and letting it roll. Although this may seem like a basic skill, the fact that some practitioners do not yet demonstrate on-camera competence is why we address it here. There are still plenty of examples of poor lighting, distracting backgrounds, awkward positions in the camera frame, too much headroom, blurred gestures, no eye contact, or a facilitator looking away at another computer monitor for much of the duration, to name a few. Although it's often a matter of not knowing what one doesn't yet know, this new digital literacy is an essential core business skill for the 21st century.

This chapter is designed to help you develop your facilitator presence with on-camera knowledge and skills. Developing this capability will help you convey a sense of presence with learners while sharing space online. Growing in this area will also build your on-camera presence as credible, competent, and professional facilitator. When done well, it contributes to how closely and attentively learners decide to listen to you, because credibility—especially in the training topic area—is even more important online than in the traditional classroom. With synchronous classes, there are myriad potential distractions for learners, as we've addressed. Overall, mastering the facilitator presence capability will help you take your virtual training to the next level.

In this chapter, we'll identify proven practices for effective and professional camera use and call out ineffective techniques as well. This chapter goes beyond the basics of turning on your webcam to see if you can pull it off somehow. It explores the benefits and challenges, offers specific guidance about when and when not be on camera, and discusses appropriate backgrounds, the technical aspects of lighting, nonverbal on-camera cues, proper angles, what clothing colors work best on camera, and framing yourself in the lens. So, let's jump in and roll the camera.

 THE BIG IDEA

As facilitators, be on camera with proper Background, Lighting, Expressions, Angle, Clothing, and Headroom (B-L-E-A-C-H) during purposeful connection moments.

Facilitating on Camera

Because most people are uncomfortable being on camera, in the past virtual trainers have sometimes opted to keep cameras turned off. When video technology was still evolving, many of us only taught with audio or just displayed a still photo of ourselves in the upper corner of the virtual platform. Back then, bandwidth was extremely limited, which presented additional challenges for video. The thinking was that an instructor's photo could at least connect learners to the human being behind the disembodied voice. But because video technology, bandwidth, and virtual training platforms have significantly improved, displaying a still image of a virtual trainer for the duration of training has become old school.

We live in a world with growing demand for video. In modern learning environments, we have the capability and improved technology to incorporate quality video on most platforms. There is no doubt video has emerged as the dominant communication medium. In 2020 alone, 500 hours of new videos were uploaded to YouTube every minute, and 1 billion hours of YouTube videos were watched daily (Smith 2020). The video revolution is here.

Notably, in 2020 and 2021 the COVID-19 pandemic boosted widespread use of webcams by creating an unprecedented need for remote work and connection. This also affected formal training, as organizations rushed to convert traditional in-person training to online learning using video conferencing and virtual training platforms. Many online training offerings experimented with greater use of webcams for both facilitators and learners (Figure 5-1).

There are certainly exemplars of instructional models where webcams are not used. Khan Academy, for example, employs a generous and hugely successful virtual learning model without showing instructors on video. Founder and CEO Salman Khan created a virtual learning academy to provide free world-class education to anyone over the internet. Instead of on-camera video, he and his instructors record spoken audio while illustrating onscreen as they teach.

So, it appears you can still achieve learning objectives without a video of a facilitator's face, but are there any other compelling reasons to use it? And how often are webcams currently used among virtual facilitators worldwide? According to virtual training expert Cindy Huggett's *The State of Virtual Training 2020* global survey, 83 percent of facilitators reported

Figure 5-1. Example of On-Camera Facilitator

Reprinted with permission from SkillPath.

using webcams in virtual training and 66 percent reported using webcams more in 2020 than they had in previous years (Huggett 2020). In addition, 48 percent reported using them for the entire duration of their virtual training classes, and 36 percent said they used them for at least some of the class. This data was collected from nearly 900 respondents between May and July 2020.

The next question we might ask ourselves is: Just because virtual trainers can use live video, does this mean we should? Let's examine the benefits and challenges webcams offer to see if we can discover some answers.

On-Camera Benefits

Two large-scale field studies out of Stanford University studied the impact of incorporating instructors' faces with video versus providing virtual instruction with audio only (Kizilcec, Bailenson, and Gomez 2015). They found no significant differences in learning outcomes between whether the instructor's webcam was shown or not. However, although turning on instructor webcams did not appear to significantly aid or degrade learning transfer, the Stanford study suggested it did have two additional benefits for learners:

- An improved overall experience
- An increased sense of social presence

These are significant findings. First, we recognize the importance of learners reporting improved experiences based on our discussion of LXD in chapter 2. Second, because this chapter focuses on the facilitator presence capability, we also recognize the value of establishing a sense of social presence online. The term social presence was defined decades ago in the book *The Social Psychology of Telecommunications* as learners' ability to feel like they're together with others and share a felt sense of virtual community, even though they're remote (Short, Williams, and Christie 1976).

When you are on camera as a virtual facilitator, you want to build this sense of online community, which ties into both the social and emotional dimensions of learning. So, should facilitators use their live video cameras? If including live video of the trainer improves the overall experience and increases the sense of social connection, then yes, this is something we want to use. Later in this chapter, we'll investigate more specifically when it is most optimal to be on camera.

This general sense of connectedness isn't the whole story. Further research has revealed more specifics about how on-camera presence enhances learning (Figure 5-2). In a 2021 webcam study conducted by Florida State University (FSU), more than 500 learning professionals were surveyed to determine how webcams are used and perceived. Their results identified the following benefits (Dennen, Word, and Arslan 2021). Webcam use:

- Promoted a sense of closeness
- Made it easier for the facilitator to guide discussion among participants
- Discouraged multi-tasking among participants
- Enhanced listening

These relational and communication benefits should be additionally weighed for how they engage participants through the social dimension of learning. When bandwidth is sufficient, webcams can offer added value to virtual training programs.

So far, we have uncovered multiple benefits to including a live video feed of a facilitator in virtual learning. The next question, then, is what are the challenges of being on-camera and are there conditions for its effective use?

Figure 5-2. Webcams Influence on Listening

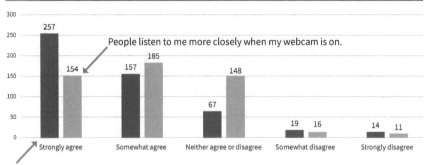

I am more interested in listening when the speaker's webcam is on.

Reprinted with permission from Professor Vanessa Dennen, Florida State University.

On-Camera Challenges

Although being on-camera appears to help facilitators better establish a sense of presence and place, feelings of closeness, enhanced listening, and improved experience, there can also be challenges to being on camera frequently. Let's explore some of the challenges to the live video feature in training platforms next.

Screen and On-Camera Fatigue

If you facilitate several virtual training sessions a day, you may experience varying levels of fatigue. Virtual participants are not exempt from this either. When either you or your participants are on camera, people may feel like they are in the spotlight or feel the need to act differently (and not be themselves). As a result, they may intentionally try to be more facially animated or nod more frequently to show they are listening. However, if this is not their normal state of being, it can be taxing after a while. It is always exhausting to project something that is not who you really are. As Clemson University Professor Marissa Shuffler adds, you realize everybody is looking at you when you are on camera. Because of this, some people feel social pressure to perform like they're on a stage, which can be even more stressful and fatiguing (Jiang 2020). According to Professor Gianpiero Petriglieri, when we communicate through live video, we also work harder to interpret nonverbal cues like vocal tone, facial expression, and body language. Because we are devoting more attention and processing resources to action, it consumes more of our energy (Jiang 2020).

Another mentally taxing piece is the scanning and processing people do to all the live, individual video streams of participants and their backgrounds. One solution for this is the Together Mode feature in Microsoft Teams, which uses artificial intelligence (AI) to digitally place participants in a shared background. This view requires less mental effort because it brings all participants on camera into a singular and visual, virtual space. This view is also controlled by each participant individually. Zoom's Immersive View also allows hosts to display shared background scenes for all.

So, there appears to be a need for balance and recommendations regarding webcams for virtual training. We know that long durations of use can be especially taxing for participants, and sometimes even for facilitators, depending on the frequency. But there's also another challenge with being on camera. Sometimes, it can feel unnatural.

Being on Camera Can Feel Unnatural

Because virtual training can capitalize on the on-camera medium, how you show up on camera can set the stage for your relationship building, presence, credibility, connectedness, rapport, attention holding, and more. However, most people feel uneasy on camera. They may report feeling like everyone is looking at them, as if they were giving a presentation. Just because we're facilitating from behind our computer screens doesn't mean public speaking anxiety fades away.

One way to think about being on camera is to reframe it. Although it may feel like the pressure is on you as the facilitator, the reality is the video is not there for you. You turn on the webcam for your learners. Your goal is to establish an on-camera presence as their facilitator. This provides a visual way for learners to connect with you. We know from extensive research in online learning that a guide on the side, an avatar expert, or a pedagogical agent can provide supportive and helpful assistance to learning. Learners respond well to expert guides. And of course, an instructor's video camera can provide more visual cues than learners would otherwise receive through audio alone. So, remember, the reason we turn on the camera is not for us, it's for learners. It helps learners discern a sense of place, a sense of person, and a sense of presence.

Drawn to Self-Views

Interestingly, many people tend to use their webcam self-view like a mirror. They watch their own live video more than others. According to FSU's 2021 *Webcams at Work* study, 75 percent of more than 500 learning professional participants said they watched themselves when they were on camera (Dennen, Word, and Arslan 2021). You have likely observed people fixing their hair or preening on camera. Maybe you have even done this yourself. If you find that you gravitate toward watching yourself and it becomes distracting, most platforms do allow the option to turn off your self-view. As Professor Shuffler adds, it's very difficult for people not to be drawn to looking at their own face as if it were an onscreen mirror, or to be more conscious of what they're doing in front of it (Jiang 2020).

In short, there are certainly some challenges with webcam use that include screen fatigue, feeling unnatural on camera, or even being mesmerized by the view of oneself to which we are naturally accustomed with mirrors. However, as previously established, there are also benefits that are compelling reasons for use. So, how do we balance it all? Let's identify some practical guidelines next.

When Should Live Cameras Be Used in Virtual Training?

We know that when a facilitator is on camera, it can improve the experience for learners and increase their perception of a facilitator's presence, which is important for learning. On the flipside, it can also distract attention from where learners need to focus if not done well, and it can be fatiguing. Weighing these benefits and challenges, the next vital question is when and how should webcams be used for virtual training?

Clearly, just because we have access to a feature doesn't mean we should use it all the time. Balance is usually the best way to go. Think of the number of fonts and features available to use in a PowerPoint presentation. I recall looking at a colleague's work in which she had attempted to use multiple fonts on the same slide, just because she could. What you're thinking right now is exactly right. It was Overkill with a capital O.

Applying this to webcam use with virtual training, one common temptation for instructors is to leave webcams on for the duration of an entire virtual class. It is easy to see why. To begin, it is certainly easier. For example, facilitators can turn on their video cameras, let them run, and not worry about them again until their session concludes. However, is this the best option for all parties involved?

Intermediate and advanced facilitators are mindful of where they want learners to focus during instruction and have a pedagogical rationale for doing so. When we approach on-camera use from this perspective, learners do not always need to be looking at facilitators on camera, or themselves, or their colleagues. For example, you do not need to be on camera when you are no longer talking after introducing a guest expert or subject matter expert who's joining your class. If you continue to talk and direct questions to an expert in an ongoing dialogue, then it makes sense to stay on camera. However, if you are observing and listening only, you do not need to compete with the other visuals onscreen for learners. In this way, we use the camera's on/off switch to direct more attention and focus. Think about it as foreground and background. When you are the background and your learners are leading activities, a guest expert is sharing, or the group is working on the whiteboard together, you can go off camera.

We want to use video when it serves a purpose. I recommend turning your camera on during purposeful connection moments. These are the moments when the focus of the interaction is interpersonal and it's essential for learners to see your nonverbal cues and facial expression. For example, when you lead a discussion with an open-ended question prompt, turn off your slides and invite learners to turn on their cameras. If a learner prefers not to come on camera, you should never force them, but as a preventive measure do set expectations in your pre-class communications for learners to be camera-ready to increase the likelihood of them doing so.

Here are some examples of what I call purposeful connection moments. These are times to optimize interpersonal connection and turn on your camera as facilitator:

- Welcoming and greeting participants
- Introducing the facilitator, producer, guests, or learners
- Large-group discussions
- Small-group breakouts
- When you share a story to illustrate important training topic points
- Explaining instructions for more complicated activities
- Modeling or demonstrating something

- Role plays
- When learners present or teach-back on something as a learning activity
- To emphasize key points
- When you close the training, as a bookend to how the session began

There are also times to explicitly turn off your camera. Webcams, for example, should be off when you step away from your desk before class starts or during a break. On one occasion, I logged in early to a virtual training class, and observed the trainer finishing up his technical setup and prep; then he proceeded to leave on his webcam and leave the room. As a result, my first impression, along with my colleagues who joined shortly thereafter, was being greeted by an empty chair.

Another time to remain off camera is when you want to direct focus: "Use webcams on the front-end to establish presence and place, but then you can turn them off to focus and direct attention to other visual points of focus" (Howles 2015). For example, if there is a complex diagram or visual that learners need to process, or if you want to focus exclusively on a whiteboard activity, turn off your camera to direct focus to the visual or whiteboard. You might also turn off your camera when you are training people how to use a new system by demonstrating the software or platform. For the same reason, you want to direct their visual focus to the elements onscreen while your audio fills in the explanatory gaps to supplement what they're seeing.

However, in some cases, evidence-based research suggests that when concurrently screen sharing supporting visuals, a small video image of the facilitator, trainer, or instructor is more effective for learning (Pi, Hong, and Yang 2017). So rather than going off camera entirely, you can make the explanatory slides or supporting visuals large, while your camera becomes smaller. A small image is just enough to establish facilitator presence without competing with other visuals onscreen. This research from Central China Normal University studied the effect of multimedia with an instructor's image and accompanying supporting visuals for video lectures. They discovered that "learners gained more knowledge from the video lecture with the small image of the instructor, and they experienced more satisfaction with it" (Pi, Hong, and Yang 2017).

All in all, facilitators can be on camera during purposeful connection moments to leverage the benefits discussed in this chapter. This balancing act recognizes that an all-or-nothing approach is not the best fit; instead, find the right times to aid learners by turning on your camera during opportune times.

Next, let's look at what you can do to project the best on-camera image during those purposeful moments.

Clean Up Your On-Camera Image With BLEACH

Up to this point, we've explored the value an on-camera facilitator can add for learners and learning experiences. We've also clarified the conditions under which webcam use for facilitators is most optimal and when to consider turning it off. Now we'll turn our attention to specifically developing your facilitator presence when you are on camera. So, what are the things you most need to do? I've identified six key elements to help you come across effectively and professionally. I use the acronym BLEACH to remind you and others how to clean up your professional image in the camera frame. BLEACH stands for background, lighting, expressions, angle, clothing, and headroom. As demonstrated in Figure 5-3, all these elements work together to present you in the most credible and professional way. Let's explore each in more detail.

Figure 5-3. B-L-E-A-C-H: Good On-Camera Example

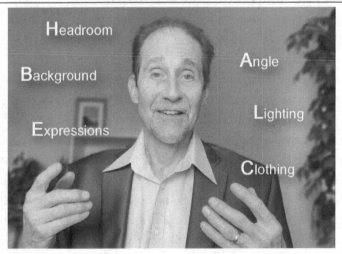

B Is for Background

To begin, the visible background behind you matters. Why, you ask? Because the camera frame subconsciously signals to learners that everything within this frame should be closely examined. It directs attention to its contents.

Think about what captures your attention the most. Is it something novel? Is it something interesting to you? Something surprising? Or is it movement, as we explore in chapter 8? It may, in fact, be all of the above. We, as human beings, are wired to pay attention to stimuli. Unfortunately, in virtual training, stimuli can also be distracting, like a ceiling fan visible right above a facilitator's head.

A busy, cluttered, bright, moving, or odd background can call attention to itself and distract learners away from where they should be focused. Fortunately, there are several things we can do to pick an appropriate background. Whether you use a real green screen, a virtual green screen, a blurred image of your real physical room, a backdrop, slides as your background, or a virtual background, the measuring stick during your selection process should be to ensure that your background is secondary, not primary, and that it supports you and your topic, not the other way around.

PRO TIP 30
Minimize or remove visual distractions from view in the camera frame.

Tidy What's Visible in Your Physical Room

If you choose to use your real, physical environment as your background, find a pleasant room or background in your environment that looks professional (for example, a makeshift desk or work area is preferred over a kitchen sink in the background). With video, it's even better to show a little depth behind you. You want to avoid being right up against a wall, if possible, which can come across flat. Try to show more of a room, home, or hallway to create more open space behind you for more depth. You can also purposely place things in your background to make the environment more appealing, such as simple artwork or a plant or two.

Some virtual instructors may not realize their background is distracting. For example, you've likely seen some people on camera whose backgrounds seem to be overflowing with storage items, crowded bookshelves, gigantic piles of papers and binders, or messy closets. These visual elements compete for viewer attention and direct learners away from key training concepts. Sometimes, it's just a matter of removing the busyness on the wall behind you. Instead of eight plaques or picture frames hanging on the wall, consider simplifying it to a few. Avoid clutter as indicated in the poor example in Figure 5-4, and clean up the area because this can present you in a more professional light. Our job as virtual facilitators is to minimize or eliminate those background distractions so learners can focus their attention on the core learning objectives.

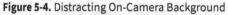

Figure 5-4. Distracting On-Camera Background

People can also be curious and start noticing things in your background and then stop listening to you. For this reason, real estate agents advise house sellers to empty or at least minimize the books on their shelves when they place their homes on the market. Why? People can be drawn to look at the book titles because they're curious about what the homeowners might be reading. Instead, agents want homebuyers' focus to be on the house. In a similar vein, we want to direct learners away from the background, as illustrated in the opening story, and instead direct their attention to what you're saying as the facilitator. Attention is a precious commodity and we only have so much of it.

It's also important to keep a designated space that's free of clutter and ready to go. And you want to choose a space that reflects professionalism for your virtual training programs. For example, one of my clients who is an attorney was delivering a virtual legal message; after carefully considering the best backdrop for him and we decided that legal office best supported his professional message. However, if dedicating an entire room to be clutter-free is too difficult or not possible, as long as what can be seen on camera is tidy it's OK if the rest of the room is a disaster.

Blur Your Background

Some virtual training platforms allow you to blur your background. This can add a very professional touch to your backdrop because it makes you, the facilitator, visually pop. This blurring capability also allows you to maintain your real environment with less concern about what's, such as your colleagues behind you at the office walking by, or your kitchen, bedroom, attic, laundry room, or any other space you prefer not to professionally showcase.

Purchase a Backdrop

Another solution is to purchase a physical backdrop to place behind you. There are a variety of photo backdrops available. This provides a way to quickly cover your background if it's not possible to tidy or declutter the space beforehand. Backdrops can be placed in such a way that all learners see is you, which neutralizes the background and still supports you as the feature on which we want learners to be focused (Figure 5-5).

Figure 5-5. Professional On-Camera Background

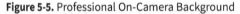

Use Slides as Your Background

Several virtual training platforms also allow facilitators to project slide content behind their own video feed as a backdrop. This way, learners see an integrated image of both you and your slide as the video feed is overlaid on your slide. For example, in Zoom you can silhouette yourself with your slide behind you. Your content slide then becomes your backdrop. If you use this feature, ensure important data on slides is not hidden from view by your silhouette. Practice ahead of time to know how gestures will come across with this backdrop and how best to interact with your content by strategically pointing when you are visually integrated into your content. Be ready to redesign slides once you test them out as needed.

Microsoft Teams also offers facilitators the ability to use Presenter Mode. This allows the facilitator to choose from several formats, which would project differently for learners based on what they select. For instance, with a Standout format, facilitators are silhouetted with the slide behind them. In Reporter format, facilitators can use the slide as a visual aid over their shoulder, as you might see in a traditional television newscast, and then the side-by-side option allows the facilitator to be in a separate frame with their slide content in a frame adjacent to them.

Explore a Virtual Background Option

Most video conferencing platforms have virtual backdrops from which you can choose. As technology evolves and improves, we will see many more customized options become available. The challenge is that backgrounds can also upstage facilitators and draw learner attention to the background instead of content material.

Ideally, a professional virtual background would provide a neutral scene or color that does not compete with you in the foreground. Be cautious of virtual backdrops that may be "fun and cool," but could also be distracting. For example, if a background includes video movement like an ocean tide with waves that continuously crash onto a shore, it may draw learners' attention away from you.

Overall, select a background that is truly a background, so you become foreground as you provide feedback to learners, offer explanations, ask for follow-up, share a professional example of a concept you're teaching, and more.

L Is for Lighting

Video requires lots of light. Lots. One of the most common on-camera errors is poor lighting, either because the facilitator's image is too dark, one side of a facilitator's face is too bright, or one side of the face is in shadow. In virtual training, your learners want to be able to see you and your entire face.

An added benefit of good lighting is that it can even make you look younger. If that's important to you, read on. With poor lighting, wrinkles are more visible. But proper lighting has a smoothing effect that can hide wrinkles. Not a bad perk, right? Fortunately, there are several things you can do to improve your lighting and help elevate your facilitator presence to the next level.

Light From the Front

First, always light yourself from the front. This means placing your light source in front of you, not behind you. So, avoid sitting or standing with a window directly behind you. As you can see in the poor example in Figure 5-6, when you are backlit, the light will either bleed in through the window like a halo-effect or cast you in silhouette. Natural light from a window in front of you does work well though. It's about paying attention to how well-lit your face is. Good lighting will also separate you from the background. You'll want to turn off visible ceiling lights as well, because these can become bright distractions that stand out and create shadows.

Figure 5-6. Examples of Poor Lighting

Soften Lighting

It's also best to ensure your light source is not too harsh, like direct light from a side window on a sunny afternoon. You can either close your window shades if the daylight is too bright or use soft lamps on either side of your computer. You can also bounce light off a wall to diffuse or soften it. There are very affordable collapsible light reflectors you can keep on hand for just such a purpose. This can be handy if you find you are frequently training near a side window when bright light streams in.

I have light sources on both sides of my computer, which helps prevent casting a shadow on half of my face. One of them is an Elgato Key Light Air, and I access the Control Center app for it from my smartphone. The app allows me to power the light and off, as well as control the brightness and color temperature based on the time of day and the current lighting in my home office. Daylight tends to be more blueish and incandescent light tends to have a more reddish-orange hue. It's best not to mix these different types of light, so depending on the amount of sunlight streaming into your space or whether the shade is drawn, you can appropriately adjust the light in the room. With a little effort, you can significantly improve your visibility and create a higher quality image with good lighting.

 PRO TIP 32
Light yourself from the front with plenty of soft, even lighting.

E Is for Expressions

In addition to elevating the professionalism of a facilitator's video image, your nonverbal expressions can play a role in your onscreen effectiveness. The camera can reveal personality, physical attributes, facial expressions, upper body language, and multiple other nonverbal cues that we would otherwise not be able to interpret in an audio-only space. It might be a nod of the head, a head tilt sideways, looking interested, or direct eye contact through the camera lens that hits a message home to learners. Thus, virtual trainers should ensure their facial expressions, eye contact with the lens, hand gestures, and other body movement all work together to create an engaging and professional facilitator presence.

Facial Expressions

Leverage your camera to convey your facial expressions, specifically your smile, as this can help learners connect with you. According to educational neuroscientist Janet Zadina, "A smile lights up the reward center of the brain" (Howles 2020). It also reduces stress by producing positive reward chemicals. When content-appropriate, allow yourself to smile naturally. This can also communicate that you are approachable (important if you want learners to ask you questions) and friendly. This does not mean you should shine those pearly whites throughout your entire training regardless of context. However, when it is appropriate to what you're saying, smile in a way that is friendly, relaxed, and pleasant. Other facial expressions—such as raising your eyebrows, widening your eyes, and more animated expressions—can help build rapport with learners, especially as they first settle into virtual training. Based on a facial expressions study from China Normal University, video lectures where the instructors used a heightened level of expressiveness promoted better student arousal levels and learning satisfaction than conventional instructor expression or audio-only (Wang et al. 2018).

PRO TIP 33
Be facially expressive in a natural way to aid learning.

As the virtual trainer, you may feel that a cold, impersonal lens does not bring out your personality. In fact, video has a way of depleting energy for most people. However, there are ways to keep your energy up. Natural nervousness will fuel excitement, which can be channeled as energy. Additionally, energy decreases when you are sitting, so some find that placing their computer on a standing desk increases their ability to muster extra energy naturally. If you come across without enthusiasm and passion, your learners—even on the other side of the screen—will feel it too. If you only focus on the reality of the situation—that is, that you are speaking to a cold, camera lens in a room by yourself far away from everyone else—your training facilitation can also come across without connection.

Camera Lens Eye Contact

You are likely familiar with the basics of looking at the camera lens for virtual eye contact. However, as we discussed earlier, being on camera is unnatural for most people. In fact, many people forget to blink when they look at a video camera lens (almost like a deer in headlights). As one optometrist shared with me, most people naturally blink 20 times per minute, but when looking at computer screens (or cold, impersonal camera lenses), some people only blink five times per minute. So, remember to blink!

Obviously in the virtual space, trainers and learners alike do not have the benefit of direct eye contact. However, we can create the illusion of eye contact by looking at the camera lens when we can. Online instruction and teaching still is very much about relationships, and even though learners may seem invisible, eye contact is a way to help establish this direct connection. As the adage reminds us, eyes are the windows to the soul.

Looking into a camera lens when it is feasible to do so while training does not come easy to most people, even experienced virtual trainers. I've tested my desktop computer and used the front-facing camera and video recording feature to look at myself locking eyes with the camera in three different ways. Then I played back the video to determine among all those points of focus when it really looked like I was looking at the camera. Then marked this spot with a small X made of tape on my computer screen so I would know exactly where to look when I wanted to communicate with direct eye contact. Obviously, there are other places you need to look as well while teaching—for example, at chat, at participants on camera, and at the whiteboard. But for openings and closings, discussions, and key points, or when responding to participant questions during those key connection moments, you want to look directly at the camera lens.

You might be thinking, it's not realistic for me to do that all the time. The point is to do it when you can. Sure, you must look away at chat or look down or search on your other monitor for the next file to share. But as you are able, come back to re-establish contact through the camera lens.

Whether speaking or not, where you choose to look is still visible to learners. If your eyes dart around or look down or to the side, learners will wonder where you're looking. Your eye contact is not only a powerful way to connect to your viewing audience, but a useful tool for directing focus. Learn to leverage the power of eye contact with the camera lens.

PRO TIP 34

Adjust yourself to be more eye level with the camera, and when instructionally feasible, look directly at the camera lens.

Hand Gestures

Hand gestures are another form of expression. Some wonder if we should even use hand gestures on camera. I and many others say yes because gestures are a natural part of communicating and they help others interpret what we are saying. According to communication coach Nick Morgan (2021), hand gestures can help communicate emphasis, comprehension, and even conviction, so they should still be included in online video communications. One research study on gestures in video lectures found that instructors' use of gestures—specifically pointing gestures—not only influenced learning, but also improved teaching (Yang et al. 2019). However, most facilitators believe they can just talk and use their hands in a virtual setting like they have always done. That's not always the case. For example, you will need to make sure you are sitting a bit farther from your computer to ensure your hand gestures are still visible.

While being on camera enables you to use movement and gestures to engage your learners, video is just a series of still frames played in rapid succession to give the impression of movement. When we view a series of still images at a set speed, it gives the appearance of moving video and the illusion of movement. Video technology cannot capture every movement in real space. Think of it like animation. You see the individual drawings with slight changes in each drawing. When those same drawings are flipped in rapid succession, you perceive the illusion of movement or animation. It looks like movement, but it is really a collection of slightly different still images.

You may have heard the term *frame rate*. Frame rate specifies the speed at which still images are displayed for you, usually indicated as "frames per second" or fps. Each frame consists of one still image. Let's say, for example, you view a live volleyball game on television at 30 fps. This means you are really seeing 30 unique, still images in one second. Surprising, right?

Why is it important to realize that video is a collection of still frames? Because knowing this helps us understand how we should move on camera. Although there's not a lot of high motion when presenting on camera or meeting with webcams, there are still guidelines that apply. For example, professionals inevitably use their arms and hands to gesture, not realizing the impact it can have on viewers. For example, if we move too fast with our bodies or gestures, the movement can become a blur and call attention away from the central message. You can liken this to excessive and repetitive *um's* from in-person presentations that call attention to themselves.

Because of the current frame rate with web conferencing technologies, make your hand gestures significantly slower when they are visible in the frame. Movement naturally grabs our attention, but on camera, we need to slow down overall movements to avoid jerky, distracting blurs (Figure 5-7).

Figure 5-7. Example of Blurred Gestures With Fast Hand Movements

There's another aspect to gesturing you should be mindful of as well. If you have had to address a big audience on stage, you know that you fill the space available. In person, we do this by gesturing larger and bigger to fill the space, whether it's an auditorium or the TEDx stage. We move physically—albeit staying within the red circular carpet—and we gesture bigger. On camera in virtual training, we can still work to fill the space. But we must be mindful of the amount of real estate we have and how we fit into it.

When I took screen acting classes in Chicago, we were trained to ask before filming a scene, "How big is my frame?" Would it be an extreme close-up, a close-up, or a medium shot, to name a few? This informed your acting. With live video, we should still be very aware of what is in the frame and what's outside the frame. Are my gestures not visible because they're out of frame? Should I move farther away from the computer? Where should I raise my hand gestures so they can be seen? This is why I call it a camera frame, because it frames you.

It's best to frame yourself before participants join on camera to identify the height your gestures should be to stay visible in the frame. Then learners will see them as you intended, rather than watching your hands appear and disappear out of camera frame. Also, remember to use gestures sparingly. Constant gesturing creates chaotic movement that can be distracting to viewers. Avoid using of the same gesture over and over. And avoid pre-calculating what to do with your hands at certain times. This can come across as artificial and disingenuous. Instead, just let your hands naturally support what you want to say by letting them freely move inside the camera frame.

Other Body Movements

Beyond hand gestures, there are several body movement principles to keep in mind for virtual training. Body posture makes a difference because everything inside the frame makes a difference. Facilitators may not realize they're slouching. Imagine a string pulling you up from the top of your head. Envisioning this should lift your posture to an upright position. A facilitator with good posture has better breath support and sends a message of confidence that, in turn, enhances your credibility. Also, keep your shoulders even and balanced and slightly lean forward to communicate you are engaged and alert. This will help you stay relaxed, keep you grounded, and look more natural.

If you are sitting, your movement on camera should include slight side-to-side shifts, never front to back. The reason for this is because as you move toward the camera (downstage), you or your head or your hands appear to grow exceptionally large on camera (Figure 5-8). Instead, it is best to maintain equal proportions and keep movement in the same plane, equidistant from the camera. When standing, try to avoid pacing, which may cause you to move on and then off camera while facilitating.

 PRO TIP 35
Avoid significant front-to-back body movement on camera; use slight side-to-side movements instead.

Figure 5-8. Hands Grow Gigantic Moving Toward Camera

A Is for Angle

You have likely seen others on webcams during virtual training with odd camera angles. Perhaps it felt like they were standing way above you and looking down, or their mouth wasn't visible because the screen cut off under their nose, or their head was cut off from the top, or worse. These odd camera angles can be distracting because it's not our natural way of viewing and interacting with others and it draws attention to how the facilitator looks, not the content.

When you facilitate virtual training, make sure you come across credibly and professionally with a proper camera angle. It's best to position your webcam to be level with your face. This means you will need to distance yourself appropriately from the computer. Avoid camera angles that give the impression that learners are looking up at you as this can be an intimidating posture. As author and social psychologist Amy Cuddy (2015) shares in *Presence: Bringing your Boldest Self to your Biggest Challenges,* when people seem or appear bigger, it's an expression of power and dominance. Applying this to facilitator video, the viewer feels small and submissive when a figure looms above them. For better rapport, move the device, adjust your chair, or prop your computer or camera up so that the lens is level with your hairline. Sometimes I prop up my laptop with something sturdy so it's even. This will help your eyes get closer to eye-level with your camera.

Notice how in Figure 5-9, not only does the facilitator create an intimidating posture because it feels like the learner is looking up at them, it's also just an awkward camera angle. The ceiling fan doesn't help either because it becomes a distraction in the background. This is something I observe more often than you might think. Sometimes, that ceiling fan is even on, which is even more distracting because it looks like a spinning hat.

Figure 5-9. Example of Ineffective Camera Angle

Other Awkward Angled Movement

I also recommend not facilitating with a computer in your lap as this can cause the camera to move up and down as you type or otherwise use the device and make learners dizzy. Instead, make sure your device is on a flat, even, steady surface. Another point to keep in mind with camera angles is to avoid excess movement, such as if you are swiveling in your chair when on camera. (Some people have been known to sit on a large bouncy ball while they facilitate, which I don't advise.) We want to focus learners on the message and content, not distract them from it.

C Is for Clothing

What virtual trainers wear on camera contributes to perceived credibility. In the past, I've worked as a professional voiceover artist and on-camera talent. In television commercials, we would bring a selection of clothing options to wear to the shoot, and the hired stylist or director would select the final outfits. They often preferred those brilliant, solid blues and greens because they popped on camera.

Solid, muted colors such as blue, teal, turquoise, green, tan, and browns work best on camera. Solid colors are best because they pop in the camera frame. You've likely observed professional journalists and news anchors often wear solid colors for TV broadcasts. (If you know you're going to be sitting the whole time and not visible elsewhere, what you wear on the bottom can be completely up to you.) But non-business attire is not appropriate, because as facilitator you always want to be dressed a step above your learners. You should look professional to enhance your credibility.

PRO TIP 36
Dress in solid colors on top, so you can visually pop.

You also want to create a contrast that sets you apart from your backdrop. So, wear light colors on a dark backdrop and dark on light. This is the also the same principle that works well developing PowerPoint slides with font color and backgrounds. What this means is that if you're up against a dark background, wear a lighter, solid color. If you have a lighter background, it would be better to wear a darker, solid color. What I see a lot is people wearing white shirts with a white background or a gray shirt with a gray background. This washes you out. Instead, a blue shirt would pop nicely on a light background.

Also avoid wearing thin stripes, busy or loud patterns, or distracting logos. Thin stripes can appear wavy and shimmery on camera. Large, distracting jewelry can call attention to itself. Watch out for jewelry that is noisy when you use the keyboard or rest your arm on the desk. I've advised clients in the past to remove their watch, bracelet, or necklace if they are very large and boisterous.

PRO TIP 37
Contrast the color of your clothing with your background—light on dark, dark on light.

H Is for Headroom

Next, let's touch on how to frame yourself in the camera. Most people do not know what they don't know when it comes to being on camera, and this includes headroom. Face-to-face environments offer binocular and peripheral vision. In the real world, we have so much longitude in our ability to see near and far, move our heads in all directions, and expand our visual field. We even have the freedom to turn our body and change our perspective with 360-degree movement if we so choose.

But when we look at a frame, its two-dimensional boundary provides closure and directs us to study everything inside the frame. Let's take a great piece of artwork, for example. Claude Monet's water lily painting invites us to take in every stroke, color, and technique, as well as the artistry of the whole. The framed perimeter directs our focus to everything inside the frame.

When we look on-screen at a facilitator in a box or circle or other shape, the two-dimensional visual window remains constant and the border calls attention to its contents. In the same way, when you are on camera we see you, everything to your side and top, and everything behind you. Make sure anything that is visible in the frame is in sync with you and your profession. What is visible must support you and not distract or call attention away from you.

Adjusting Headroom

It is quite common, but not advisable, to see a huge amount of room above one's head. Unfortunately, it is also common to see the head cut off at the hairline. Here are a few important tips to keep in mind about headroom. Frame yourself in the camera by either raising your device, lowering or raising your chair, or stacking something even and sturdy under your device to raise it up. Ideally, you should give yourself a small margin of space right above your head inside the frame.

Be wary of showing excessive amounts of headroom above you as well as truncating your head at the top. Often, people will leave most of the real estate in their camera frame to headroom and then their head is cut off at the chin at the bottom of the frame (Figure 5-10). In this example, all the real estate above your head is wasted on empty space. You want to fill the real estate in the camera frame to feature you. Ideally you would include more than just your neck and head in the frame. Better to see some of your upper body and hand gestures too.

Figure 5-10. Example of Excessive Headroom

There is also such a thing as being too close to the camera. As you'll notice, the closer you move toward camera, the larger your image becomes. We discussed this with movement and hand gestures. If your face is too close to the camera, those watching you will feel like you are up close and personal, but this distance is usually reserved for intimate relationships or conflict because it can feel like someone is invading your space. To avoid this distraction, extend your arm from where you are either standing or sitting. Your fingers should be able to touch the screen from this distance. If not, move back or forward to align yourself so that your fingers just reach the screen from where you are. Sitting or standing approximately an arm's length away from the screen will serve you well.

You'll want to place yourself in the center of the webcam. Make sure the spacing to your camera left and the spacing to your camera right are equal. This way you don't appear lopsided by being too far left or too far right. Most people are unaware of where they might be positioned in the frame. However, it makes a difference because of how you come across.

The Three-Finger Rule for Measuring Headroom

To properly frame yourself, use the three-finger rule as a measurement guide. The amount of space these fingers create is an appropriate amount of headroom to leave above your head or from the top of your hair. Essentially, hold up your index finger, middle finger, and ring finger together like you're counting to three. Lay them sideways so they are horizontal and place them right on top of your hair or head. Line up yourself in the frame, so that there is a three-finger margin of space between your head and the top of the frame.

If you are using a USB external microphone, you may think you need to be closer to the microphone, but it's better to see more of your body than just a head shot. Ideally, we want learners to be able to view your head and upper body so they can see more of you and your nonverbal movement.

Most experienced photographers learn to imagine the frame of the photo in thirds and place items where those thirds merge. When you are working with a webcam, centering yourself in the middle third of the frame is a good place to start. To help get comfortable, practice looking at yourself on camera, as uncomfortable as this might be, so you can see yourself as others see you.

PRO TIP 38
Center yourself in the camera frame with a small margin of headroom using the three-finger rule as a measurement guide.

On-Camera Participants

We've discussed at length how to develop your on-camera presence as a virtual facilitator. What about your virtual participants (Figure 5-11)? Should they also be required to be on camera during virtual training? According to virtual training expert Cindy Huggett's *The State of Virtual Training 2020* global survey, 55 percent of participants use webcams during virtual training either for the entire time or part of it (Huggett 2020).

As a guideline, you can invite or request learners turn on their cameras, but ultimately they should be able to choose whether to turn them on or keep them off. We are simply not privy to all the reasons participants do not wish to come on camera. (For example, they may have stayed up all night finishing a project, their camera isn't working right now, it's early hours in their time zone or middle of the night, or they're not feeling well.)

Figure 5-11. On-Camera Participants

Photo by Chris Montgomery on Unsplash.

To a certain extent, participant webcam use appears to be influenced by what their colleagues do. For example, nearly 70 percent of respondents in FSU's webcam research study reported feeling pressured to turn their cameras on when other people did (Dennen, Word, and Arslan 2021). But note that the study also found that as the size of the virtual event increases, "fewer people are comfortable having their webcams on."

Another reason to allow participants to remain off camera is because of screen fatigue. A compromise can be to give them advance notice before training day to be camera-ready on their top half and invite them to be on camera for certain parts, like introductions and breakouts. As facilitators, be cognizant that we unconsciously tend to focus more on participants we can see on camera, and it's human to sometimes forget to call on or talk directly to those we cannot see. We must make a note to deliberately include those we cannot see on-screen. So, when you ask a discussion question, make sure you call on others who are not on camera first to balance airtime with those who are. You might ask, for example, "Jon, we haven't heard from you yet. What are your thoughts?"

Individuals who know they are expected to be on camera tend to take two distinct actions before the live event. In FSU's 2021 webcam study, respondents said that if they anticipated they would be on camera, they would spend more time grooming beforehand and tidying their workspace surroundings. In fact, 82 percent of the more than 500 respondents said they groomed more carefully beforehand, and 79 percent said they tidied their surroundings first (Figure 5-12; Dennen, Word, and Arslan 2021).

Figure 5-12. Grooming and Tidying Affect the Decision to Be On Camera

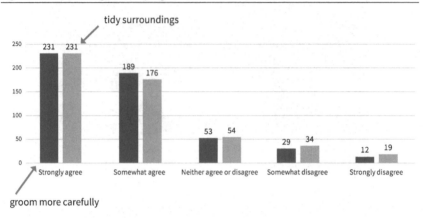

Factors affecting the decision to turn one's camera on

Reprinted with permission from Professor Vanessa Dennen, Florida State University.

Grooming and tidying workspaces are just two factors affecting a person's decision to turn on the camera. Respondents were also asked what their decision was influenced by, whether they were in virtual training, meetings, or online in general, and the top reason was the individual's degree of involvement in the live event. Other factors included what others do, attention, how many people were there or class size, and other related factors. Reference Figure 5-13 for percentages by factors.

Figure 5-13. Other Factors Affecting the Decision to Be On Camera

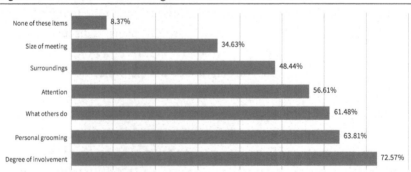

Reprinted with permission from Professor Vanessa Dennen, Florida State University.

For these reasons, if you know you'll invite participants to come on camera during the parts of the training that are most relational (such as introductions, group discussions, and breakouts), set those expectations for participants well before class day. For example, you could communicate this either through your LMS's automated messages, instructor welcome video, or pre-class email. In more robust virtual training programs where you meet multiple times over the course of several weeks or months, it's important to invite all to come on camera for initial introductions to build those relationships. Inviting—although not forcing—participants to come on camera for introductions can help to facilitate relationship building.

If, however, learners are working on the interactive whiteboard collectively or annotating on slides, you may invite them to turn off their cameras. Do share the rationale with them: to help them focus on the whiteboard or slides. To decide whether to encourage participants to turn their cameras on, ask yourself where their attention focus should be. If there is too much competing with the primary focus of an extended whiteboard activity, for example, you can invite them to turn cameras off. However, we also don't want to incur webcam whiplash by turning them on and off again repeatedly. Use your discretion to invite them to turn on cameras for extended activities like breakouts or large group discussions. Then, invite them to turn cameras off so they can focus better on the slide content, if they're annotating slides, or when you are explaining complex material. It is the responsibility of the virtual trainer to gently suggest when it might be a good time to go on or off camera and why.

Summary

Overall, establishing a sense of facilitator presence and place is an essential capability for virtual trainers. One of the main ways we can effectively project this is through our on-camera competence. As we have seen, there are many aspects that contribute to building professionalism and rapport through effective webcam use. These include instructor framing, nonverbal on-camera cues, and technical aspects such as audio quality and lighting. Because there are so many distractions that compete with learners' attention in today's modern learning environments, focused attention is critical. And so, it is our responsibility to do everything we can to eliminate and minimize distractions with video technology and leverage it as a relationship-building and connection tool to support our learners' virtual journey.

Ultimately, we want to be on camera with proper lighting, background, and framing during purposeful connection moments. These are the times when the focus is interpersonal connection. This can help to effectively establish a facilitator's presence for learners. Also, remember to use the acronym BLEACH to help you remember to clean up how you come across in the camera frame: B for Background; L for Lighting; E for Expressions; A for Angle; C for Clothing; and H for Headroom. In the next chapter, we will continue to build on this capability by exploring the various elements of vocal delivery. Projecting through live video and audio work together to establish a sense of place and presence for learners. All these components build toward a proficiency and competency in these areas.

So, the next time you are on camera and training others virtually, remind yourself that you are connecting with real people in real time, across space and distance. They just happen to be . . . on the other side of the camera.

Pro Tips for Developing Facilitator Presence through On-Camera Competence

TIP 30	Minimize or remove visual distractions from view in the camera frame.
TIP 31	Select a virtual backdrop that does not call attention to itself.
TIP 32	Light yourself from the front with plenty of soft, even lighting.
TIP 33	Be facially expressive in a natural way to aid learning.
TIP 34	Adjust yourself to be more eye level with the camera, and when instructionally feasible, look directly at the camera lens.
TIP 35	Avoid significant front-to-back body movement on camera; use slight side-to-side movements instead.
TIP 36	Dress in solid colors on top, so you can visually pop.
TIP 37	Contrast the color of your clothing with your background— light on dark, dark on light.
TIP 38	Center yourself in the camera frame with a small margin of headroom using the three-finger rule as a measurement guide.

"*Be congruent in body and voice.*"

—Elaine Biech, talent development expert and author

CHAPTER 6

Enhancing Facilitator Presence Through Audio and Vocal Delivery

It was a small virtual training class, only eight or nine learners (including me) and the facilitator. Our facilitator was a gentleman located in a big city in the US, and I remember when he turned on his video camera, he showed us the view out his window from a skyscraper. But what I remember most from that class was his genuine and enthusiastic voice. He spoke in a lower range. He emphasized certain words. When he said, "We're going to have fun today," he meant it. He varied the rate at which he spoke by slowing down in important places and speeding up in less critical points. He also was extremely conversational and called on us occasionally as he reviewed the assignments we had turned in from the last live online class with him.

In virtual training, you can do without certain tools or a missing worksheet, but your vocal instrument is irreplaceable. So why is it that as facilitators of virtual training, we take our voice for granted? Well, we use it every day, all day. However, we often give more attention to the technology operation than our vocal performance. It may be tempting to think we should not have to think twice about speaking, much less view it as a skill to professionally develop. Nothing could be farther from the truth. Your voice is one of the most powerful instruments you possess as a facilitator.

In virtual learning spaces, your voice is even more important than in the traditional classroom. With in-person classrooms, participants are privy to many visual cues in addition to an auditory voice. These cues help learners interpret the meaning of your words. But virtually, there are fewer visual, nonverbal, and physical cues available to interpret. This makes learners more reliant on the anchor of voice to develop a sense of the facilitator's presence.

In this chapter, we continue with the capability of facilitator presence, which helps learners gain a sense of the person they're being led by and the place where they are located (because learners are often curious about where facilitators are connecting from). In chapter 5, we discussed how you can effectively manage your on-camera presence. Now, we'll cover this capability from the angle of how to develop voice proficiency and ensure good audio quality. If done well, facilitator presence conveys a sense of sharing a space regardless of time or geographical distance. When you successfully pair voice and camera, you might even hear participants say, "I feel like we're really together."

In this chapter, we'll explore vocal elements, global languages, verbal messaging, paraverbal messaging, vocal care, and audio equipment. Let's dive in!

 THE BIG IDEA
Enhance your online presence as facilitator by elevating the quality of your audio and vocal delivery.

Audio Distractions in Virtual Training

Audio is an integral part of live online learning. Yet one of the most common challenges with virtual training is getting the audio right. As most audio visual specialists agree, poor audio can be even worse than poor video. This is an instance where rationalizing that your "sound is good enough" can have a serious negative influence on the training. If learners are not able to hear you well because of static, echoes, feedback, background sounds, or other noises, this can distract learners. Additionally, large pieces of jewelry hitting the desk, accidentally tapping your desk with your hand, or even the noise your headset cord can make when you turn your head can all be easily picked up by a microphone. All these distractions call attention away from where the focus of learning should be. In addition, ambient noise can present serious challenges to people who are hard of hearing or neurodivergent. Take this under consideration when using elements such as background music in videos, as well, since this may make it harder for those with hearing impairment to discern your speech.

Back in the early days of virtual training, we used a landline telephone to connect with audio and then a separate connection via the internet for the virtual training platform. Computer audio, or Voice over Internet Protocol (VoIP), was available then but far inferior in quality. Today, computer audio has far surpassed other audio options for virtual training. However, that doesn't mean ambient noise is always automatically eliminated during your live online learning sessions.

At one time, when I was near the end of facilitating a virtual training class from my home office, a neighbor's tree specialist crew arrived and proceeded to chop down some rather large trees with extremely noisy equipment right next to us. Fortunately, my husband was home that day and had the awareness to run outside and ask politely if they would mind waiting another 10 minutes before they continued and explained why. Luckily, they agreed. Thanks to his quick thinking, my virtual training concluded with just that brief disruption.

Thanks to noise-cancelling audio equipment and today's virtual training platforms, this is much more manageable. Fortunately, some virtual training platforms like Cisco Webex allow you to silence ambient noise like pets, kids, and even keyboard typing sounds. If you do not have the luxury of a virtual training platform that removes background noise, find a space to facilitate your virtual training class that is a quiet and free from distraction. For example, I always shut my windows and home office door to minimize any unwanted background noises when facilitating a virtual class. Do what you can to control the noise in your environment. If working from home, place pets in other rooms, shut your office door (if you have one), and alert others in your living space about when they should be extra quiet and why. Place a sign that says "Do Not Disturb—Class in Session" on the closed door to your room or reserve a separate conference room away from your work area in the office.

Once, I was training a virtual class in the middle of a winter night in my time zone because my learners were international participants and it was daytime for them. I was using an external microphone, and my home office at the time happened to be in a finished basement. Midway through the session, my furnace turned on. The heat vents were in the ceiling directly above my desk and the metal in the vents reverberated loudly and distractingly when the furnace was on. So, when I gave my virtual attendees a break, I ran upstairs to turn down the heat. I learned from that point on to warm up the basement first and then turn the heat down right before training sessions to avoid the constant noise interference. This is an example of how virtual trainers need to adapt quickly to unforeseen circumstances and how they need to thoroughly think through their environments to anticipate possible distractions. Do your best to first predict, then minimize, and, when possible, eliminate competing noise.

While most of this chapter focuses on your voice in virtual training, it's important to also touch on the voices of your learners. Some virtual training practitioners recommend participants stay muted during live online learning. What you need to remember though, is that muting can also inhibit conversation. If you have a smaller class (10 or fewer) and they do not have a lot of background noise in their environments, you can ask them to keep their microphones on. As noises emerge, they can mute as needed. This allows for more fluid conversation. Even when you have a large class, for small group discussions like breakouts, ask participants to remain unmuted, if possible, to keep the conversation flowing naturally. Pre-class instructions should be sent to all participants encouraging them to find a quiet space free from distractions to attend the training, as we established earlier in chapter 3. This can help set the stage for muting less often. Again, this is primarily important for those in an environment with ambient noise where you want to be careful not to disrupt the flow of the live session.

 PRO TIP 39
If your virtual training platform does not have the ability to silence ambient noise, use noise-cancelling headsets or an external mic in a quiet space.

Vocal Elements

Our voices can communicate several things in a variety of ways. For example, they can communicate enthusiasm or lack thereof, inflection, rate of speech, and more. It is often the energy in our voice and passion for the topic that can inspire others.

To aid your growth as a professional facilitator, the rest of this chapter helps you be more vocally aware. Together, let's explore various components of voice and tips for effective delivery. Some schools of thought divide voice between language and paralanguage. Language, of course, is the words we use, and paralanguage includes all the other ways we communicate without words; for example, nonverbal gestures, body movement, and tone. In our virtual training context, we will focus specifically on the verbal (what we say) and paraverbal (how we say it) elements.

Global Languages

First, I want to touch on a universal consideration for international audiences. Over the last decade, our virtual classes have become increasingly global with participants attending from multiple countries. If you work for an organization with several locations around the globe, this influences the words you choose and your rate of speech as a virtual facilitator. For example, you may facilitate virtual sessions in a language with non-native speakers located in other countries. If you facilitate in English, Darlene Christopher (2011) of World Bank recommends doing your best to use international English that is free from slang, idioms, and other references unique to one country or another.

Overall, it is helpful to speak slower, enunciate more clearly, and use plain language easily understood by all. If learners do not recognize the spoken words, they cannot ascertain their meaning. Another option is to use a virtual training platform that automatically provides live translations in multiple languages. Virtual platforms like Digitell offer automated closed captioning services that provide language translations for learners, who can select from multiple language options. Webex and Microsoft Teams also provide closed captioning and language translation. Offering live language translation in virtual training platforms will continue to become more widespread. This is a very important accessibility feature for individuals who are deaf and hard-of-hearing as well.

Verbal Messaging

Even though we likely take our verbal delivery for granted, there are several nuances that can help us be more vocally effective when facilitating live online classes. To improve vocal delivery in virtual training, we can focus on breath support, pausing, rate, pronunciation, enunciation, emphasis, inflection, and more. One research study from Amsterdam, Netherlands, and Canada examined the skills for successful synchronous facilitation and identified necessary communication skills that included "clear, appropriately paced, engaging and articulate speech" (Phelps and Vlachopoulos 2020).

One of the best ways to get a sense of your vocal delivery is to record one of your virtual training sessions and listen to the playback without watching the visual part. Close your eyes and listen to the audio of as if you were a learner. This is a unique opportunity to understand how others might experience your facilitation. Almost everyone finds it difficult to listen to themselves, but if you do so with a trusted confidante, they can also help point out opportunities for improvement. Celebrate your strengths and be open to areas for professional growth. Some of us use excessive vocalized pauses, other talk too fast, and still others unintentionally swallow consonants.

In this section on verbal messaging, we'll tackle the following topics:

- Breath support
- Vocalized pauses
- Brief pausing
- Speaking rate
- Pronunciation
- Enunciation

Breath Support

The voice is all about breath. We would not be able to speak without breath support. The greater the breath support, the more resonant and powerful your voice will be. Breath comes up from the abdominal areas in our diaphragm to vibrate your vocal cords in the larynx (your voice box). Tongue placement and how we shape our mouths then forms consonants and vowels that become our speech. When we fully support our voices with breath and a relaxed larynx, magic happens when we facilitate online.

You may be accustomed to projecting good volume during in-person classes, but even when you facilitate virtually, ensure that your breath support is still coming from your diaphragm. This way you will have more air behind your voice. And if you have more air, you have more control. To ensure you are breathing properly from your diaphragm, try this experiment. When you go to bed tonight, lay on your back and place your hand on your lower abdomen. Observe how your body naturally breathes. When you lie on your back, your body will naturally breathe in this fully supported way. Use this awareness to inform supported breathing when you facilitate virtual training events. Alternatively, if you notice your shoulders rising and falling when you speak and train online, this is shallow breathing. This is designed for quick breaths like after exercising when you need to catch your breath.

Body alignment also makes a difference vocally. Sit or stand upright when you facilitate virtual training, with your shoulders back and a straight posture. This allows you to best support your sound and can also help provide an energy boost as your voice rises and moves out.

PRO TIP 40
With upright posture, breathe from your diaphragm when you facilitate online.

Vocalized Pauses

Vocalized pauses are the filler words we use habitually to fill awkward silence. We use them because we are uncomfortable with silence. They fill the gap while we think of what we want to say next when speaking. They're formally called vocalized pauses because you vocalize where you really should pause.

It is common in many languages to use filler words between sentences. These filler words become so entrenched that the more we repeat them, the more they're reinforced. With more heightened awareness—which is the first step to reducing them—you may begin to recognize vocalized pauses you already use in your native language. In the English language, for example, some common filler words are "um," "uh," "like," "right," "so," and "OK."

Because vocalized pauses are common, using them is not completely taboo. Occasional vocalized pauses interspersed throughout your facilitation is fine. However, when used excessively, they can draw learners' attention away from content and become distracting. It becomes problematic when learners begin paying attention to the vocalized pauses instead of listening to what you're saying. This is especially the case when learners start counting how many *ums* you say rather than what you are saying.

As facilitators, work to minimize vocal distractions with the following steps. First, identify your unique filler word. We all have idiosyncrasies and usually have a few filler words that we tend to repeat over and over. It's very likely your over-used filler word is very different from mine. Because you might not even know what filler words you use or if you have any, there are two ways you can identify them. One way is to listen to the audio of a recorded virtual training session you led. This will be eye-opening for you. I realize people rarely want to see or hear recordings of themselves, but it is honestly the best way to learn what needs to be improved. This gives you the unique opportunity to sit in the shoes of your learners and experience what they do. Another way to identify your unique filler words is to ask a trusted colleague to watch a recording or sit in on one of your virtual training sessions to listen specifically to your speech patterns for the sake of professional improvement.

The second step to becoming aware of what unique fillers you use is to ask a trusted colleague to listen for frequency. Rehearse your virtual training while your colleague logs into the platform to listen to you. Speak from your notes as you normally would and accelerate through the learning activities where learners would normally be doing something. Then, every time you say your filler word, they can raise their virtual hand. This way you can get a sense of frequency and whether it's excessive.

The third step is to catch yourself either right before you try to use the vocalized pause or while you're doing it. To change this behavior, you first need to replace it with something. For example, every time you are tempted to use "so," "like," or "um," you can swallow instead, if it's comfortable to do so. Or you can close your lips instead and make a short hum as a replacement behavior. You will learn very quickly how frequently you might be tempted to use a filler word.

From here, the ultimate goal, of course, is to phase out the swallowing, closing lips together, or brief hum replacement behaviors and instead permanently replace them with a silent pause.

PRO TIP 41
Work to eventually replace vocalized pauses with a real pause.

Brief Pausing

Pauses are an inherent part of nature's rhythm. In the physical world, there are many polarities: day and night, action and rest, sound and silence. Pausing is natural.

There are also times to speak and times to pause. For example, as you are facilitating virtual training class, you may try to compress a lot of information into a brief speaking time: "So that wraps up this section on how you can identify priorities at work. What questions do you have? I know this can be challenging when it feels like you have a million projects hitting you at once. OK, so next we want to address SMART goals. Has anyone written these before?"

It can be easy to be so focused on what you need or want to say that you forget to pause and allow participants to process what you've just said. Intersperse pauses after questions and even when you transition to subtopics. As author Darlene Christopher (2015) points out, participants need time to process thoughts, type responses in chat (and even more time if typing in a second language), and time to remember how to un-mute their audio connection to speak. Thankfully, many platforms now provide more attention-getting reminders when either a learner or facilitator forgets to unmute and inadvertently speaks while muted.

Our own physical bodies provide a helpful metaphor. When your body is in the rest and digest stage, your digestion system works better. In contrast, when you eat in a state of high stress, this is not helpful for digestion. Likewise, for learners to best digest content, absorb new concepts, and connect to their prior knowledge, providing pauses as a brief "rest period" can help facilitate this. Briefly pausing while facilitating not only helps learners process what was just said, but also reminds you to slow your rate. Leverage brief, natural pauses as you facilitate live online learning. Purposeful silence has a place.

PRO TIP 42
Pause briefly between sentences to create space for learners to process what you just said.

As mentioned previously in chapter 4, silence is called dead air in radio broadcasting. Some practitioners suggest it is to be avoided at all costs with virtual training. Extended, unannounced silence makes us think something went wrong, such as a technical difficulty. Although this is certainly true for radio, virtual learning is not radio. When you ask a question, and there is only silence, it just means you need to wait a little longer for the first person to speak up. Sometimes this means holding your tongue or placing yourself on mute. Brief silence commands attention and allows for learners to think of how to respond.

Speaking Rate

Movement naturally captures our attention, as we explore more deeply in chapter 8. So, how might this influence our vocal delivery as facilitators? When a virtual trainer says several phrases rapidly and then slows to deliver a different phrase more slowly, what happens to the learner's attention? This subtle change, varying the speaking rate, draws attention to the novelty of the speech pattern. For example, the virtual trainer might say quickly, "Everyone, scroll to page 11 in your digital workbook. Let's focus next on the four types of behavioral styles." Then you might slow down as you explain what each of those four main styles are.

Have your virtual training evaluations ever pointed out that you talk too fast? Perhaps that feedback surprised you. Some people are naturally fast talkers, and think their speaking rate is fine; it's as normal as breathing. This is understandable. Fast talkers are conditioned over a lifetime of speaking. In my experience, fast talkers are often also fast thinkers. The downside to this is that learners may be left behind. If you speak rapid-fire during a virtual training session (especially without pauses), your learners will soon tire of the accelerated pace. They simply cannot keep up, and as a result, they may disengage and start doing other things.

Participant attention is a precious commodity and essential to learning. We do everything we can to minimize distraction and appropriately direct attention. So, how might this be remedied?

If you try to remind yourself to slow down, it might work initially but eventually you will find you are back to the races again (that's conditioning!). However, there is a solution that works even better. If you are a natural fast talker, slow your rate by speaking in phrases—not sentences. This new rhythm will naturally slow your pace. Speak a phrase, pause very briefly, speak a phrase, pause very briefly, and so on. You can even leave yourself notes on your monitor to remind you to do so. Yes, it will take practice to recondition yourself over time, but it works. Do not separate every word, just insert a brief pause after a short, spoken phrase. Deliberately slowing your speaking rate also gives non-native speakers more time to recognize, translate, and understand what you are saying.

For example, in your virtual training session, let's imagine you say the following as an instruction before a breakout activity: "You will need to read the scenario in your participant guide and designate one person in your group to summarize the actions you decide to take to address this situation." To slow your rate by speaking in phrases, you would instead say, "You will need to read the scenario—in your participant guide—and designate one person in your group—to summarize the actions you decide to take—to address this situation." This way, your rate of speech is organically slowed down because you are speaking in phrases. Be wary of sounding too robotic though; keep that conversational style.

Also, do a self-check before you begin a virtual session to gauge your state of being. Be wary of adopting an accelerated speech rate if you feel like you have a lot of material to cover, feel behind schedule, or sense that you don't have a lot of time. It is never worth it to rush. Learners will pick up on your nervous energy and feel rushed too. This even shows up on evaluations as the feedback, "felt rushed." Breathe in slowly, breathe out slowly, and remind yourself that a non-rushed pace is better for participants and learning.

 PRO TIP 43
To slow speaking rate, speak in phrases—not sentences.

Pronunciation

Pronunciation is speaking a word correctly with the appropriate emphasis according to the cultural norms for saying that word. If you are facilitating in a non-native language or are unsure of how to pronounce certain words before you train, there are many apps and YouTube videos available to help you.

When I facilitated a virtual training session with participants from Japan, I held the session in the evening in my time zone, so it would be daytime for my learners. The client informed me that they also spoke English and I could train in English. I do not speak Japanese, but I knew the importance of pronouncing their names correctly. And, as we discussed in chapters 3 and 4, I also knew the importance of using participant names throughout the training. As a result, I enlisted the help of a Japanese teacher from my family's school at the time. This high school teacher graciously agreed to create an audio recording of how to say each of my participants' names from a class roster. I listened to her recording beforehand and wrote out their names with notes on emphasis and syllables to remind myself how to pronounce them. This way, I was able to say their names aloud with confidence when I affirmed their comments in chat or when they came off mute to share. I was only on camera at the beginning of the session, so I was able to check my roster and notes on pronunciation frequently without them seeing me look down. I had an expedient way to recognize their name in chat and then could call attention to it aloud.

If you are not sure how to pronounce something during your rehearsals, look it up online to hear playbacks of certain words so you can feel confident saying them.

Enunciation

Enunciation is different than pronunciation. *Enunciation* means clearly articulating consonants and vowels. If you have been told that you do not clearly articulate all your words or that you swallow some of your consonants, it could be that you are holding back air or not fully shaping sound with your mouth. For most virtual trainers, if you have conditioned speech patterns such as slurring certain consonants when you speak, you can discover them by recording one of your virtual training sessions and listening to the playback.

Your speech can also be affected by your thoughts. For example, if you're trying to hide a lisp, you don't like the quality of your voice, or you're just trying to get to the finish line of your virtual training session, it will affect your speech. Be proud of your voice and let it shine. The prescriptive tip about speaking in phrases will not only slow your speech rate but can also help with enunciation and inflection too.

You can also practice over-articulating certain consonants or words before your virtual class begins to warm up your enunciation if you are someone who may not articulate as clearly. Ideally, we want to hear all vowels and consonants to correctly interpret the words you speak and their meaning as you intended.

PRO TIP 44
Vary your rate of vocal delivery for emphasis and as an attention-getting technique.

Now that we have addressed the verbal aspect of vocal delivery, let's focus on the paraverbal elements.

Paraverbal Messaging

A key part of your vocal message as an online facilitator is what you say. However, how you say what you say can even be more important. As discussed earlier, verbal delivery is what you say and the paraverbal is how you say it. I used to work as a professional voiceover talent and on-camera talent for commercials, multimedia productions, film, and other media. We used many techniques as voiceover artists to be effective and create interest. Many of these elements can also improve your delivery as a virtual trainer or online facilitator. Let's take a closer look at each:

- Tone
- Conversational style
- Nervousness
- Pitch
- Vocal inflection
- Energy

Tone

Think about when you last visited the grocery store or an open produce market. At the end of the transaction, did the merchant say, "Thanks. Have a good day"? If you isolate those words by themselves, they are pleasant enough. But what happens when those words are said to you with an apathetic tone? Immediately, you know the merchant doesn't mean it, and is not wishing you a good day. When there is a mismatch between what someone says and how they say it, we instinctually know to not believe the message. Thus, how we say something can either negate or reinforce what we say.

When we apply this to virtual training, remember that everything you say is more powerful when the how and the what are in sync. If they're not, your tone will negate the meaning of your words. For example, if at the start of a virtual training session you say, "I'm excited to be here and to have all of you here," but your tone communicates you aren't excited at all, you just cancelled the message's meaning. You also missed a window of opportunity to build credible rapport. Learners can tell when tone contradicts your message. They also know to believe tone over words when they're in conflict, and they're right to do so.

As a live online facilitator, be genuine and speak authentically. When you facilitate live online learning, listen carefully to how you say what you say. There is an element of more taxed listening required of you here. Another way you can help yourself is to listen for your own use of emotionally charged phrases like "My pleasure," "No problem," or "That's great." If you assist someone in the training class and then you say, "My pleasure" but your tone sounds like "That was a waste of time," we know it certainly wasn't your pleasure. If you say, "No problem," but you sound irritated, your tone will communicate that instead. And if a learner shares something and you say "That's great," but your tone makes it sound like you really don't care, once again, your tone negates your verbal message.

There are some awareness questions you can ask yourself to be more attuned and in sync. Ask yourself, "How am I coming across?" "What is my tone?" Check your tone by watching the visual expressions of your participants on video or by intentionally listening to hear if how you say something is in sync with what you say. The biggest tip is to be real and genuine. If you really are excited to be there and you say that at the front-end, your tone will naturally convey your excitement. If you say, "I can't wait to show you all the great goal setting tips we're going to learn today" and you don't mean it, learners can tell as well and they'll match your lack of enthusiasm.

Conversational Style

At some point, you likely have attended virtual training where the facilitator read verbatim from a script. From a virtual trainer perspective, we understand why this might be tempting. Quite simply, it's easier—but it is not best practice. Everything is thought out ahead of time and written down exactly the way it should be elegantly said. This way, you do not have to worry about finding the right words in the moment. When this happens in the context of virtual training, however, learners either check their smart-phones, send text messages, shop online, or drift away.

When we speak during live online learning, it should not sound rote or like we're reading verbatim. Learners do not want a monologue. Instead, to be most effective, use a conversational speaking style. Speak in dialogue, not a monologue. I recommend you not read a script as a virtual facilitator, unless you have the very rare ability to sound like you are not reading. Sometimes, I will script my closing statements to make sure I hit all the points, because let's face it, at the end of a virtual training, you're tired and may not be at your eloquent best anymore. But I do work hard to make it sound spontaneous and conversational regardless.

Speaking in a conversational style is also supported by evidence-based research for most effective learning. Richard Mayer coined the term *personalization principle* based on his leading multimedia studies. This principle states that people learn better from a conversational style than a formal style (Mayer 2014). Conversational style means you're speaking extemporaneously and choosing the words you use at the time that you speak them. It should also feel like we're sitting in your living room having a conversation—albeit, hopefully an energetic conversation.

 PRO TIP 45
Speak with a conversational style using informal language.

Another way to speak in a conversational tone is to use personal pronouns like "you," "us," "we," and "let's," which makes it feel more like the speaker is talking directly to participants (Mayer 2014). Using first- and second-person pronouns when we facilitate aids learning. When pronouns such as *he, she,* or *they* are used, learners tend not to pay as much attention. With second-person pronouns and a conversational speaking style, however, learners pay more attention because it feels like the facilitator is talking directly to them. Remember, if someone speaks directly to you, you listen.

One tip that helps me be more conversational is to allow my hands to gesture naturally when I speak. Hand gestures are a natural part of organic communication. I've noticed they also encourage more vocal variety, inflection, emphasis, and many of the other elements we discuss in this chapter. Just as when a violinist, pianist, or vocalist might use their body language to move to the music as they perform, when the whole body is in sync with communication, it naturally boosts our overall effectiveness. Experiment with this technique for yourself to see if your speaking style becomes even more conversational.

There is much research to support the value of conversational style in learning, and how it creates heightened listening on the part of the learner. As Ruth Clark (2020) advises from consistent evidence-based research, you can "promote deeper learning by addressing learners in a conversational manner using first- and second-person and polite phrases." This demonstrates that live online facilitators should absolutely speak in a conversational style because it is more effective for learning.

Nervousness

When we are nervous while facilitating, it is normal for there to be shakiness in our voice or to sound out of breath. As a physiological reaction to stress, your heart may start to beat faster, which causes you to breathe faster. However, if you breathe from your belly, you will have greater breath support, especially if you're nervous. When we experience stress, we tend to unknowingly hold tension in parts of our body, including our vocal cords. When we are nervous, this tension cuts off our full breath support and could cause us to speak softer or in a higher, strained pitch.

To help remain calm, try a set of three repetitions of a breathing exercise before your virtual training class begins. Inhale for four counts in through your nose, and exhale for eight counts through your mouth. Physiologically, your body will realize it is not in danger if your breathing is slow and steady. This is how you trigger the rest and digest state, instead of the fight or flight response.

Additionally, rolling your shoulders can help to relax your body. Humor, of course, is a great way to release tension, and yawning can also be a healthy release. Sometimes, chatting with your producer ahead of time after the platform is prepped and ready to go can help you relax and settle in before participants arrive.

Pitch

There is a wide variety of voices and speaking styles among individuals. Some speak with high-pitch ranges, others have lower voices, while still others are somewhere in between. Without having to sacrifice your own speaking style or change your voice, you can still benefit from finding a pitch range that is most comfortable for learners listening to you.

For those with high pitches, my recommendation is to become comfortable with your full range, especially your lower register. One easy tip for finding the lowest part of your register is to pretend like you're answering a question. When someone asks you if you're a virtual facilitator and you say "uh-huh" as a yes, you will discover that you usually answer in the lower part of your register. From there, continue to speak, allowing your voice to drop deep into your belly and with supported breath speak from this place. Ideally, it's best to use more of your vocal range, high and low, which introduces variety and helps garner interest. For those with boomy bass voices, you also want to strike a balance with variety and use more of your range with natural inflection. Maintaining a balanced voice can also contribute to credibility.

If you record one of your virtual training sessions and listen to the playback, you may notice other patterns. For example, some online facilitators have a pattern of speech where, at the end of every sentence, their voice rises as if they were asking a question. This rising inflection can inaccurately and unintentionally communicate insecurity or that they're asking a question when they're not. While in Western cultures, it's appropriate for the pitch to go higher when you ask a question, and it's better to let the pitch of your voice drop at the end of a sentence. This, of course, depends on your culture and native language, as many intonations can change the meaning of words across different languages, which provide exceptions.

Vocal Inflection

As Aristotle wrote well over 2,000 years ago, the right management of the voice "to express the various emotions" with varying pitch and rhythms suitable to various subjects "we cannot do without." In other words, we need inflection. *Inflection* is the movement of our voice using a variety of pitches (low, middle, and high). Have you ever noticed that when a person's pitch stays the same when they talk, you tune out? We are wired to notice things that do not stay the same. Again, the magic is in the mix. As online facilitators, we want to strive for variety with inflection.

One of the most popular radio shows from old-time radio was *The Shadow*. It first aired in the 1930s and ran until 1954 as a 30-minute program. It's worth asking why audiences were so riveted for decades by only audio. One potential reason is because of how much the characters used inflection, especially in the main character's trademark laugh. Their voices went up and down in pitch and used emphasis and varying rates.

Even when we are not on camera during virtual training, using a variety of inflection can still help hold your learners' attention. When coaching one of my clients who later taught both virtually and in-person, we recorded his vocal delivery. As we listened to the playback together, I asked him to draw a diagram of how much inflection he heard in his delivery. I drew a diagram too. When we compared our drawings at the end, we were surprised to see that they looked almost identical. We had both mostly drawn a static line with a few small ups and downs. This was a great way to illustrate what he had not realized before. It was a great segue for us to begin incorporating more inflection into his vocal delivery for his learners' benefit.

Monotone is the opposite of inflection. This is when someone's pitch stays relatively the same while they speak. If we facilitate with monotone delivery, it is underwhelming for learners, and they will tune out quickly. Monotone delivery certainly does not help you connect with learners.

If you tend to facilitate with little inflection, one technique you can experiment with is rehearsing to music. Music naturally rises and falls. During rehearsal, play instrumental music that rises and falls to encourage yourself to use more fluctuation in your own voice. However, the inflection should not be contrived. When I used to record voiceover narrations in studios, sometimes the sound engineer would play the music track for me that would be added later for the final production. Doing a practice read with the music playing in my ears helped me create more energy and inflection, so that when we did the final recording, the takes were so much better.

One classic exercise you can do to help generate more inflection is to think about saying "yes" in different ways. First, say "yes" like you are angry, then surprised, then shocked, then sad, then bored, then happy. When you exaggerate this skill at first, it can be a venue to help you explore more inflection in your own voice and then start incorporating it in your virtual training sessions.

PRO TIP 47
To create more interest, vary your vocal inflection.

Energy

According to Darlene Christopher in *The Successful Virtual Classroom* (2015), learners can read a facilitator's level of energy from their voice, and whether to be interested in a topic because of what the facilitator projects. Our voices reveal energetic levels. The best virtual facilitators are energetic, enthusiastic, and passionate. Perhaps you have seen "great energy" typed on your evaluations for virtual training. Smiling can also convey a more pleasant and energetic tone for facilitators. Learners can hear the smile in your voice even if you're off camera.

Energy is contagious. If you watch videos of people laughing on You-Tube for approximately four minutes, I guarantee you will be smiling, if not laughing by the end. Why? Because you have mirror neurons in your brain. When you see someone else smiling, you smile. When someone else yawns, you yawn. When someone else laughs, you laugh. When you facilitate online, if you bring positive energy, your learners feel it. The inverse is also true. If you bring negative energy to your synchronous sessions, your learners feel this too.

I advise virtual facilitators to generate twice the energy they would normally have when they are training. There are two main reasons for this. First, energy takes a hit when it is transmitted through technology either via computer audio or the virtual training platform. Second, we are not able to play off the natural energy we would normally experience with an in-room dynamic—think of the energy level of the audience at an in-person stand-up comedy show, for example. Therefore, we must work harder to convey energy transmitted through technology and multimedia. Facilitating a session while standing instead of sitting may also help you deliver with more energy.

I used to drive my father to special sessions at Gilda's Club where they generously provided emotional support, cancer education, and hope to those fighting cancer. On one such occasion, I dropped him off for a laughter class. My father knew intuitively that there was something to the axiom, "laughter is the best medicine." When I returned to pick him up an hour or so later, to my surprise, the entire class was uproariously belly laughing—including my father. I could not help but smile when I walked in. His energy had spread to me instantly. As I drove my father home, I asked him what was so funny, and he smiled and said, "I have no idea." There was so much positive energy in that room, and all those mirror neurons were at work.

Obviously, I'm not suggesting we make our virtual learners belly laugh during a virtual session, unless, of course, that happens naturally. The point is that your energy—positive or negative—is contagious. It emanates from your presence, personality, and voice. To help you bring this energy to your virtual training you can remind yourself of the bigger role you play and the higher purpose behind developing others to help your organization accomplish its vision and mission. You also are hopefully excited about the training topic naturally. This way your learners will be as well. If you aren't, try to dig deep and find at least one thing about the training topic that you are genuinely excited about. Start there and your enthusiasm may grow. Obviously, if your training topic is how to manage unacceptable employee performance, that is not a go-getter topic for anyone involved. However, you can dig deep to discover the motivation for you in the topic to help your organization succeed and bring that natural energy to your training. It must be real.

The virtual training takeaway for us is that we must strive to lead the creation of healthy, supportive, positive climates that nurture learning as we discussed in chapter 3. We do this through effective vocal delivery and positive energy. We show up as our best selves and with our whole person to help learners be successful.

Vocal Care for Virtual Facilitators

Because we rely so heavily on our voices in virtual training, we are essentially vocal athletes. Our vocal cords are muscles like other muscles in our body, so they, too, benefit from a warm-up before extensive use. Otherwise in extreme situations when you're talking at length for several days and this is outside your normal routine, you risk straining your voice, temporarily losing your voice, or going hoarse. Staying hydrated is particularly important beforehand. Contrary to popular belief, you actually need to drink water several hours before training to hydrate your vocal cords. Ice-cold water can usually shock vocal cords, so drinking room-temperature water during online classes is better. I also find that warm, herbal tea can soothe my vocal cords and remove mouth noises like clicking when I speak. Caffeine can also dry out the larynx, so be judicious with caffeinated beverages before a session. Ideally, we want to keep our voice box hydrated and relaxed to produce the best sound.

Some days you may have several virtual training classes and will be using your voice more than usual. On these days, you will want to vocally warm up beforehand. This is especially helpful if you facilitate first thing in the morning in your time zone. Let's look at some vocal warm-ups you can try:

Humming.

- Simply humming is a great way to ease your vocal cords back into use in the early morning, and is one of the best ways to warm up your voice. You can hum a scale or a tone or a few notes.

Sirens.

- Begin at the very top of your vocal range projecting a resonant sound and then let you voice drop to your lowest register. It should sound just like an ambulance siren going by. Then reverse the direction and do the same thing—going from the bottom of your range to the top of your range. After a few times, you will hear how it opens your voice for your entire register.

"Aluminum, linoleum, aluminum, linoleum."

- This is a standard vocal warmup. If you say these words repeatedly and over-enunciate them, it helps you warm up your ability to shape sounds with your mouth and more clearly enunciate consonants so learners can understand everything you say.

Audio Equipment

Before facilitating, always test your equipment before class day. For example, the unique circuitry of different devices can result in a high-quality microphone working well with one device, but not with another. Every computer can react differently to a microphone pairing, so always check your equipment ahead of time and have someone else join you on a tech check to let you know how it sounds and if there are any issues. Work with your producer, colleague, or trusted confidante to thoroughly test audio quality before your live event. This will also reduce your stress level. If you are testing it yourself, record part of your speaking portion and listen to the playback to assess quality.

With live online delivery, everything a facilitator says in real time must be communicated through a microphone. If using an external microphone, ensure it is set to the cardioid setting, which looks like an upside-down heart. It's also helpful to train in a carpeted room filled with furniture, curtains, and other material that can help absorb sound, so your audio doesn't bounce and reverberate. And be wary of buzzing sounds from monitors or overhead lights. When using an external mic, you may need to use other lighting, switch computers, or change rooms.

Noise-cancelling headsets and other devices as mentioned earlier in this chapter can be a great remedy for ambient, environmental noise. Noise-cancelling headsets work best with lower sound frequencies. You can significantly improve your audio quality by using a USB external microphone, headset, earbuds, or air pods. Thankfully, transmitting background noise through your microphone is less likely with headsets. As a best practice, avoid using your device's built-in microphone because it can make your voice sound like it is bouncing off the walls in a cave or large room.

To optimize audio quality, where you place an external microphone and headset mic also makes a difference. If you place it too close to your mouth, you can sound too breathy and it might pick up breathing and other clicking mouth sounds. If it is too far away, learners may find it difficult to hear you. For an external microphone, elevate it so it is approximately at chin level but still out of camera view. Do not position your mouth within inches of the microphone or directly aligned with it. If you do, it will create distracting pops of air (plosives) and learners will be able to hear your breathing. This can be distracting and make it more challenging for learners to clearly hear what you're saying. Position the microphone slightly to the side of your mouth to avoid these popping sounds. For headsets, place the mic above your mouth to avoid plosives or farther below your mouth, aligned with your chin. These are the sweet spots where you will not be too close to pick up unwanted breathing sounds, yet at the same time you're not too far away to magnify sound.

In terms of vocal volume, adopt the mindset of projecting your voice to fill the space and not unintentionally shrinking your voice because you have a microphone. Remind learners to let you know if they cannot hear you. They usually let you know in chat or your producer will let you know if your audio drops mid-session. It is always best practice to set levels and check audio with your producer at least 30 minutes before the live session begins, even if you met for a tech-check on a different day. This buffer also provides an extra window of time in case you need to troubleshoot anything else technically.

Summary

Vocal delivery is just one way to enhance facilitator presence with learners. There is always room for professional growth. We have established that the voice plays a significant role in communicating intention, care, attention, energy, enthusiasm, professionalism, pace, rapport, how much learners pay attention, and more. We've also established that how you say something is just as important as what you say, if not more important.

Elevating your energy, varying your inflection, minimizing vocalized pauses, using proper breath support, and speaking with a conversational style all help to build your capability in facilitator presence. In addition to developing your online presence as a facilitator, it's also important to develop your technical fluency. In the next chapter, we'll look at how you can best leverage your platform's technical tools for virtual training.

As a professional virtual facilitator, continue to enhance your online presence by elevating the quality of your audio and vocal delivery. Keep polishing your facilitator presence skills to take your virtual training to the next level.

In the next chapter, we'll explore the many tools available to you in virtual training platforms.

Pro Tips for Improving Facilitator Presence through Vocal Delivery

TIP 39	If your virtual training platform does not have the ability to silence ambient noise, use noise-cancelling headsets or an external mic in a quiet space.
TIP 40	With upright posture, breathe from your diaphragm when you facilitate online.
TIP 41	Work to eventually replace vocalized pauses with a real pause.
TIP 42	Pause briefly between sentences to create space for learners to process what you just said.
TIP 43	To slow speaking rate, speak in phrases—not sentences.
TIP 44	Vary your rate of vocal delivery for emphasis and as an attention-getting technique.
TIP 45	Speak with a conversational style using informal language.
TIP 46	Intentionally use personal pronouns to promote deeper learning.
TIP 47	To create more interest, vary your vocal inflection.

"vILT tools offer features that enable instructors to optimize the learning experience, helping learners retain information and collaborate, potentially increasing employee engagement, and driving revenue."

—Josh Bersin, global industry analyst, thought leader, and author

CHAPTER 7

Leveraging Your Platform's Technical Tools

When I worked for a large US corporation, one of the leaders often updated the entire division through synchronous web conferencing. Although most staff were on-site at desks, others were remote or in field offices. Unfortunately, even though the platform offered many interactive features, these sessions did not take advantage of them. The communication was one-way, absent of any interaction. Attendees only heard this leader's live audio and viewed slide after slide for what seemed like a millennium. Sound familiar? I'm sure you may have had a similar experience at one time or another. As you can imagine, there were literally paper airplanes flying over cubicle walls during those virtual sessions.

With virtual training, online facilitators must play an active role to continually refocus learner attention. As we established earlier in this book, thoughtful experience design, cultivating a welcoming and psychologically safe environment, elevating your virtual facilitation skills, building your on-camera competence, and optimizing vocal delivery are all ways to direct focus and support learning. In this chapter, let's turn our attention to how to use virtual platform tools to capture attention and engage learners.

What is remarkable about video conferencing and virtual training platforms is their ability to integrate multiple media formats seamlessly. This is evident through the integration of video, internet content, application sharing, audio, collaborative whiteboard tools, live polls, and chat. By discussing these tools, we introduce the next capability, technical fluency. *Technical fluency* means upskilling your proficiency in all things digital related to virtual training. This means modern virtual trainers and professional online facilitators must be well-versed in a variety of rapidly changing platforms, virtual tools, on-screen interactions, and updated hardware and software. Naturally, during the COVID-19 pandemic, features and functionality improved rapidly as high customer demand exploded globally. These marketable product improvements will likely continue into the foreseeable future.

Although some facilitators use a variety of virtual tools in their online training, others may not. And other practitioners are not always confident about how best to use them and why. There is a current skill and knowledge gap in this area. In a fall 2020 survey, 83 percent of higher education IT leaders reported that their top priority was to improve usage of instructional tools for synchronous learning (Pelletier et al. 2021). As mentioned earlier, still others may have a variety of features on their virtual training platform but do not regularly use them in virtual training. According to ATD's 2021 research report on leveraging virtual training technology, some tools like chat, screen sharing, and hand-raising prompts were commonly used. For example, out of the 430-plus talent development respondents, 93 percent reported regularly using chat, 90 percent used screen sharing, and 82 percent used hand-raising prompts. However, less-used tools included reaction feedback from participants, annotation tools, and virtual whiteboards. Only 49 percent reported regularly using reaction feedback indicators, 52 percent regularly used annotation tools, and 59 percent reported regular use of digital whiteboards (ATD 2021).

By developing your technical fluency capability, not only can you more confidently start using more tools but you'll also improve your knowledge about when and how to use them. Doing so makes you more likely to be part of a high-performing organization. "Failing to leverage every tool offered by a virtual classroom platform represents a lost opportunity for talent development. On average, high-performing organizations use a significantly higher percentage of the available features than other organizations" (ATD 2021). Let's explore the variety of technical tools available to you in virtual training to elevate your fluency.

 THE BIG IDEA
Strategically leverage virtual platform tools at the right time with the right activity for the right reason.

Leveraging Virtual Tools

We are fortunate to have all the affordances of today's technologies to aid online learning. Because we can observe patterns from the past, we know that live online technology will continue to improve in quality and in ease of use. However, just because something is available doesn't mean we should use it. And when we do use it, we need to be mindful of guidelines for using it well. For example, in chapter 5 when we explored on-camera competence, we learned that there's more to using video judiciously than just turning on a camera.

I remember when having the option to choose more than one font first emerged in word processing. My colleagues began typing documents that used many different fonts all on one page. Why? Because they could. I remember reading a colleague's work, where she proudly showed me how each paragraph had key words in a different font. Multiple fonts were new technology at the time, and she was naturally excited to try them out. Professionals have since discovered that using an excessive number of fonts distracts readers more than it helps them. Just because we have dozens of fonts available, doesn't mean we should try to use them all, especially in the same document.

The same is true for technical tools. Just because a virtual training platform has live polls, does not mean we should poll our learners every five minutes. At some point, learners would habituate to them. Polls would become old hat, and their overuse would weaken their power to captivate attention, as discussed in chapter 4. Likewise, just because you have so many tools at your disposal doesn't mean we overload learners by jumping from using one tool to another without explaining connections, key points, and transitions. We want to use them, yes. Tools help us explain, illustrate, discuss, process, reflect, or practice. So, how should we effectively leverage the tools available to us in virtual platforms? The answer begins by referencing those initial learning objectives and allowing your performance and knowledge objectives discussed in chapter 2 to drive the selection of learning activities.

 PRO TIP 48
Once learners successfully use a virtual tool, the more likely they are to use it again.

For our purposes, we will assume that live video and audio platform features are a given. Facilitator video and audio have also been addressed extensively in previous chapters. Although music is not addressed specifically below, some platforms do allow for music to be played and broadcast to all participants. When I was a virtual trainer for SkillPath, our producers would broadcast upbeat music through Adobe Connect during breaks. This was a great way to infuse energy into the session, and there is plenty of non-proprietary and royalty-free music available for you to use.

So, let's look at some of the most common virtual training tools. Most platforms offer many of these tools, although they may vary slightly by interface or location on the platform. I have organized them into the following categories to provide a more manageable approach: basic, intermediate, and advanced:

- Basic tools
  - Chat
  - Virtual hand raising
  - Reaction feedback
  - Screen sharing
  - Document upload
  - Randomizer
- Intermediate tools
  - Annotation tools
  - Live polling
  - Video clip playback
  - Countdown timer
- Advanced tools
  - Virtual whiteboards
  - Breakouts

Basic Virtual Tools

In this category, we discuss the tools that are easier to use, and perhaps because of this, more commonly used. They are also more intuitive and self-evident. Although I once had a virtual learner who I noticed was not participating in chat. After the session, he connected with me and helped me understand that he wasn't clear on which button to click to send his chat posts. This taught me once again to be careful about making assumptions about what learners do and don't know how to do. The tools we'll address in the basic category are chat, virtual hand raising, reaction feedback, screen sharing, document upload, and randomizer. Let's begin with chat.

Chat

Chat allows for text communication in real time by all parties. Over the years, it's been referred to as the chat panel, *chat pane, chat pod, chat queue*, and now, just *chat*. This tool is a great way for facilitators and learners alike to send instant text communications either publicly to all attending or privately to select individuals. In the chat log in Figure 7-1, you can see learners greeting each other and reflecting on the pre-test they took before attending this virtual training session on emotional intelligence. Notice the conversational feel and the flow back and forth between chat responses. Also observe their honest reflection as they discuss how to manage their emotions in response to the facilitator's question prompts.

What you might be surprised to learn is that chat is an oral medium. It may seem like written communication because you are typing. But the immediacy of the back-and-forth responses, the casual tone, and the conversational style demonstrates all the elements of orality. One of the affordances of chat's real-time interaction is that virtual facilitators can observe the stream of consciousness from their learners. This provides a window into how learners are thinking about the conversation at any moment, which is something you were not privy to as a traditional in-person trainer. Additionally, chat gives voice to all learners at any time, as long as chat is enabled. For example, if your pet suddenly appears in the video frame behind you, several learners will likely ask its name or breed or comment on how cute it is. Then, you will likely see other learners' comments about having the same type of dog breed or that they used to own a pet like that. Side conversations such as these can help form connections, and help learners move along the different stages in the 5 Cs Pyramid from chapter 3.

Chat can also be leveraged for intermittent check-ins. This gives you a quick pulse on where learners are coming from. As you see their responses to your question prompts, invite them to share their ideas or work with them closely on problem solving a challenge together. Chat incorporates the social, cognitive, and emotional dimensions of learning. If users are excited about

Figure 7-1. Chat Example

Diana: Welcome, everyone, to Emotional Intelligence training . . . we'll be starting shortly!

Anna: Good evening from Prague, Czech Republic

Jacob: Hi everyone, joining from sunny Tampa, FL!

Kip: Hello everyone! Joining from Lagos, Nigeria

James: Hi from British Virgin Islands

Matt: @Jacob – Hello from Florida too!

Sarah: Hi everyone

Seth: It looks like I'm ok with intrapersonal, and have a little work on interpersonal

Anna: I'm same with Dave.

Sumit: Lower self-awareness than I expected, although some of that might be related to anxiety

Matt: It was interesting to see how the score turned out. I had a different view going into it.

Jacob: Lower self-awareness than I expected as well

Evelyn: sure made you think

Matt: Anger

Hege: anger

Seth: jealousy

Clara: anger, frustration

Gabriela: jealousy

Matt: frustration

Anna: jealousy

Clara: Understanding your triggers and reading other triggers

Gabriela: The ability to read emotions

Sarah: being able to manage your own emotions and be aware of and manage others as well

Matt: the ability to maintain balance in high-stress situations

Seth: knowing what makes you react with emotions

Jacob: Being aware of the nonverbal messages

James: IKR

Kip: Tiny traumas are still traumas

Clara: Putting yourself in their shoe

Hege: Robot, no feelings

Sarah: WOW!!

Sumit: lol

James: the individual actually cares about my issue

Jacob: They understand what is going on

Evelyn: Still mad but I don't want to take it out on the person on the phone any more

Gabriela: how do you work with people and not become judgmental and difficult yourself?

Kip: 100% yes

Matt: @Gabriela definitely

something or highly motivated, you see this emotion through their punctuation with exclamation marks, all capital letters, or smiley faces.

The cognitive dimension—the bedrock of the learning dimensions—is at play here as learners think about their responses and use mental resources. We used to have to show learners how to use chat during the platform tour at the beginning of training. We also used to have to tell them to type in what city, state, or country they're connecting from, and they always would when prompted. But after the global acceleration of virtual tool use during the COVID-19 pandemic, most learners will now automatically chat about where they are connecting from without being prompted.

Chat is also a way to discover more about the learners. Watch their comments for hints about where they're struggling, where the content is resonating, or where they might be slightly off and need a bit of course correction. Sometimes, learners will pose a question they're puzzling over in chat, and one of their peers will respond and answer their question, so it's a great way to crowd source.

This is not something we could do in an in-person classroom, unless learners connected with their own devices to contribute to a word cloud or provide responses that were then projected on a screen in the room. In a traditional classroom, when a facilitator speaks, they are not immediately privy to the inner thoughts and reactions of learners. So, this is a clear benefit the virtual space provides that traditional in-person training or classrooms do not.

When to Avoid Chat

Chat has an undercurrent of immediacy. For this reason, it is not conducive for lengthy responses. For example, if you say, "Tell me about a time when you experienced your greatest creativity in your professional career." This is something that could be hinted at in chat but is better shared in richer storytelling format via discussion in the large group or in breakouts.

Let's explore this further. Stop and think about how a learner uses chat. There is pressure to respond immediately because of the oral nature of the medium. There is also a natural lag. After the facilitator asks a question, the users must think about it and then type before the response is visible. In this rush, there is no time for deep thinking. In fact, you'll often see spelling errors in chat, which testifies to the immediacy of typing fast and the rush to post quickly without proofing. For richer discussion when you can go much deeper and explore the nuances of something, live oral conversation is best. Some learners will inevitably feel more comfortable contributing in the less anxiety-ridden medium of chat, however, so always keep that option open for them as well.

Best Practices for Using Chat

Chat is good for crisp, short answers. For example, imagine we're training on the topic of leadership, and as facilitator, I say, "Think of some of the most effective leaders you've met or observed. What is it that they do well that makes them a good leader?" This question tees up participants to share brief responses very appropriate to the fast medium. The following phrases might start appearing in chat: "sets clear vision," "actively listens," "influences others," "builds good relationships." All of these are phrased responses that are perfect for chat because they are just a few words—easily typable for the sender and easily scannable for the reader.

You can also use chat for participant responses to a starter activity. Jane Bozarth (2016) recommends displaying a slide where you show learners the beginning of a sentence that participants then complete. For example, "The best negotiation tip I know is . . ." Additionally, you can conduct round-robins via chat where learners take turns adding their ideas to a common goal, improving a process, or expanding on an idea by following the order in the participant panel (Bozarth 2016a).

Here are some additional best practices for chat:

- Use chat when seeking succinct responses to open-ended questions. For example, if you are training on assertive communication skills, you might ask participants to let you know in chat "What are some examples of aggressive communication phrases?" They might type, "I don't care how you get it done. Just get it done." Finally, you can ask them to let you know in chat some examples of assertive communication. For example, "I need to report on this tomorrow. Would you be able to complete it by mid-afternoon today?"
- Encourage and affirm responses when you see them, especially in the beginning. It feels great to be recognized and have your

question heard and addressed aloud. This can encourage engagement because you make it rewarding to do so again. If you have a co-facilitator or producer and they are experts in the subject matter, they can address some questions through chat if you've missed them or don't have time to address them.

- Call out names when referencing their chat. Reference it by calling out an attendee's first name; for example, "Casey is sharing . . ." or "Wenche adds that . . ." or "Ursula says . . ." This recognizes participants, while encouraging more of this behavior because you have rewarded them.

- Read some comments aloud, or paraphrase if you're sure you interpreted the meaning correctly. It's important to read a few comments out loud because this communicates that "I see you and I hear you." Inexperienced facilitators may just answer the question aloud without the context or crediting where that question came from. However, saying "Ali is asking about tips for coaching staff. Let's throw that out to the group. What are your thoughts about effective coaching tips?" is an opportunity to weave Ali and their question into the session, and organically gives them more ownership in it.

- Quickly scan and strategically select which comments to read aloud. Avoid randomly reading aloud the first three responses you see. Be strategic: Which ones tie into the main points you want learners to walk away with? Which ones trigger new but important questions? Which ones hit the bull's eye? Which ones are an opportunity for corrective feedback? You want to call these out to reinforce key points.

- Do not read all chat responses. It gets old if you read every single comment. To keep things interactive, highlight a few. Participants can scroll and read the rest of the comments if they wish.

- Use paired chat. For some activities, you can use private chat for participants, which pairs them with a partner in class. This works best if the facilitator arranges and communicates these pairings. This way, the conversational chat can only be seen by the two individuals as they discuss and brainstorm and problem solve depending on the communicated task.

PRO TIP 49

Leverage chat for immediate responses to prompts that a learner can answer in a brief phrase or with a few words.

Virtual Hand Raising

The icons shown in Figure 7-2 are traditionally found in participant panels where you can see if a virtual learner has raised their hand. Learners might raise a virtual hand to ask a question or make a comment. We understand the symbolic meaning from our own schooling, because we were conditioned to raise our hands in formal settings before asking a question. You can use these icons when learners have questions, a comment, want to share without speaking over others, respond to yes or no questions, have finished an exercise and are letting you know, or return from a break.

Figure 7-2. Adobe Connect Example of Hand-Raising

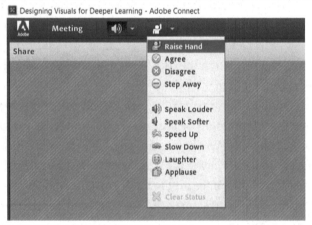

Adobe product screenshot reprinted with permission from Adobe Inc.

Virtual hand raising uses the cognitive dimension of learning because there is usually a comment, question, idea, challenge, or objection behind the hand raise. Using this tool also relies heavily on the social dimension because the facilitator and learners are reacting with each other in the group context and learning from one another.

For more orderly verbal discussion, it can work very well for participants to raise their virtual hands when they have professional experiences to share, such as stories or insights for comment. However, when you aim to establish a flow with back-and-forth-discussion, it can work better to invite all to come on camera and come off mute, stop sharing any other applications, and keep the verbal discussion flowing by just looking at faces on live video. This way you avoid the stop-start pattern of raising hands, waiting to be called on, and finally, unmuting to share.

PRO TIP 50
Request learners use the raise virtual hand feature for quick responses or when they have a comment or question.

Reaction Feedback

Virtual training platforms have always had some options for participant reaction feedback. These are the wide variety of icons that allow participants to quickly communicate to facilitators or other participants how they are doing and feeling. In the early days of virtual training or web conferencing, we called participant reaction buttons *status indicators*. As this name implies, these button options (which now include emoticons) help communicate a participant's status. For example, if a learner steps away to get a cup of coffee, they might click the coffee icon. If they agree with a question, they can click the green check. If they disagree, they can click the red x. If they applaud a peer's practice role play on a training topic, they may click the thumbs up icon.

The best time to use reaction feedback is for closed-end questions. For example, in a leadership class, if you asked, "Are you new to supervisory leadership within the last year? If yes, click the green check, and if no, click the red x." This is a great way to collect quick responses and you avoid the string of yes and no in your chat. One of my colleagues shares scenarios with learners and stops at critical decision points. He asks learners to vote on what they might do next. A green check means they approve of the character's choice and a red x means they would intervene. In the participant panel, he can then quickly scan this simultaneous feedback to get a pulse on the group's responses.

Animated gestures are another type of reaction feedback (Figure 7-3). Gestures have always been an integral element of human communication. They help convey and clarify the meaning of our intended messages. They enhance what we say and how we say it. Animated gestures bring in the emotional dimension of learning because of the joyous nature of applause, celebration, and thumbs up or other emoticons that might reflect a learner's state emotionally. Usually, when one learner shares a thumb's up or an applause animated icon, others will follow. As a result, this can also bring in the group dynamic and social dimension.

Figure 7-3. Cisco Webex Example of Animated Gestures

In Cisco's Webex platform, for example, there is hand gesture recognition, which translates user hand movements in their video frame to a matching icon. This enhanced communication technology is also customizable to respect different interpretations of gestures within regional cultures. For example, if you give a thumb's up in real life with your webcam on, Webex's artificial intelligence (AI) will convert your own gesture into an animated image of a thumbs up onscreen. Or if you clap, an applause icon will appear. Unmuting or using the mouse or keyboard is not required for this functionality to work. These also provide fun, additional ways to share nonverbal and text-based feedback.

The addition of emoticons and animated gestures have only expanded the palette for participants. The older Microsoft Office Live Meeting platform included a visual seating chart grid where learners had options like "proceed" (which was green) and the ability to change their color and their status. This tool could provide instant and simultaneous feedback from multiple learners to the facilitator. Other feedback buttons or icons include emoticons, applause, went to get coffee, or away. For example, I often ask participants to select the green check once they're back from the break and ready to go. Alternatively, I ask them to use the green check when they are done working on a quick individual exercise because I cannot see them lay down their pen or stop typing; this is the signal they give me when they've completed the assignment. With today's modern platforms, we now have animated options as well. For example, some icons that are distinguishable as shapes are preferred over colored dots because colorblind individuals may not be able to tell the difference between the colored dots. They would, however, be able to discern a check or an x.

PRO TIP 51
Encourage learners to use reaction feedback to communicate in real time in a fun way.

Screen Sharing

When application sharing first emerged in this field, we used to only be allowed to share our entire desktop. Back then, it was important to close everything else on your desktop before activating this share feature. With current tools, we can select exactly which document or application to share, while also being able to select desktop or monitor 1 or 2, if needed (Figure 7-4).

Figure 7-4. Zoom Example of Screen Sharing

To effectively screen share, ensure you:

- Close all other applications on your desktop that are not relevant to the session. Even if there's less risk people will see something you don't want them to see, applications you don't need to have running will eat up your bandwidth as you are sharing your screen with other participants.
- Select to share system audio when appropriate. In MS Teams, for example, you need to select that you will be sharing system audio if you are going to play a video through the app. Make sure you select this before sharing to ensure in-app audio (besides your speaking voice) works correctly.
- Give verbal cues when you are transitioning between screen shares. Let learners know what you're doing, because they have no visual cues to see what you're doing or what's coming up next, as discussed in chapter 4.

Here are some examples of when you might use this tool:

- Sharing slides via screen share where you can alt/tab to find your other open windows and then resize them accordingly so that you can share two open apps on one screen.
- A game show-like review game on slides for review of content knowledge.
- Share an application for a live software demo.
- Share slide visuals for a case scenario challenge with still shots setting up the scenario and its choices.
- Share a desktop application document or digital workbook that attendees were provided ahead of the session.

 PRO TIP 52
Leverage screen sharing to share clarifying visuals, provide examples, or illustrate the instructional content.

Document Upload

Document uploads are a way to pre-load documents, slides, or PDFs. The convenience of an upload is that the document remains in your platform and is ready for you well before class day. It's always a good idea to go through your documents or slides after uploading them to ensure that nothing has changed in the upload process in terms of visibility, font size, animations, or anything else. In some platforms, your animations may "flatten" so only the final state of the slide is displayed; if you want to include gradual builds, you can alternate in-app slide visuals with screen sharing a presentation app such as PowerPoint.

Overall, document upload is a great way to place multiple documents that you'll need for your virtual training class into the platform. It allows for you to have them all in one place, and ready to go on the virtual training day. Additionally, you can sometimes store additional prepared elements near your document uploads.

In the example in Figure 7-5, in addition to uploading slides into the platform, the facilitator also placed multiple whiteboards that were prepared ahead of time so they are ready to be used throughout the training. This provides an easy and convenient way for facilitators to switch from a whiteboard to slides to a different whiteboard.

Figure 7-5. Cisco WebEx Training Center Example of Slide Upload

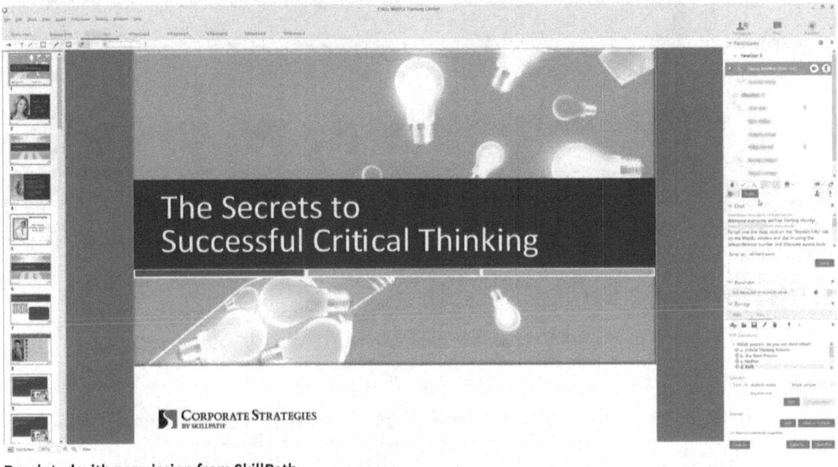

The Secrets to
Successful Critical Thinking

CORPORATE STRATEGIES
BY SKILLPATH

Reprinted with permission from SkillPath.

PRO TIP 53

For large group discussions, close slide sharing and invite all participants to come on camera.

Randomizer

The Randomizer extension in Adobe Connect allows for the facilitator to randomly select an attendee during the session and display the selected name for all who are online to see (Figure 7-6). Always give learners a heads up when you will be using the randomizer. Adult learners, especially introverts, may feel uncomfortable being put on the spot. I always give learners the option to pass if they are selected and I give them lots of time up front to prepare their answers if called upon. In all my years of virtual training, I've only had one adult learner request to pass. Randomizers are also great for selecting a name for prizes at the end of the session.

Figure 7-6. Adobe Connect Example of Randomizer

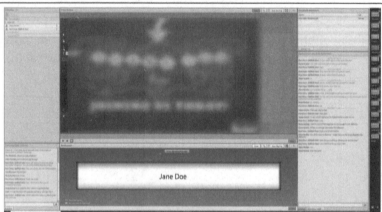

Adobe product screenshot reprinted with permission from Adobe Inc. Also reprinted with permission from SkillPath.

Intermediate Virtual Tools

In addition to the basic virtual training platform tools, there are other tools that may take some practice and a bit more nuance. As you grow in technical fluency capability, you will also become faster, more creative, and confident using these tools. So, in the intermediate category, we will explore annotation tools, live polling, video clip playback, and using a countdown timer.

Annotation Tools

Annotation tools are the drawing tools, which facilitators and learners can both use on virtual platforms. They allow both parties viewing and editing to access a shared screen where they can create and erase illustrations. In many platforms, these drawing tools can be found in an annotation toolbar or in a drop-down menu (Figure 7-7). They are a great way to not only direct learner focus, but also clarify which part of the visual you're explaining at the time you discuss it. This way, the learner does not have to waste precious working memory resources searching for the part of the image you're explaining. By the time they find where you are, you may be done talking about that part.

Sometimes, however, annotations can disrupt virtual sessions if they're not managed well. For example, learners may start drawing on shared visuals at inappropriate times if the tools are enabled and the annotation toolbar is accessible. Younger family members of participants have even been known to draw with them, although not realizing everyone else could also see them. In these situations, you would need to verbally address this issue right away, as well as clear the drawings quickly. In Zoom, for example, you have a more advanced option to specifically clear viewers' drawings, clear your drawings, or clear all drawings. If your design does not plan for whiteboarding or annotation—although I recommend you leverage both—you may keep it disabled for participants. But make sure annotation is always enabled for facilitator use. It's best to enable annotation for learners, of course, to be more interactive. Whiteboarding, which we'll discuss later in the advanced tools section, especially relies on learners using the annotation toolbar.

In some platforms, annotations also need to be cleared before advancing to the next slide. Still other platforms allow annotations to remain on a slide, but then do not carry over to the next. You need to understand which way your training platform operates before starting your virtual session. If you are not aware that annotations carry over to other slides during your

Figure 7-7. GoToTraining Example of Annotation Tools

Reprinted with permission from LogMeIn, Inc.

session—or how to erase them either individually or clearing them all at once—this can cause disruption. In chapter 9, we talk specifically about preventive actions you can take to ensure this doesn't happen to you. I always advise clients to play with and practice using annotation tools with a remote colleague. This way you can ensure you know how they work in a live training session.

An easier way to avoid the potential disruption of uncleared annotations in Zoom, for example, is to use the vanishing pen. As an advanced annotation tool, Zoom's vanishing pen allows you to circle—with the color of your choice—a visual or object on the screen. The drawing or highlight—if you're calling attention to something—will display for approximately three seconds before it automatically disappears. The elegance of this annotation feature is you don't have to worry about clearing your annotation, but learners still experience the benefit of you highlighting what is visually important or using it as a form of emphasis. Along with the vanishing pen in Zoom, you may also use a variety of stamps with stars, arrows, checkmarks, and question marks, as well as ready-made customizable shapes and freehand drawing. You can also save the screenshot or annotated image as a PNG on your device, if needed.

For prescriptive tips, adhere to the following best practices:

- Well before your class day, rehearse with the tools exactly how you will use them. This includes turning them on, setting colors, drawing width, circling, highlighting, and using arrows, the laser pointer, or any other elements.
- Test with your producer acting as the attendee to ensure your annotations are enabled before you request attendees annotate. Permissions, rights, and correct role assignments as organizer, host, or presenter, as well as enabling or disabling functionality mean everything in virtual training platforms. Sometimes, a single little permission can make the difference between successfully using the platform the way you need it to work and struggling to find something that has not yet been enabled.
- Use annotation tools but use them sparingly to draw the learner's eye and focus attention. The annotation movement draws focus, as we discuss in chapter 8. Use it strategically to highlight the most

important points and where learners should be looking during your explanations.

- Always pre-determine how to clear all annotations on a slide. Some platforms carry over annotations to the next slide. Others leave them on the slide where you entered them but do not carry them over. You need to know ahead of time. The most important thing to remember about the drawing tools is how to turn them off, and how to get your cursor back once you've turned them on.

Consider the following example from one of my clients who was training medical staff in a healthcare context. She shared her screen with imaging on a slide, and as facilitator, used annotation tools to type the anatomy on her slide visual as text labels (for example, compacted and non-compacted). She then asked learners to identify the proper place in the imaging where the walls began to uncompact. This was an opportunity for learners to also use annotation tools. Learners used their drawing tools to add the white x's you see on Figure 7-8. Learners also were asked to draw lines of noncompacted myocardium and another line to identify compacted myocardium. The facilitator then used live annotation to add arrows pointed to any errors. This active use of annotation by both facilitator and learners was a great way to clarify, check knowledge, provide immediate corrective feedback, and ultimately help virtual learners determine whether they could diagnose left ventricular noncompaction.

Figure 7-8. Example of Annotation

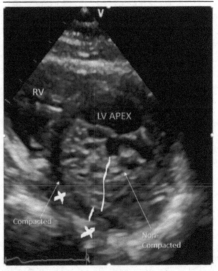

Printed with permission from Melissa Albrecht at Advocate Aurora Health.

PRO TIP 54
Use live annotation such as highlighting, circling, arrows, or the laser pointer to direct learners' focus to key elements of a supporting visual.

Live Polling

Live polls are prepared questions posed to all participants for immediate voting (Figure 7-9). You can also use them to share results with all participants in real time. Polls are a great way to collect information from your participants quickly. For example, you can find out how much they know about a topic, whether they're using behavioral style assessments or something else at their organization, and more. Polls also work well when you want to ask closed-ended questions with yes/no responses (Clark and Kwinn 2007). I like to use polls to review content with learners to take a quick pulse on whether or not they're comprehending the material and if it's resonating with them and making sense. Not all platforms have polling features, but many integrate other surveys or apps as an alternative way to poll your learners.

Figure 7-9. Adobe Connect 11 Live Poll Example

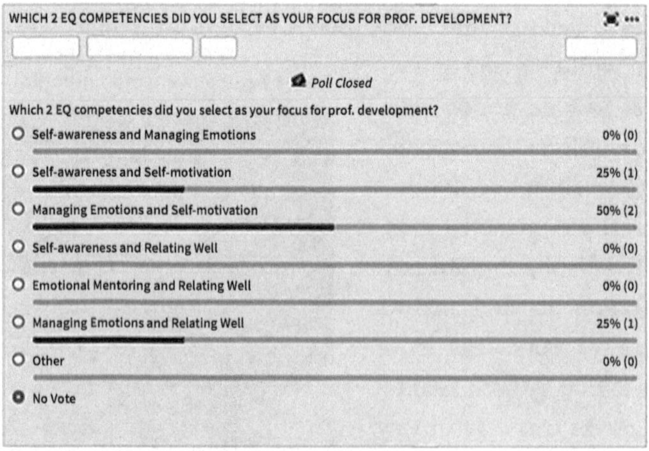

WHICH 2 EQ COMPETENCIES DID YOU SELECT AS YOUR FOCUS FOR PROF. DEVELOPMENT?

Poll Closed

Which 2 EQ competencies did you select as your focus for prof. development?

Self-awareness and Managing Emotions	0% (0)
Self-awareness and Self-motivation	25% (1)
Managing Emotions and Self-motivation	50% (2)
Self-awareness and Relating Well	0% (0)
Emotional Mentoring and Relating Well	0% (0)
Managing Emotions and Relating Well	25% (1)
Other	0% (0)
No Vote	

Adobe product screenshot reprinted with permission from Adobe Inc.

Novice facilitators may use a poll for the sake of using a poll or just trying to insert a question for the sake of adding interactivity. However, the most effective use of polling is to collect data on your audience's opinions, experience, attitudes, knowledge, or behavior. Intermediate facilitators then either remember or jot down the top two most popular answers so they don't forget them, and then refer to the data as they move forward with their virtual training class. You can also use polls as a pre-test or post-test to measure baseline knowledge with your participants on the front-end and then compare this to what they've learned or demonstrate that they know at the end.

The poll questions themselves should be tightly interwoven and relevant to the subject matter. For example, if you are training a virtual class on how to facilitate online training, one of your opening polls might ask which virtual training platform they use. Multiple choice answers might include GoToTraining, Webex, Adobe Connect, Microsoft Teams, and Zoom. Dependent on how participants respond, you would continue to build that information into the rest of your training. For example, when you discuss virtual tools, you might say, "Since most of you let me know in our poll that you primarily use Adobe Connect, make sure you know how to . . . " This is one way to reference back to the information you collected from the polls.

Because participants take the time to vote their opinion, always broadcast the results of the poll so they can see their responses. If for some reason, you experience technical difficulties and are not able to visually share the results, summarize them verbally so participants receive closure for their investment in the activity. There are certainly occasions when the poll feature may not load correctly and therefore not work appropriately. In these instances, be ready with your backup plan. I always try to have a printout of all my whiteboard questions and poll questions and answers just in case the technology has glitches. This way, you can pose the questions verbally and ask them to vote A, B, C, or D in the chat. Alternatively, you can have a pre-prepared slide with poll questions that you can use instead as your Plan B, which we'll talk more about in chapter 9.

And as always, make sure to practice using the poll beforehand. Practice opening a poll, sharing a poll, closing a poll, sharing results of the poll, and moving on to your next segment. To ensure all goes smoothly, you need to know the process.

Video Clip Playback

Many virtual training platforms have built-in video players where you can share videos and watch them together live during virtual class. Using the built-in video player will offer more qualitative viewing than if the video was shown as part of screen sharing. For example, in Zoom, facilitators may click share screen, then switch to the advanced tab and select video.

From there, they can select the video they wish to view and click open. This way the video is not only opened within the platform itself but also playable from there for all participants to view (Figure 7-10).

Because playing videos online often seems fraught with technical challenges (there's almost always someone who cannot see or hear them or the video freezes due to bandwidth issues), I often assign videos to be viewed beforehand through pre-work assignments. This way it stirs their curiosity on the topic, and they have more time to think about it before coming to class.

You can also place links to a video in the chat, invite learners to view the three-minute video on their own right now, and then prompt them to come back to the session in five minutes, so the group at large can discuss it. Regardless of whether you show it live, they view the video beforehand, or they mute their mic to view on their own and then rejoin the session, you always want to prepare their viewing. In other words, let them know what they should be watching for. For example, "As you watch this video, notice what the manager does to demonstrate they are actively listening, and see if you can identify the impact on the employee." This is a way to prime the learner for what to pay attention to, and it can also help them focus on key aspects that you'll bring into the discussion debriefing after viewing.

Figure 7-10. Zoom Example of Annotating a Video Clip

Countdown Timer

Countdown timers display a visible clock for all participants to see (Figure 7-11). Timers can usually be set for any amount of time and count down from there. They are available on some, but not all virtual training platforms. Timers are useful for setting time limits for certain activities, which frees the facilitator from being timekeeper. For example, when learners work independently on exercises in their participant guides or digital workbooks, timers can communicate how much time to devote to the exercise. Countdown timers can also be used during breaks to clarify when it's time to return, especially if there are differences across time zones for participants. Facilitators may also use timers to set time limits for reflection exercises or allocate time for learners to start working on action plans. I like to use them for brainstorming exercises with a group at large, when appropriate to the content.

Figure 7-11. Adobe Connect Example of Countdown Timer

Adobe product screenshot reprinted with permission from Adobe Inc. Also reprinted with permission from SkillPath.

Advanced Virtual Tools

Next, let's look at the advanced virtual tools, which include whiteboards and breakouts. I've placed these two in the advanced category because they are inherently more complex. They require more skill and knowledge on the part of the facilitator to successfully manage. Please note that partnering with your producer when using these virtual tools can also be extremely helpful.

Virtual Whiteboards

Many participants and facilitators resort to drawing shapes and words and pictures on whiteboards and seem to be unclear how best to use them (Figure 7-12). Although this might be fun socially, there are also ways to bring more purpose that ties into the learning objectives and supports your training concepts. Not knowing how to best use digital whiteboards is common and widespread in secondary education, academia, professional education, and online learning. Let's explore some tips now.

Figure 7-12. Adobe Connect 11 Example of Virtual Whiteboard

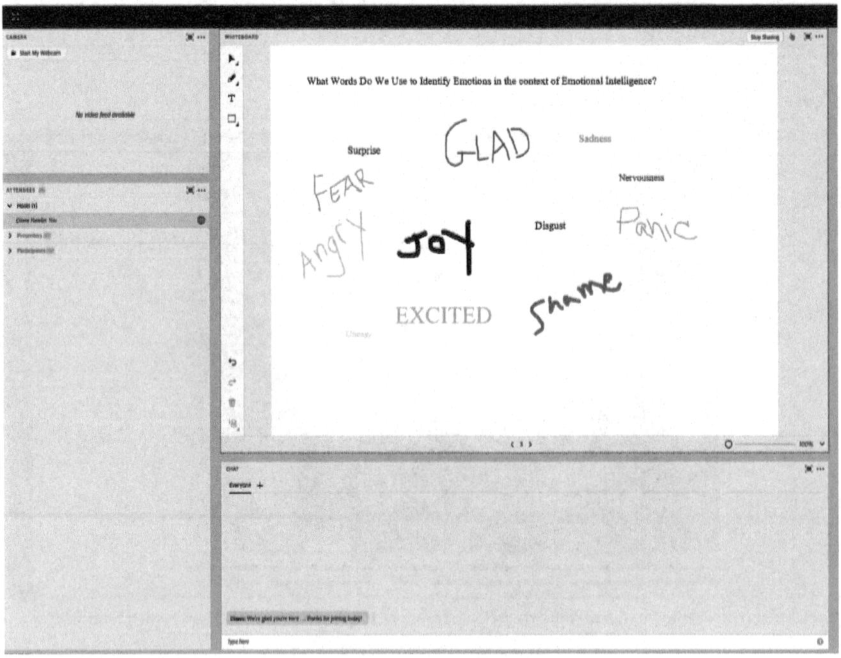

Adobe product screenshot reprinted with permission from Adobe Inc.

If you facilitate a virtual training session for call center staff on how to improve customer service, for example, you could begin by displaying a quadrant on the whiteboard. In the top left, you could title a space for characteristics of poor customer service skills, and in the top right, characteristics of good customer service skills. Frame the exercise so that participants are thinking of themselves as the customer. Ask them to think back on their own experiences shopping for retail items, speaking to a phone service provider, or receiving service on a vehicle. Ask them to type responses to identify pain points of poor customer service they've experienced, as well as aspects of good service to make it more tangible. Use this as a stepping stone for a larger discussion about improving customer service at the call center. Next, request they consider and type in responses in the bottom quadrants related to improvement opportunities and strengths with the call center's current level of service to customers.

Whiteboards can bring in the behavioral dimension of learning because using them involves doing. If the overarching learning objectives are knowledge based, the whiteboard can serve as a conduit for checking knowledge, summarizing what they currently know, or comparing concepts. Annotating on the whiteboard also integrates the social dimension because of the level of learner-to-learner interactions while participating.

Here are some considerations for virtual whiteboards:

- Prepare whiteboards ahead of time if your platform allows. Not all virtual platforms allow you to prepare whiteboards ahead of time or to prepare multiple ones. However, it can be very tricky to do this on the fly. Some platforms only allow you to create the whiteboard right before your session begins. If this is the case for you, think through and draw out what you want your whiteboard to say before the class begins using it. You can either have your producer create it by sharing your design with them ahead of time, or you can plan it so that you start with it right after a break so you can use your break to set it up and have it ready to go.
- If your platform allows, tell learners not to worry about their typed text overlapping and that you will spread it out for better visibility. Although this is not a feature on all virtual training platforms, it is very helpful to avoid visual clutter. You can select the text they typed and then slide it over to an open space, so all contributions can be easily viewed and read.

- Design your learning activity so learners have something meaningful to annotate on the whiteboard. I like to draw columns down the middle and have participants compare concepts. Additionally, I have them type one takeaway at the end that they will apply right away.
- Practice and familiarize yourself with the idiosyncrasies of whiteboards. Sometimes there are limitations for features and platforms. "Some have quirks—like limiting the number of users who can write on a board at a time—so that's something important to know" (Bozarth 2016b).
- When appropriate, keep contributions on the whiteboard anonymous to increase participation. On some whiteboards, learners are identified with a name inside an arrow where they type or draw. However, if you hide their names and keep their contributions anonymous, you may see greater participation from the class, depending on how well a group knows each other. In this case, it's also important to stress that their activity and participation is anonymous. Sometimes this can be key to participants feeling safe to share, especially if their supervisor or manager is also attending. External whiteboarding tools like Mural, Miro, and Padlet can also add to your whiteboarding palette of options. Many of these tools offer integrations and built-in templates for added sophistication where appropriate.

PRO TIP 55
Leverage whiteboards for synchronous brainstorming and for activities that involve contribution by multiple participants concurrently.

One of my favorite activities for virtual whiteboards is to have participants record their progress and ideas while working in small groups. In Figure 7-13, the virtual training platform was Adobe Connect. Learners were divided into breakouts to identify and discuss what they had used as successful strategies to work more effectively with challenging or difficult co-workers. Each breakout had their own whiteboard to collect responses and anchor discussion. Once everyone returned to the main

Figure 7-13. Adobe Connect Example of Breakout Debrief on Whiteboards

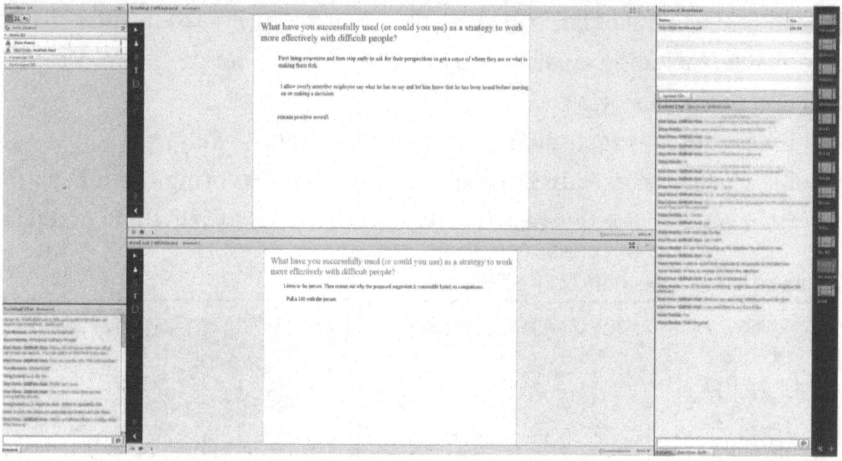

Adobe product screenshot reprinted with permission from Adobe Inc. Also reprinted with permission from SkillPath.

session, those whiteboards could also be shared to facilitate a debrief with the whole group.

Breakout Groups

Breakouts allow us to divide participants into small groups for discussion and collaboration where they can share documents, screen share, chat with each other, and see and hear each other on video and audio. I think back to how cumbersome it used to be to conduct audio breakouts with an audio bridge when we facilitated virtual training in 2000. We were required to press multiple number combinations and the hashtag into our analog phones to enter an audio-only breakout, and then press another combination to be returned to the main session. To conduct breakouts, we had to manually divide people by name and then tell them what group they were in and the respective number combination each group would need to enter into their phones. This meant the audio connection was separate from the visual connection to the internet.

Today, Adobe Connect, Zoom, Webex, and other virtual training platforms have made it astonishingly easy for us to click a button and enter small group breakouts with quality video and audio (Figure 7-14). Small-group breakout sessions are common now in most web conferencing platforms. According to the 2021 ATD virtual training research report, more than 80 percent of talent development professionals reported small group activities (like breakouts) as the top learning activity. Breakouts offer many affordance, including small group discussions, collaboration, brainstorming, and problem solving.

Breakouts can create anxiety for some facilitators who worry about not placing learners correctly in groups or being able to bring them back to the main session. For this reason, I work with clients to help them practice

Figure 7-14. Zoom Example of Small Breakout Group

© Zoom Video Communications, Inc. Reprinted with permission.

breakouts during their teach-backs. This way they learn how to manage them in a safe, small environment and then they realize can do it. Later, some even comment about how fun it is to pop into learners' breakouts and see how they're doing.

Breakouts primarily emphasize the social dimension of learning. Together in small groups, learners can collaborate with one another. Breakouts also incorporate the cognitive dimension of learning as participants use their mental resources to work on activities. As mentioned before, the behavioral dimension is the doing. So, if the breakouts involve an activity where learners are creating an action plan, writing a report, evaluating a presentation, solving a challenging scenario, or doing a skill practice of delivering constructive and positive feedback, all these activities are doing. This then would bring the behavioral dimension of learning into breakouts.

InSpace has created a platform used by academic institutions and businesses alike to provide an intuitive, more free-choice option for navigating in and out of breakouts as a collaborative learning arena (Figure 7-15). For example, InSpace allows learners to independently move in and out of various breakouts. They can also come out of a breakout to ask the instructor a question and then return to their breakout (Figure 7-16).

Figure 7-15. InSpace Example of Breakouts

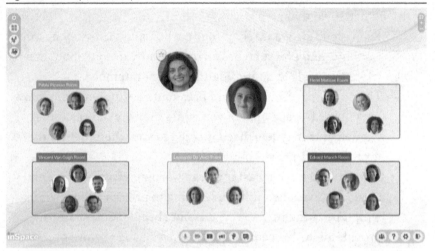

Reprinted with permission from InSpace.

Figure 7-16. InSpace Example of Self-Navigated Breakouts

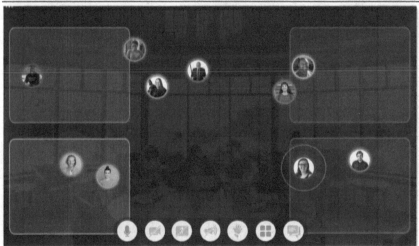

Reprinted with permission from InSpace.

Here are some basic best practices for breakouts:

- Clarify an appropriate timeframe based on the activity. This way, learners clearly know how long they have to complete an activity. Allow more time than you think participants need to give them the buffer to greet each other, get acclimated to working together, and make conversation. One of the most common errors I see beginner facilitators do is assign too many things for a group to do in a breakout with too little time in which to do them.
- Keep group size to three or four participants. This way no one can hide, and everyone has an opportunity to contribute in a space that feels less intimidating by sheer number.
- Throw them a lifeline before breakouts begin. Let them know how they can get a hold of you while they are in breakouts. Participants may feel disconnected to you when they go there for the first time without you.
- Always send a broadcast message warning when you will end sessions. Give a two-minute warning to prompt conversation wrap-ups so the breakout end is not abrupt. Some platforms provide 10- to 30-second countdown warnings before breakouts are closed.

Here are a few more intermediate best practices for breakouts:

- Allow those who would prefer it the option to work alone (without calling them out as introverts). This can be better for learning if someone is anxious about working in a group and would learn more working independently.
- Strategically pick group facilitators depending on the activity. I handpick leaders based on my observations of their earlier participation (they do not realize this). I watch for demonstrated leadership and then ask aloud for their permission to facilitate the group. This saves precious time, so that people don't use up all their breakout time deciding how to get started. Instead they can jump into the exercise immediately if a selected leader is already identified. If you have a learner who early on

demonstrates a poor attitude for being there, they would not be the best pick for leading the breakouts.

- Ask the group to choose their own facilitator; this plays off the learner agency we discussed in chapter 4. If you do this, build in extra time, because it can require a little time for a group—especially if they don't yet know each other—to select a facilitator. In other instances, you may not need a facilitator because a learner is practicing their virtual presentation with a partner. So, it depends on the type of activity in the breakout as well.
- Give crystal-clear instructions three times, three ways. Author Kassy Laborie (2021) also separates the technical instructions from the activity's instructions to help communicate both more clearly.
- Allow independent choice for which breakout to enter when your platform allows. The more autonomy we can provide learners, the better. This means learners are allowed to enter and exit breakouts as needed.
- Always build in time during the first breakouts with a given class for learners to at least say hi and share their first name. Even if you don't tell them to do this, most will do it naturally.
- Do pop in occasionally to visit breakouts, check on completion status, and ensure conversations are on track.
- Debriefs are often more important than the breakouts—so almost always include them. This is the opportunity to connect what they're learning with the real world or their work back on the job.

PRO TIP 56
Ensure breakout activity instructions are clearly understood before starting them, and always debrief afterward as the connections realized are often even more important.

Table 7-1 shares a list of suggested activities for each virtual tool. Let's take a moment to review these tools.

Table 7-1. List of Suggested Activities and Ideas for Virtual Tools

Virtual Platform Tool	Description	Activities and Ideas
Chat	This is a dedicated instant messaging space that allows participants, facilitator, and producer to send typed text messages publicly or privately to each other in real time.	Use chat to collect multiple ideas from a wide variety of learners by posing open-ended prompts to them. For example, for a virtual training leadership course, ask participants to post in chat some of the qualities they've observed in effective leaders. Always provide an example to get them started. For example, you might say "visionary" or "influential."
Virtual hand raising	Learners click a hand raise icon to indicate to facilitators that they have a question or comment, or they've raised their hand in response to a question.	When you first introduce learners to a topic, use the "Raise Your Hand If . . ." activity. Ask three or four questions related to the topic and tell them, "I'm going to say a statement and if it's true for you, raise your virtual hand." You can even make the last statement a joke or something that makes them laugh. For example, if you are training on emotional intelligence, you might say "Raise your hand if you've ever lost it emotionally with anyone. You can lower those hands now." "Raise your hand if you know what EQ is. I see those hands going up, you can lower them now." "Raise your hand if you can explain the difference between EQ and IQ," etc.
Reaction feedback	Based on the various virtual training platforms, these vary widely but include icons, emoticons, animated reactions, green check, or red x to quickly communicate participants' reactions.	You can have a lot of fun with the gesture recognition animations, emoticons, and even animated gestures like thumbs up. In the middle of training (as a pick me-up energizer), ask learners to use their emoticons to tell you how they're feeling about the content and if it makes sense to them. Emoticons can help you discern if they're confused, and thumbs up tells you things are going in the right direction. It's a way to keep a pulse on the group.

Table 7-1 (cont'd)

Virtual Platform Tool	Description	Activity/Ideas
Screen sharing	This allows facilitators and/or participants to share their current view of documents, files, systems, videos, and websites from their own device with everyone in the virtual class.	When you train learners on technical systems or teach them procedural content, you can take advantage of screen sharing. Either in large groups or small breakouts, learners can practice the how of what they are learning by taking turns sharing their screen and practicing in the system. It's very important to set them up for success by explaining and slowly modeling it for them first. If they have access to a testing environment, they can take turns sharing screens and each walking through another part of the process as review and practice. If there are junctures where learners are unsure what to do next, the group at large can assist by deciding what to do next. This is a great opportunity for repetitive practice and corrective feedback, both of which boost learning.
Document upload	Instead of sharing your screen to show PDFs or slides or other files and documents, they can be uploaded ahead of time and conveniently stored in the platform. This way they are ready for you to select and share at the time you need them.	Almost everyone loves review games. The energy of competing on teams or even working as a large group to see if they can play for points always adds a nice edge to the training and builds helpful recall time for working memory too. You can create a separate slide deck building off popular game shows to come up with slides that ask questions related to your training topic for a review game.
Randomizer	This tool once clicked can randomly select a name from a participant list in real time and display it for all to see in a matter of seconds.	Use the randomizer to select a participant's name for a drawing or giveaway. For example, everyone who submits their action plans by the end of class will be included in a drawing for a prize. Then at the end of class, use the randomizer to select the winner.

Table 7-1 (cont'd)

Virtual Platform Tool	Description	Activity/Ideas
Annotation tools	These are commonly called drawing tools and allow a facilitator and participants to annotate or highlight, draw, point, use arrows, erase, clear all annotations, and more on whiteboards, slides, and videos, depending on the platform.	When you are teaching a topic like business writing or business grammar, display a slide for learners that is a paragraph they can easily read and see. Then instruct them to use their annotation tools to find all the business grammar errors in the sample writing displayed onscreen. For a more orderly collaboration, you can have them take turns in small groups as they find additional errors that need correcting in the sample.
Live polling	Allows participants to respond to survey questions where results are collected and may be shared with participants in real time and saved for future reference.	One of the best ways to use polling for learning is to leverage it as a check-your-knowledge quiz as you go along. This provides a built-in way to measure whether concepts are clear, learners are grasping the content, or where correction is needed. Create polls ahead of time for easier management and always broadcast results with the group. Participants will be curious about where they stand with everyone else.
Video clip playback	Depending on the platform, video clips can be played back for participants to view either through built-in video players for better quality or by sharing one's screen of the video.	I recommend offloading videos as viewing asynchronous assignments before coming to class. This way, the video stimulates their thinking on the topic beforehand. However, if you want to reinforce parts of the video again or show brief clips, you can also annotate right on the video in some virtual training platforms. Feel free to start and stop to allow for group discussions on the video topic in between collective viewing.
Countdown timer	This tool is a convenient way to set a timer for any activity that can be shared and visible to everyone in class as it counts down.	Countdown timers are helpful for timed independent exercises and can also be set when class adjourns for a break. Set the timer for five minutes, for example, so everyone is clear on the break start and end time across time zones.

Table 7-1 (cont'd)

Virtual Platform Tool	Description	Activity/Ideas
Virtual whiteboards	This is a digital empty white space used for free drawing by participants and facilitators. They can type text, draw, create tables, erase, and more. In most platforms, facilitators can also move typed text around to be more clearly read. It is used in tandem with the annotation toolbar. In many platforms, whiteboards can be saved for future reference as well.	Using the annotation toolbar's straight lines, draw a line down the center and a line across the top making a "T" intersection. In the left column, request learners type a key takeaway they're going to start doing from the training. In the right column, ask learners to type something they were already doing that the training validated or reinforced for them.
Breakouts	Enables a large group to divide into multiple smaller groups to discuss and collaborate with audio, live video, shared documents, whiteboards, shared screens, and more.	Give each small breakout the option to select from one of two problem-solving scenarios. Using the concepts and techniques learned in the training, they need to decide as a group how they're going to address the problem and resolve the situation.

Summary

You have many interactive tools to leverage for virtual training. When used strategically, they can optimize learner engagement, increase participant attention, and promote deeper learning. Using these tools strategically starts with having a rationale for when and why the tool is used. We want to move beyond the basics of using something just because it's there. Rather, we aim to have a thoughtful rationale for when, why, and how we might use a tool to support the intended outcome and learner goals.

Basic tools like chat, raising virtual hands, feedback options, and more provide opportunities for building online community and connection. Intermediate tools like polling and video as well as advanced tools like whiteboards and breakouts allow for real-time interaction and collaboration. And some tools—like the annotation toolbar—use movement as its ally.

In the next chapter, we'll uncover the dynamic principle, another strategy to captivate and focus attention. All these tips and strategies work together as one to captivate, direct, and focus learners so that they can absorb, and ideally transfer what they've learned to the workplace.

Overall, developing your fluency with virtual technical tools gives you the knowledge and skills to understand their unique affordances and optimize them for learning. As you continue to raise the bar as a virtual facilitator, challenge yourself to leverage platform tools while observing what works best and reflecting on why. Keep up to date on the latest enhancements and evolving technologies, as these improvements inform our future designs. Developing your capability in technical fluency is not only a core business skill, but will also significantly improve your ability to deliver interactive and engaging virtual training programs.

Pro Tips for Practicing your Technical Fluency Skills

TIP 48	Once learners successfully use a virtual tool, the more likely they are to use it again.
TIP 49	Leverage chat for immediate responses to prompts that a learner can answer in a brief phrase or with a few words.
TIP 50	Request learners use the raise virtual hand feature for quick responses or when they have a comment or question.
TIP 51	Encourage learners to use reaction feedback to communicate in real time in a fun way.
TIP 52	Leverage screen sharing to share clarifying visuals, provide examples, or illustrate the instructional content.
TIP 53	For large group discussions, close slide sharing and invite all participants to come on camera.
TIP 54	Use live annotation such as highlighting, circling, arrows, or the laser pointer to direct learners' focus to key elements of a supporting visual.
TIP 55	Leverage whiteboards for synchronous brainstorming and for activities that involve contribution by multiple participants concurrently.
TIP 56	Ensure breakout activity instructions are clearly understood before starting them, and always debrief afterward as the connections realized are often even more important.

"Every body perseveres in its state of being at rest or of moving uniformly straight forward, except insofar as it is compelled to change its state by forces impressed."

—Sir Isaac Newton, physicist and mathematician

CHAPTER 8

Following the Dynamic Principle of Engagement

Imagine you have joined a virtual training session on emotional intelligence. Your eyes scan the screen on your device to see who else has joined. You hear the producer welcome everyone, go over a few ground rules, and then introduce the facilitator. The facilitator at this point proceeds to provide a rather lengthy introduction about their own experience on the topic.

As slide sharing begins, you notice the first slide is quite text heavy. The facilitator says the purpose of this training is to learn how to manage emotions well when working with colleagues and customers. They proceed to drone on in a monotone voice. Five minutes later, the initial slide still displays, and the facilitator begins to explain the different types of emotions. You glance toward the virtual platform's chat and see no activity.

Finally, the slide changes to another one but is just as full of text and bullet points. After a while, all the slides begin to look the same. So, you decide to respond to a few emails and finish prepping for that meeting you're leading later. As you work, you keep a partial ear open for anything that might be of interest, and, of course, in case they happen to call on you. You begin thinking about what to make for dinner, and suddenly remember you forgot to schedule your pet's grooming appointment. Clearly, your attention has drifted to a galaxy . . . far, far away.

Sound familiar? Would you want this virtual training to come to a theatre near you? Unfortunately, when virtual training doesn't grab our attention, something else will. Boredom for live online learners translates to disengagement. We lose their interest. We lose their attention. We lose them.

When a learner disengages, they seek out other stimuli. For example, instead of sitting through a training they find boring, they might check their phone for messages, shop online, or respond to email. In today's world with a workforce that works from anywhere, the myriad distractions can pull learners' attention away from learning. Even in office buildings, we can experience distractions from colleagues, fire alarm tests, loud meetings, and so on. Because of smartphones, people also have immediate access to email and work projects just a hand's distance away. In the context of virtual training, their focus should be the visual and audio stimuli through virtual training platforms.

As mentioned previously, the top thing virtual facilitators seem to repeatedly seek an answer to is the age-old problem of how to engage learners. Virtual trainers will ask, "How do we prevent learners from multi-tasking?" "How do we make sure they're paying attention?" or "How do we keep them engaged?"

Unfortunately, there is no silver bullet for completely eradicating learner distractions. Instead of a single strategy, it's often a combination of different strategies that works most effectively. One strategy is to set expectations at the outset of virtual events for participants to close email, minimize any unrelated open apps, and silence smartphones if not used during training. This is just one suggestion. In a live online setting, facilitators compete for learner attention with the number of virtual training platform pods on a screen at a given time. Because of these multiple potential distractions, "Instructors must work harder to capture learners' attention, encourage interaction, and reinforce the key points from the session" (Bersin 2020).

Moreover, attention is a precious commodity because it is a critical brain process for learning (Zadina 2014). According to educational neuroscientist Janet Zadina (2014), "Attention is the act of selectively attending to some stimuli rather than other stimuli . . . it does not mean taking in more information: it means taking in less. . . . Attention is the mechanism by which the brain conserves its resources and focuses on specific information. This affects what we actually see and hear." This poses a fundamental challenge for virtual facilitators and adult educators. Attention is vital to virtual training because it is essential to focus, which is needed for learning. To effectively train online, we must capture and direct learners' attention.

So, how do we draw virtual learners in and keep them engaged when multiple distractions compete for their attention? Quite simply, learner engagement is dynamic. In this chapter, we'll explore the dynamic engagement capability and how it can help us draw in learners' attention. We can also improve engagement by leveraging the four learning dimensions (cognitive, emotional, social, and behavioral) as discussed previously. Before we get into dynamic principles, let's explore some cognitive neuroscience concepts that are important for engaging learners: habituation and working memory.

 THE BIG IDEA
Leverage the power of movement in multiple ways to engage learners throughout virtual training.

Habituation in Live Online Learning

Once, when I was coaching a client, our first meeting was in a room in a building where he worked. The room happened to have overhead fluorescent lights that buzzed loudly and a clock on the wall that made an incessant and obnoxious ticking noise. We continued to use the same room weekly. Nearing the end of six weeks, I was surprised to discover that I didn't even hear the buzzing or ticking anymore. They were still there, but I had gotten used to them. I was able to tune them out.

This phenomenon is part of our built-in survival instinct to be alerted to new noises in our environment. It's because we need to determine whether they are a threat to our well-being whether (Zadina 2014). Once we determine a new stimulus is not a threat and become accustomed to it, we stop paying attention to it. Meet habituation.

What Is Habituation?

According to psychologist David Myers (2014), habituation is the "decreasing responsiveness with repeated stimulation." This means we pay less attention to a stimulus in our environment the more exposed we are to it. Not only is it part of our survival instinct, but it's also part of our adaptability. Once we determine a stimulus is not a threat, over time we are able to pay less attention to it. It's an adaptation gift. With repeated exposure, a stimuli's ability to elicit a response is reduced (APA 2020). Eventually, we may even tune out the stimulus altogether.

To help us better understand this concept, let's look at another example. Let's say you move to a new neighborhood near an airport. The noise from the airport is new for you and keeps you awake several nights in a row. However, after a while, you find you've become desensitized to the noise and your sleep improves. Eventually you notice you have completely tuned out the airport noise.

Habituation is an important concept we can also apply to the learning process. As Julie Dirksen (2012) explains in *Design for How People Learn*, "Habituation means getting used to a sensory stimulus to the point that we no longer notice or respond to it" (Dirksen 2012). This is what I was able to do over time in the noisy room.

Applying Habituation to Virtual Training

So how might habituation apply to live online learning and why is this important? When learners are repeatedly exposed to the same stimulus, there can be a decrease in their response to it. In live online learning, there are many opportunities for a stimulus to become stagnant and not change. For example, virtual learners might disengage because of monotone delivery, long introductions, static slides, and never-ending lecturettes. When this happens, learners can habituate and stop paying attention. Table 8-1 identifies some of these potential habituation examples in virtual training and how to address them.

To remedy the effect of habituation, experiment with ways to bring more dynamic variety into live online learning (Table 8-1). As discussed in chapter 6, our voices can demonstrate movement inflection. Additionally, multiple speakers or a producer who also works as a facilitative assistant can provide another voice to the mix. The greater the contrast between voices (for example, deeper versus higher), the more interest it generates as well. Even introducing a podcast-like format to the virtual training, where you interview a guest expert and ask them questions for part of the session and take questions from participants, can inject lots of movement. In addition to leveraging strategies to avoid habituation, let's explore how to capitalize on working memory with dynamic engagement.

Table 8-1. Habituation Examples in Virtual Training

Potential for Habituation	How to Address
Single slide shown too long	Only spend a few minutes on a slide visual.
Monotonous facilitation delivery	Vary vocal delivery with natural inflection that rises and falls.
Static content on slide	Progressively build slide visuals with animation. Annotate by circling or highlighting key content.
All slides are bullet points or text heavy and look the same	Vary how content is presented. Use diagrams or charts for descriptive content and bullet points for factual content.
Lecture-style delivery	Look for opportunities to interject a variety of activities, including interactive ones, relevant to content and learner goals.
Mostly one voice talks for the duration	Leverage a producer as a second voice with more of a co-facilitative role, or work with co-facilitators to add two voices. Incorporate large group discussions and breakouts where participants are actively sharing.

 PRO TIP 57
Employ strategies to avoid learner habituation.

Working Memory

Working memory is your active thinking. It is "a central element of human cognition responsible for active processing of data during thinking, problem solving, and learning" (Clark and Kwinn 2007). It is what you are using right now to read this book. For any of this information to be encoded into your long-term memory for later retrieval, it must first go through your working memory.

The most important thing you need to know about working memory is that it has a limited capacity. This might seem odd to you, but it has a purpose. With limitations, it must be efficient. Working memory's job is not to store everything you were ever exposed to for all of time. Instead, "working memory has a relatively short duration and limited capacity, but you use it pretty much constantly throughout the day" (Dirksen 2012). In addition to a limited capacity, it also has limits with the duration of storage. This has ramifications for learning. As Ruth Clark and Ann Kwinn

(2007) clarify in *The New Virtual Classroom: Evidence-Based Guidelines for Synchronous e-Learning*, "Because humans have a very limited working memory, instructional professionals must diligently conserve students' memory capacity for learning purposes."

Cognitive Load

Because working memory has a limited capacity, at times learners can become overwhelmed while learning. This is cognitive load, or the amount of mental processing or brain effort required by working memory. There are three types of cognitive load: extraneous, intrinsic, and germane (Sweller, van Merrienboer, and Paas 1998). Extraneous load comes from how we present content. It can impose extra mental work irrelevant to the learning goal and by doing so wastes mental resources that could have been used for germane load (Clark, Nguyen, and Sweller 2006). An example is when when we include extra nonessential information on a slide visual. Intrinsic load is the internal complexity inherent in the content itself. Attempting to understand the complexity can also use up learners' precious working memory resources. Germane load, however, is the good stuff. This is the load we want to impose on learners because this is when they are actively engaged in creating mental models, forming new schemas for the content they are learning about, and attaching it to their prior knowledge on the topic. As Clark and Kwinn (2007) summarize, "Cognitive load can come from the difficulty of the instructional content, the manner in which instructional materials are organized and displayed, and the mental processes required to achieve the learning goal."

As a result, we want to free up as much working memory resources as possible for germane load, and to do this, we must reduce extraneous load and manage intrinsic load. Thankfully, both are under our control as facilitators and developers. For example, we can remove nonessential visual elements on slides. We can also introduce complex content with just the overarching structure first and then gradually share more details to scaffold the complexity. Additionally, Clark and Kwinn (2007) recommend the following to manage cognitive load in virtual training, "keep sessions relatively brief, heavily interactive, and reliant on visuals explained by instructor narration to deliver content."

We also want to adhere to evidence-based principles, like the redundancy principle that reminds us to avoid adding a lot of text to slides that is repeated with the facilitator's live audio (Clark, Nguyen, and Sweller 2006). Instead, allow the facilitator's verbal explanation to supplement the imagery and diagrams illustrated on a slide with key text phrases or words. By avoiding this redundancy, you improve learning for virtual participants. As we keep the flow moving and keep sessions highly interactive with effective supporting visuals, we leverage dynamic movement to minimize overloading learners' working memories.

The Dynamic Principle of Engagement

Movement naturally calls attention to itself. This truth is the underpinning for what I call the dynamic principle of engagement. It is when facilitators use movement of various means to intentionally engage learners and their virtual participants. This principle implores virtual trainers to creatively think of ways to purposefully and strategically use movement, variety, and change to draw in learners and capture and sustain their attention. As international consultant David Sousa (2011) summarizes, "You cannot recall what you have not stored." So, how do we entice learners to be attentive so they can actively encode new information?

Imagine for a moment that someone just walked into the space where you are. What do you do? You likely turn and look toward the new movement. But why? Why did you turn and look? We turn because it's novel, it's a change in our current environment, and we're curious who it is and from where the sound originated. More importantly, we're also wired to notice new stimuli in our environment as part of our survival instinct. "The human brain is wired for detecting motion" (Bersin 2020). When something changes in our view or in our environment, our survival instincts kick in and we pay attention to determine whether it is a threat. As author Nancy Duarte (2008) notes, "When things move, the eye is drawn to them like a moth to light. It's unavoidable. Humans are hard-wired to look when things move, primarily from the innate fight-or-flight instinct. They will process what moves and make sure they're not in danger."

Because of this, we can introduce strategic movement to call learners' attention. The goal, however, with live online learning is to incorporate balanced movement. By this, I mean that there is a point when movement is too excessive. Excessive movement weakens its power as an attention-getting tool. Just as using too much salt for seasoning food spoils the taste but when used in moderation greatly improves it, so also we can spoil the effect if movement is excessive.

We want to leverage this instinct to fully focus on any new type of movement for learning. Our virtual training sessions should be dynamic, not static. In other words, we can use movement to gain learners' full attention throughout virtual training. And the reason we want to capture and sustain their full attention is because attention is critical to learning. If learners are not attentive, they cannot absorb, process, and retain the new content or create new mental schemas. Let's now apply the dynamic principle to some other aspects of virtual training.

 PRO TIP 58
Keep the flow of live online sessions dynamic, not static.

Applying the Dynamic Principle to Vocal Variety

As we learned in chapter 6, selective word emphasis and varying your pitch or speaking with natural inflection are ways to create movement and thus learner engagement. For example, what you choose to emphasize and how you do so when delivering virtual training can have an outsized impact on whether learners pay attention throughout the session or tune you out. Simply put, what's best for keeping learners engaged is variety. You can slow down on key points and even repeat them for added emphasis, while speaking faster (but not too fast) on the things they already know a bit about. Throughout all of it, use vocal inflection (leverage the natural ups and downs in your vocal range). Building on this, let's explore some additional ways to add vocal variety and movement into your virtual training programs by inviting learners' voices, using multiple facilitators, and elevating the producer role.

Invite Learners' Voices

Hearing from learners and inviting them to share either aloud or in chat not only aids their ability to process the information but can also be more interesting for others because of the vocal variety. But what can a facilitator do when learners are quiet? Let's explore next how you might incent learners to talk and share. It's important to note that chat is also an oral medium, as we discussed in chapter 7. As you may have noticed, some learners (especially introverts) may feel more comfortable contributing in chat only. This is certainly acceptable because in this way they still have a voice. To add greater vocal variety, however, for those who do wish to speak aloud, how can you incent them to talk? Here are some tactics you can apply:

- **Assign pre-work or pre-class activities.** These assignments can whet learners' appetite, so they are more prepared to converse on the subject and have formulated questions on the topic that pique their interest. For example, you might have them view a video or read a published article.
- **Overtly invite their expertise.** Learners recognize the unspoken authority of a facilitator in the presumed hierarchy of a class. They may assume that the facilitator is the authority on the subject. Yet learners also bring insights, professional experiences, great questions, and expertise to every virtual class. When we genuinely and overtly say, "I want to hear your great ideas" or "You all have professional experience with this. What are your thoughts?" learners are more likely to share.
- **Place them in breakouts early.** In a breakout of three to four individuals, people are not able to hide or passively participate in virtual training. They get into a flow after getting over their initial inertia, as we discussed in chapter 4, and begin to enter fluid conversation. The beauty is that when they return from breakouts, they are now warmed up. You may even observe elevated energy levels. Because they were just talking, they're more likely to talk again. I strategically place thoughtful discussion questions a short time after breakout debriefs while the open exchange is still flowing.
- **Modify your course to be a blended learning solution.** While chapter 11 is dedicated to this very topic, let's touch on it briefly here. A blended learning virtual training program incorporates both asynchronous and synchronous elements. When you offer a blended solution, employees are more invested by their

participation in a previous discussion thread, after listening to a podcast they had questions about, or after completing a reflection. These offline, additional activities can spawn greater and richer sharing during the live online sessions.

- **Build working relationships.** Relational learning—where learners know you care about them and have had a chance to meet you previously—can also bolster participants' comfort level in speaking up during class. For some of my more robust programs, I offer virtual office hours or schedule brief one-on-one tech checks. Participants may feel more comfortable after viewing a welcome video from you, or if you've asked them to introduce themselves in a discussion thread inside a course management system before the first live class. The more comfortable they are with you, the more likely they are to speak up during class.

- **Pre-class conversation.** Encourage learners to join five to 10 minutes early in your pre-communication messaging. Seize the opportunity to talk with them casually and welcome a few of them by name when they join, such as, "Welcome Wei and Imani—great to have you here!"

- **Apply the wait-time principle.** We discussed this in chapter 4. After you pose a question, wait up to six seconds for a response. This gives learners time to think and craft a reaction (Rowe 1986). Allow for extra time in chat too. They need to first think about what you're asking and then type and send.

- **Give advance warning that you'll call on learners.** I always like to prepare learners ahead of time if I'm going to call on them by name. This sets them up for success. I'll let them know in a little bit I'll be calling on them and then I give them time to think about and complete the exercise before choosing individuals to share what they've discovered. For example, you might ask, "Clara, what about you? What has resonated the most with you so far and why?"

- **Be mindful of what you do after learners share.** If you say nothing after someone shares, or if you say "Anyone else?"

without some type of acknowledgment, they may feel like they were ignored. Also, when the facilitator says trite comments like "thanks for that"—especially repetitively—it can come across as rote and sterile, as discussed in chapter 4. It's better to briefly acknowledge what was shared by asking a follow-up question, paraphrasing, reacting in a way that builds on it, or making a related comment. For example, you might say "Antonio, that's a great example! Tell us more about how you think that might work." Learners are watching how you treat others, knowing they will be treated in a similar way if they decide to share. This impacts their interpretation of a safe space free of ridicule and their willingness to also come forward.

- **Model sharing first.** Tell an on-topic story from your professional experience. The rules of reciprocity are at play here. When you divulge one of your own professional experiences tied to the topic at hand, it opens the space for more vulnerability and sharing. Then others are more likely to follow and share too. For example, when I was teaching a class on assertiveness, I shared a story about how I was once refused a jewelry repair even though I was told the piece would have a lifetime guarantee of repairs at the time of purchase. I asked my learners what they thought a passive customer response and an aggressive customer response might look like in this scenario. Then I shared what I did at the retailer by applying the assertive techniques we were discussing. As a result, the jeweler agreed to let me select another item as a replacement. After sharing that story, others came forward with their own assertive stories from which we could all learn.

Use Multiple Facilitators for More Vocal Variety

Adding multiple facilitators is another way to add movement through vocal variety. This is contingent naturally on class size and available resources. When appropriate, multiple voices can be valuable because learners no longer habituate to one facilitative voice, as discussed earlier in the chapter. There are many ways you can leverage multiple voices.

These include inviting a guest expert, an internal SME, a senior leader, or a co-facilitator to assist with part of your virtual training program. Let's explore each further.

Invite a Guest Expert

One way to add greater voice variety is to invite a guest expert to briefly join your virtual class. This allows learners to hear directly from the expert in real time. For instance, if you have been studying leadership development and have been reading a leadership book as part of the course work, you might invite the author to speak for 30 minutes. Or you might ask a world-renowned expert on leadership to join your class for 15–30 minutes. And, because you are not limited by physical proximity in live online learning, your guest experts can be anywhere in the world.

Another technique that works well with guest experts is to conduct a live interview. You, as the facilitator, could begin by asking questions collected from learners and sent to the expert ahead of time on the topic. From there, learners would have the opportunity to ask live questions by coming off mute or submitting them through chat. This interview style always works well and is not only captivating but a great attention-getting technique. You can see the inherent movement built into this method as questions and answers go back and forth in real time. People are naturally baited and curious about the expert's answers to each question.

Some of the downsides of working live with someone anywhere in the world include having to carefully coordinate language translation, time zones, scheduling logistics, and technology glitches. Many platforms have language translation abilities or captions, which can help with language barriers. From a technical perspective, the best time for an expert to join is before the session begins or after an extended break. This allows time to connect with the expert and troubleshoot technology issues either before class begins or during the break, so your guest is ready to go when learners return. It is also important to ensure that the guest is informed and updated on what the learners have been discussing so far on the topic, so the guest can connect their own comments to what participants have been learning.

Invite an Internal Subject Matter Expert

You can also invite an internal subject matter expert (SME) to log in—preferably during an extended break to ensure their connection is working—and talk with learners right after the break. Depending on the topic of the virtual learning class, the SME may be able to provide not only vocal variety but also a different perspective. Let's say, for example, that you were training a virtual class on how to be a skilled project manager. You might ask one of your organization's seasoned and best skilled project managers to make a guest appearance during and share some of their best practices, lessons learned, and roadblocks to avoid, which will connect back to the techniques you discussed in class. One downside of this is having to troubleshoot for technical issues with the connection. Additionally, working through the logistics of different time zones is also worth careful thought. As mentioned previously, the SME should be informed of the key points that have been discussed in the virtual class up to this point so that they can connect their comments to what participants have been learning.

Invite a Senior Leader or Executive to Make a Guest Appearance

You could also invite a senior leader or executive to make a guest appearance. For example, if you were conducting a leadership development virtual training session, a senior leader might join at the beginning to kick off the session by thanking participants for their leadership, acknowledging the important role leaders play, explaining why this training is so important to the company, and talking about how the outcomes of this class tie into the long-term strategic goals of the organization. A downside of incorporating a senior leader is that they may be interested in staying for the duration, although this is rare for an executive. This may suppress learner engagement because they tend to be more participative when senior leaders are not present and more quiet when they're there. Sometimes, just being frank with senior leadership about this can be helpful. They may agree to come for a time and then leave to allow more openness and sharing.

Invite a Co-Facilitator to Co-Train

Another way to include more voices in your virtual training is to work with a co-facilitator who is credible and has expertise on the topic. Each of you could each take turns facilitating different portions of the virtual training, which provides a natural contrast in vocal tones for learners. I have partnered with co-facilitators and found it easier to share the work, as well as being enjoyable and fun, and certainly more interesting for learners. When we worked together, we were also able to alternate playing the producer role for each other, although you could also work with a producer who then supports both learners and co-facilitators.

PRO TIP 59
Use multiple facilitators to add vocal movement and greater interest through vocal variety.

Elevate the Seasoned Producer's Role for More Vocal Variety

Depending on your topic and their experience as a producer, your virtual training producers may even be able to play a more involved facilitative role. According to virtual training expert Kassy LaBorie (2021), facilitative producers manage the technical aspects of the training, but also play a supportive role teaching segments as needed. Depending on the skill level of producers I've worked with, I have experimented with involving them in more facilitative roles in various ways. The longer you work with a producer, the more trust you develop in your partnership and the more added duties you can explore sharing. For example, I've strategically included some of my producers as another voice not just at the beginning or end, but also during the training sessions to intentionally add more vocal interest. You'll need to discern their ability to do this, however, as novice producers may be too overwhelmed to take on extra responsibilities. In my experience, seasoned producers handle this well, provided it's later on in the training when most technical issues have been resolved and we have reached smoother waters.

One producer I had the good fortune to work with was exceptionally experienced. We had worked together so many times that I trusted her with everything and knew she could solve almost any virtual training issue. The online class I was teaching at the time was an active listening course for a Fortune 500 company. I asked my producer ahead of time if she would be willing to share a story about her experience watching the total solar eclipse in 2017. She agreed. After all, it was an active listening class. I thought this would be a great opportunity for learners to apply the listening techniques we had just discussed while a new voice shared her story. The producer explained that she was in the path of totality and saw the moon completely cover the sun for approximately 2.5 minutes. She went on to share that everything suddenly grew dark, and the crickets started chirping even though it was the middle of the day. After she shared her story, I quizzed learners on the key points of the story and it became a rich discussion example for what active listening techniques they applied and how it worked for them. Evidently, the fact that I still remember what she said all these years later shows that I was actively listening too! The point is, as a virtual facilitator, you can leverage your experienced producers to assist with things beyond just managing the technical aspects. This is a way to add movement that draws attention through vocal variety.

Another time, I asked a different producer if she would be willing to share a brief professional story during our virtual class on effective storytelling for leaders. The advantage to this was threefold. It was a way to generate more interest through a new voice, it was an opportunity to check learners' knowledge and practice recall, and it served as an example. Certainly, hearing the prominence of a new voice piqued learners' attention. Before she began, I asked them to type the one-word tenets we had learned about effective storytelling in the chat while she progressed through her story. This exercise was strategically placed right before learners practiced outlining their own stories in independent breakouts, where I could pop in and check on their progress.

By inviting learners' voices; being open to guest experts, internal SMEs, senior leaders, or co-facilitators; and elevating the verbal role of a seasoned producer, you can add vocal variety and dynamism to virtual training.

Applying the Dynamic Principle to Visuals

If you have ever attended an hour-long webinar that used a total of six static slides, you have experienced death-by-webinar. Visuals are important to clarify and explain concepts and other types of information, but when left up too long at a time or when they display something that is no longer being discussed, they lose their effectiveness. One strategy you can use is to reveal the visual at the time you talk about it—not long before you talk about it or long after you've stopped talking about it.

There is evidence-based research to support visuals' aid to learning when they are designed and used appropriately. "Effective visuals engage learners, promote learning, and help to reduce mental load" (Clark and Kwinn 2007). Creating effective visuals for your live online learning classes requires visual literacy skills. One thing you want to keep in mind is not to use a visual for the sake of using a visual. Just because your virtual training platform allows you to share slides doesn't mean you always need them. For example, during lengthy group discussions, I like to stop sharing slides and invite learners to just come on camera. You don't need to prepare a slide for everything you say or have one on display all the time. Use supporting visuals when your content calls out for greater clarity and to anchor learners to the key points you're making.

PRO TIP 60
Use visuals to add variety to your virtual training when the instructional content calls out for more clarity.

Use Progressive Builds

Progressive builds are one way to create movement. This means gradually revealing more and more complexity on a slide through animated entrances at the time that you speak about them (Figure 8-1). Instead of displaying all the content on your slide at one time (text, graphics, images, and so on), you can reveal certain elements gradually. This scaffolding movement of unveiling a new part of the slide naturally draws the learner's attention and builds curiosity for what's coming next. More importantly, it aligns with Richard Mayer's temporal contiguity principle, which states that people learn better when corresponding animation and narration are presented at the same time (Mayer and Fiorella 2014). This technique also avoids cognitively overloading your learners by only displaying the most relevant part of your slide visual at the time you explain it.

Note that some virtual platform technologies may not display progressive builds or animations on slides once they are uploaded. For example, when I trained a virtual class using Blackboard Collaborate, I had several animation layers built into my slides that I knew would aid learning. With novice learners especially, you want to gradually build in complexity by scaffolding, so as not to overwhelm them with complexity all at once. However, at the time, if I uploaded my PowerPoint slides through Share Files, it would not display my animations in this mode. Because I felt it was important to show my animations, I used Share Application instead. This way, when I chose to share my PowerPoint application onscreen, my animations displayed and then learners could see my progressive builds.

Figure 8-1. Slide Example of a Progressive Build

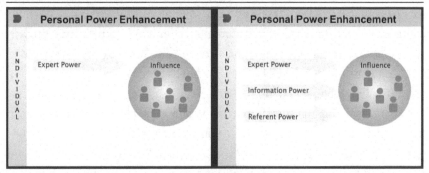

PRO TIP 61
Progressively construct complex slide visuals in real time with animated builds.

Create Movement With Annotation and the Signaling Principle

Building on our discussion of annotation in chapter 7, annotation is a very useful tool for learning. In addition to inviting learners to select the text tool from the annotation toolbar to type text or draw for any whiteboard learning activities, facilitators can also use annotation to highlight visual content as they discuss it. For example, you can use annotation to draw learners' attention to where they should focus on a visual. You could highlight the part of the slide you're referencing by drawing arrows or circling it with the digital highlighter or pencil from the annotation toolbar. In some platforms, if the annotation toolbar isn't available while sharing slides in-app, you can share your screen instead and click the bottom left of the projected slide to use PowerPoint's annotation tools. This is also a way to reduce cognitive load. We preserve limited working memory resources for the learning content by providing these visual cues to the learner.

In a research study by Richard Mayer and Roxana Moreno (2003), a narrated animation with visual media was shown along with intentionally added extraneous facts and some confusing graphics. For one group, learners were shown where to look by adding red and blue arrows to the animation in real time along with other interventions like adding clear headings to the text. Learners who received the signaled version of this multimedia presentation performed better on a problem-solving transfer test than those in the un-signaled control group. "We refer to this result as a signaling effect: Students understand a multimedia presentation better when it contains signals concerning how to process the material." In terms of adding cues to direct where to focus through highlighting or annotation, it appears to help learners select and organize information.

To aid learning, it's also important to show the visual that's relevant to your verbal explanation at the time you speak about it to anchor the content. I sometimes observe virtual trainers who talk about netiquette ground rules while their title slide displays, or they share a story while we look at a diagram that has nothing to do with the story, or they ask a discussion question while we are looking at learning objectives. It is better for deeper learning when your verbal explanations match the visual displayed. Distinguished Professor of Psychology at the University of California, Santa Barbara, Richard Mayer, calls this the temporal contiguity principle (Mayer and Fiorella 2014). It involves presenting corresponding animation and narration simultaneously, not one after another or any other combination. For example, with PowerPoint slides, when the content being shown does not match what is being spoken, there is a mismatch. This can create dissonance for learners. To fix this, a relevant visual should anchor what you are explaining at the time you explain it.

Changing the color of your annotation when you work with a digital pen or highlighter from your toolbar is another natural differentiator that will draw the eye. Any color that is not already displayed on the slide would help the annotation stand out to learners. In Figure 8-2, you can see how the facilitator is using a highlighter to circle what she's explaining, as well as using an arrow pointer. As Mayer and Fiorella (2014) explain, annotations like arrows can help highlight the key visual concepts that learners should attend to most.

Figure 8-2. Example of Annotated Trainer Slide

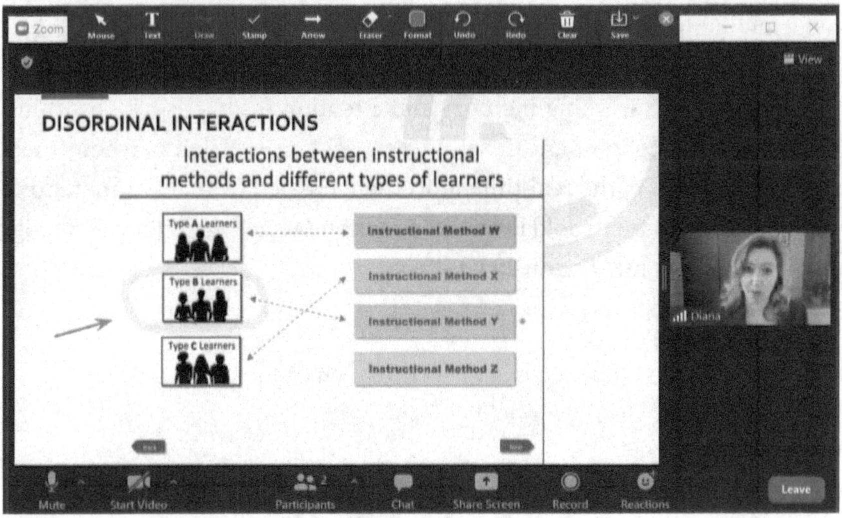

Movement, Rest, Movement

Annotation can be used by virtual facilitators to signal where learners should focus attention on any type of visual shared on a platform. What I often see novice trainers do, however, is continue to move their laser pointer, drawing tool, cursor, or highlighter in a continuous motion while they talk. This is excessive and can make learners dizzy. Instead, use the highlighter or drawing tool to draw attention to where the learner should focus and then keep the pointer still until it's time to note the next important aspect on the slide. It is dynamic, but not overdone or excessive. Movement, rest, movement—this fine balance between a variety of visual movement interlaced with rest can be leveraged as a hook to capture and sustain learner interest and attention.

Some of my clients have successfully used the cursor in place of annotation tools to guide learner focus. They move their cursor to the specific slide they're sharing via Zoom, for example, and then move it near the visual content they are discussing on the slide. This way the cursor serves as a laser pointer of sorts and helps draw attention.

In virtual training, everything on the platform is a competing visual. Chat and the live video feed of facilitators and other learners can compete for visual attention. Annotating a slide using a highlighter or pen clarifies immediately where learners should direct their focus. This assists them by reducing mental overload because they are no longer taxed with trying to figure out which part of the visual you're currently explaining. This then reserves precious working memory and attention resources for absorbing and processing content and forming new schemas, which is where their focus should be. So, the real-time movement created from live annotations not only can be used to hold learners' attention but also to reduce their cognitive load (Clark and Kwinn 2007).

 PRO TIP 62
Annotate visuals to focus learners' attention on the part you are discussing at the time you discuss it.

Variety in Visuals Based on Content Type

Movement can even be leveraged in the way visual content is depicted. Earlier we discussed how learners can habituate after viewing slide after slide of bullet points, because after a while, they all look the same. Not only does frequent changing of slides create movement, which breaks the cycle of habituation, but this is also accomplished when the slide content is illustrated in different ways. As explored previously, all forms of movement grab attention.

Decades ago, Robert E. Horn brilliantly discovered ways to structure content and visually represent it. According to him, some of the major content types include facts, concepts, processes, procedures, and structures (Horn et al. 1969). It can be helpful to know how to identify a content type because you can create more effective visuals based on it. For example, a list of grammar errors for a virtual training class on business writing is an example of factual content. Facts are best represented with bullet points. Although bullet points certainly have their place, they are not appropriate for all content. Because factual content shows no inherent sequential order or ranking importance of hierarchy, facts wouldn't need to be numbered.

Let's say you are conducting virtual training on emotional intelligence; you might use bullet points to list all the major emotions human beings can experience (such as joy, anxiety, fear, anger, and sadness). These emotions are facts, so they don't need to follow a hierarchical system and don't need to be numbered. Thus bullet points are an appropriate way to represent them on your virtual training slides.

However, let's now imagine you were training a virtual class on how to develop productive teams. You want to include a slide visual of the stages teams progress through that psychologist Bruce Tuckman developed in the 1960s: forming, storming, norming, performing, and adjourning (MasterClass 2021). Could you include all five stages as bullet points on a virtual training slide? You could, but remember, first we want to determine what type of content this is. Is this content factual? Structural? A concept? Procedure? No. It is a process because it has stages that spread over time.

Although bullet points work well for facts, they do not show the progression or hierarchy. What's important to visually show with these five stages is that they progress up a ladder, but if new conflicts emerge or team members join, you might return to an earlier stage. Bullet points would not adequately reflect this. However, if you created a slide with five rectangles containing the name of each phase and illustrate them as if you are climbing a ladder, that would be a more accurate representation. Additionally, arrows could show how teams can return to previous stages depending on circumstances like conflict or the arrival of new team members.

Concepts with definitions and descriptions benefit most from an analogy or an example contrasted with a non-example. Processes include successive stages that span over time; alternatively, procedures follow specific steps to achieve a desired outcome (Horn et al. 1969). Quick references, job aids, and other performance support tools often walk employees through procedures such as how to use project management software to track your time on a project. Visually, both processes and procedures benefit from descriptive diagrams and charts that show these steps with shapes, arrows, and workflows. To reduce cognitive load for learners, evidence-based research also suggests how you can improve learning outcomes when training procedural or process content. "When teaching processes or procedures, present and practice related concepts first, followed by the stages of the process or steps of the procedure" (Clark and Kwinn 2007).

Structural content includes the parts or subparts of a whole with boundaries (Horn et al. 1969). Because structure can be visually represented, this content benefits from diagrams that visually illustrate and clarify the overall structure and its subcomponent parts.

So, when you design your slides for visual training (see Table 8-2 for examples), first pause and identify what type of content you are trying to illustrate. Is it factual, a concept, a process, a procedure, or structural? Based on the different types of content, you can then create slides that give a sense of movement or change. Some will contain bullet points, others graphs or tables, some flow charts, and others illustrations and images.

Table 8-2. Visual Representation by Content Type

Horn's Content Types	How to Represent Content on Slide Visuals
Facts	Bullet point lists, statements, or tables
Concepts	Image representing the concept or an image and shapes representing an example and non-example combined with key words
Process	Visually illustrate stages with flowcharts, shapes, and arrows and minimal text
Procedure	Visually show procedural steps with flowcharts, shapes, and arrows and minimal text
Structure	Diagrams, illustrations, or graphics

Remove Extraneous Imagery

We also want to steer clear of overloading learners visually in your training slides. Remove content from slides that is extraneous and unrelated to the topic. I once saw someone justify adding kittens to their slides because they "thought they were cute." The kitties were cute but had nothing to do with the topic. This is an example of extraneous content. If images or text are irrelevant to the topic, they only add busyness to the slide and should be removed. According to evidence-based research, "Slides that incorporate too many decorative or unrelated thematic visuals do not contribute to learning and may even depress learning" (Clark and Kwinn 2007). Everything on the slide should support and clarify the core message of the visual. As Richard Mayer's Coherence Principle articulates, "People learn better when extraneous material is excluded rather than included" (Atkinson and

Mayer 2004). Presentation development and design expert Nancy Duarte (2008) also eloquently sums this up in one of her manifesto theses for powerful visual presentations: "Practice Design, Not Decoration."

 PRO TIP 63
How you visually depict slide content depends on what type of content it is.

Applying the Dynamic Principle to Platform Tools

As we discuss in chapter 7, the virtual trainer has many tools to use in today's platforms. It is best practice to familiarize yourself with all of them and then leverage them for variety and movement during live online learning. As global talent analyst Josh Bersin (2020) explains, "enhanced vILT tools offer a multitude of options to keep the presentation moving and learners' brains engaged." Further, according to author Julie Dirksen (2012), "Variation can be a useful tool for maintaining attention, but it should be used in a deliberate and meaningful way."

Here are examples of how you can add meaningful dynamic movement:
- **Annotation.** Highlighting, circling, or using the cursor draws eye attention.
- **Polls.** Opening polls and sharing results visually changes what's on the screen and asks learners to get involved.
- **Chat.** Chats are both a place for stream of consciousness flow from all participants and a place for them to respond to direct questions that you or other participants pose.
- **Whiteboard.** Whiteboards offer real-time attention with drawing, typing, and annotating.
- **Video.** Videos by their very nature showcase movement. Some platforms like Zoom allow you to annotate and highlight over video.
- **Breakouts.** Breakouts introduce significant movement as learners divide into smaller discussion groups.
- **Screen sharing.** Screen sharing enables everyone to collaborate on documents in real time, as well as broadcast visuals, PDFs, websites, files, and more. Live movement is also visible by gradually building complexity in slide visuals.

Take Frequent Refresh Breaks

One of my colleagues mentioned to me in passing that he didn't have time to take a break in his two-hour online session. I mentioned to him that his learners still needed a quick break and that he needed one too, even if he didn't think he did. Always give learners a break. After approximately 45–60 minutes, even a quick stretch break sends more blood to the brain and refreshes everyone's focus. Breaks offer an invaluable opportunity for learners to step away and rejuvenate before absorbing more.

In your design, you can build in 10-minute refresh breaks but never announce how long they will be until right before. This way, if you're running behind, you can reduce your break to 5 minutes on the fly. The point is to give them the opportunity to take a break from their screens even if it's brief. For this reason, I encourage them not to check their email during breaks, even though many still do.

Before sending learners to break, there are a few key points you can share with them. You always want to clarify the time on your clock, since there may be slight variances. When you have global learners, always announce the time zone you're using as a reference point. For example, if all my learners are in Pacific time, I will say what time it is in Pacific time, not where I am (Eastern time zone, for example). If needed, look up how to make that conversion in advance of your session. Before sending learners off to break I might say something like, "Alright everyone, we're at 2:45 Eastern time. Let's take a five-minute break. We'll see you back here at 2:50 p.m. Eastern. Please mute yourselves and turn off your cameras. I encourage you to get up and move around your home or office floor. Get a drink or go outside." Instruct all learners to keep connections on, but request they mute themselves and turn off their cameras. Avoid making colleagues stare at an empty chair or desk space.

You can also play royalty-free music during breaks matches the professional tone and mood of your virtual training session. Above all, remember that focused attention requires effort and is not sustainable over long periods of time. We can best maintain focused attention with ebb and flow. Interject more movement and variety by incorporating frequent breaks.

PRO TIP 65
Use breaks to inject movement into your training and to sustain focused attention.

Summary

Overall, learners run the risk of habituating from repeated stimuli when our live online sessions are mostly static. This can happen when facilitators use a monotone voice, display a single slide until the world seemingly ends, give a mini-presentation that lasts way too long, use a deck where every slide starts to look like the one before it, fail to include a variety of learning activities, or don't properly leverage training tools. Why should we care if habituation sets in? Because if learners habituate, we lose their full attention. And because attention is essential to learning, we must do everything we can to entice, motivate, show relevance, captivate, and sustain full attention online.

As we learned in this chapter, you can leverage the power of movement in a variety of ways to engage learners. Variety does not mean chaotic and rapid jumping from one thing to the next. We want to be dynamic, but not excessively dynamic. Most online experts agree that switching up visuals or activities approximately every four minutes works well. While the amount of time you take before changing it up is less important, note that there is a rhythm, and when learners are focused on static content for too long, they lose interest. Movement must be purposeful and smooth with transitions that tie everything together.

To apply the dynamic principle in your virtual training sessions, vary the rhythm using high-energy activities, independent work, and breakouts. Use signaling to highlight and cue which part of a visual learners should be looking at onscreen when it's explained. Progressively build slide visuals to support learning and create movement, adding on the complexity as you go.

Additionally, create variety in the way you present content based on what type of content it is. Use multiple facilitators to create vocal variety and garner more interest with co-facilitators and two voices. Incorporate more visual anchors as needed, based on when the content calls out for greater clarity. And leverage a variety of virtual training platform tools to keep things dynamic and moving in fresh ways. All these strategies support your development of the dynamic engagement capability.

Let's revisit this chapter's opening scenario. Only this time, let's apply the tips and techniques we've discussed. Opening scene, take 2:

Imagine you join a virtual training session on emotional intelligence. You scan the screen to check out the class landscape. You notice 11 other attendees, a few of whom appear to be on camera. The producer of the session begins to welcome everyone, provides a brief tour of the virtual training platform, and asks participants to raise their virtual hands and post the name of the country they're connecting from. The facilitator begins to share what's in it for you in this session and how this course can help you advance your career by developing your emotional intelligence.

The facilitator uses a lot of inflection and has great energy in his voice, and you can tell he's passionate about emotional intelligence. This helps you feel excited about it too. He says that after this training, you'll be able to manage your own emotions when working with co-workers and difficult customers. He shares a professional story of how he was able to stay calm during a customer service crisis after applying some of the techniques he'll be teaching today. You wonder what techniques those might be, thinking they could help you with some of the conflicts you've had recently with a team member.

Then the facilitator begins to share a slide and gradually adds more elements to each slide through animation. He uses a drawing tool to circle the part of the slide as he's talking about it. He next asks participants to type all the emotions they can think of on the digital whiteboard. You type in a few emotions using the text typing tool. Occasionally, he also asks for your responses to open-ended questions in the chat. You were hoping to respond to a few emails and finish your prep for that meeting you lead in the morning, but you decide you'll do that later.

As you can see, there are distinct differences between this scenario and the one at the beginning of this chapter. As virtual facilitators, we prioritize capturing and focusing learner attention because of one foundational reason: To teach humans, we need their attention. The front door to learners' working memory (and, hopefully, long-term memory) is attention. Dynamic engagement is just one strategy we use to help learners focus attention. Work to leverage the power of movement in multiple ways to engage learners throughout live online learning. As you continue to facilitate live online sessions, practice developing your capability in dynamic engagement.

There are also some other things we can do to help learners focus. One such strategy is to ensure the technology supporting virtual training does not distract learners. In the next chapter, we'll learn about the preventive actions we can take to minimize and troubleshoot any technical issues you might encounter. Ideally, we want to do our best to ensure we keep things running smoothly for everyone.

Pro Tips for Practicing your Dynamic Engagement Skills

TIP 57	Employ strategies to avoid learner habituation.
TIP 58	Keep the flow of live online sessions dynamic, not static.
TIP 59	Use multiple facilitators to add vocal movement and greater interest through vocal variety.
TIP 60	Use visuals to add variety to your virtual training when the instructional content calls out for more clarity.
TIP 61	Progressively construct complex slide visuals in real time with animated builds.
TIP 62	Annotate visuals to focus learners' attention on the part you are discussing at the time you discuss it.
TIP 63	How you visually depict slide content depends on what type of content it is.
TIP 64	Create dynamic movement by guiding learners to use a variety of tools in the virtual training platform.
TIP 65	Use breaks to inject movement into your training and to sustain focused attention.

"Once we truly know that life is difficult—once we truly understand and accept it—then life is no longer difficult."

—M. Scott Peck, author, *The Road Less Traveled*

CHAPTER 9

Troubleshooting and Recovering With Agility

One day I eagerly joined a virtual training session as an attendee to learn more about an interpersonal business skills with my colleagues. The producer began by welcoming us to the session, shared her enthusiasm for the topic, and then introduced us to the trainer. After the handoff, the virtual trainer shared his own background, and then transitioned to the topic for the day.

Suddenly, mid-sentence, everything went silent. We could still see the shared slides but could no longer hear the trainer or see his live camera. A few of us sent chat messages to alert both producer and trainer of what was happening on our end. The producer, clearly horrified, told us she was not sure what had happened, assured us the trainer would soon re-join, and that she would text him and get back to us. So, as an audience, we sat in silence and waited. A few attendees posted messages in chat speculating what might have happened and sharing their reactions. Moments later, we heard the producer speak again. She let us know the trainer had lost his internet connection and was attempting to reconnect. But so far, the attempts remained unsuccessful.

This is an all-too-common occurrence in virtual training or virtual anything. Anytime we use electric technology to train adults—or to do anything for that matter—there's always the potential for things to go wrong. This is the reality of working with technology. As McLuhan and Nevitt (1972) brilliantly observed in their book *TAKE TODAY: The Executive as Dropout*, when you bring in a service, you also bring in a disservice. There is a reason why help desks, technical support, and IT departments emerged after computers became widely adopted. Computers offer great services, but they also created a need to support, problem solve, and troubleshoot their disservices.

Virtual training platforms also offer a great service. They facilitate global connections with people across time, space, and distance. They provide an effective venue for staff training, and they significantly reduce travel costs and other expenditures associated with traditional in-person training. Yet at the same time, they can also provide a disservice. Even though we admire technology for its many affordances and technological advancements, we can still experience lost connections, outages, low bandwidth, latency issues, dropped audio, frozen video, distractions, and more. You have likely experienced similar challenges in your own virtual training or online adult education sessions. And if you have so far miraculously escaped such an experience, just wait. It's coming.

As learners, facilitators, and producers, we work with multiple virtual training platforms, varying connection bandwidths, and a myriad of devices all converging concurrently. The likelihood of something going wrong is high. The focus of this chapter is how to help you troubleshoot and recover when it does. So, let's explore the next core virtual trainer capability: agile troubleshooting.

 THE BIG IDEA
Use the 3 Ms Method to mitigate risk, manage the expected and unexpected, and help learners (and yourself) keep moving forward.

Troubleshooting Also Means Managing Expectations

It may seem like virtual training is a mixed bag. But once we realize technical challenges are part of virtual training, we are less disappointed when they occur. It's all about managing expectations. Not only are we less surprised, but more importantly, we are quicker to adapt. The real lesson, of course, is to learn to accept what is happening and then take necessary action. This makes us less likely to react negatively, which only makes a situation worse. By first accepting that things can go wrong in the virtual space, it equips us to respond more productively.

In one of my virtual training classes, I prepared learners for an exercise to complete in small breakout groups. For this session, my producer had graciously agreed to manage breakouts when the time came. As she started to divide them, some attendees were successfully placed, but others were not. After she made three attempts to divide everyone into their breakouts, it was still not working correctly. So, I sent her a quick private chat that we would do the activity in a different way instead. Ironically, the topic of this class was how to conduct virtual training. For attendees to experience a challenge like this in real life could be a great teaching moment. As my producer regrouped everyone into the main session, I said, "Well, we did that on purpose . . . so you could experience what can happen in virtual training!" They laughed, of course, knowing it wasn't true. Humor is a great way to diffuse tension. It also increases positive energy in any space, including virtual space.

With everyone back from the breakouts that were not meant to be, I had to be agile and decide how to proceed. Their breakout assignment included a challenging scenario for them to discuss and figure out how to resolve within their small groups. Although small-group discussions allow for greater individual participation and are preferable, I knew we had to pivot. I also knew we could still complete the assignment as a large group. So, that's what we did.

With the group at-large, we discussed various solutions to the scenario in their assignment. Some participants raised virtual hands and came off mute to share, while others posted ideas in chat. Through it all, my producer and I were able to stay calm and even joke about it with learners. We did not allow ourselves to get upset in the moment. It's important to keep a level head during class; you can always express any needed emotional release after class. Later, of course, we asked technical staff to investigate the incident further. Our conduct during class not only demonstrated to attendees how to pivot when technical issues emerge, but it turned into something more memorable. Years from now, they may not remember what we said that day, but they may remember what we did. Sometimes participants learn more from what you do than what you say.

PRO TIP 67
Use humor to diffuse tension, infuse positive energy, and redirect learner attention.

It's also important to remember that when you debrief with your producer after class, never do it using the same training session link right after, unless you're using private chat. Sometimes participants may be slow to exit and overhear your discussion. End your original virtual training session first and then reconnect separately with your producer to debrief, as needed.

When technical challenges arise, we have a choice. We can either choose to react negatively or look for opportunity. If we look for opportunity, this shifts us into problem-solving mode. For example, if a virtual tool is not working correctly for a learning activity, ask yourself if there is a different tool you could use instead. For instance, if a poll is not launching correctly, you can read the question aloud and ask attendees to post their answers (A, B, C, or D) in chat, or type the question on a whiteboard and have them circle the appropriate letter with annotation tools. When things go wrong in the virtual platform, focus instead on what you can do, not on what you can no longer do.

The 3 Ms Method

A personal method I created and have taught others to use is the 3 Ms Method (Figure 9-1). It is a framework that has helped me address the technical challenges that inevitably happen. This three-pronged method offers strategies for predicting and addressing issues before class day, when live challenges emerge during training, and how to recover and move forward afterward. The 3 Ms are:

1. Mitigate
2. Manage
3. Move forward

Figure 9-1. The 3 Ms Method for Troubleshooting

Overall, this method helps us circumvent a variety of virtual training technical issues. The first M mitigates risk ahead of time by reminding you to take preventive actions well before virtual training day. The second M helps you manage both the predictable and unpredictable when they arise during training. The final M reminds you to let things go and expedite everyone's recovery—including your own—so the training session can move forward productively. Let's examine each more closely.

Mitigate

Again, the first M in the 3 Ms Method is mitigate. Most of us are familiar with Murphy's Law. If things can go wrong, they will. To increase our chances of smooth and successful training, we mitigate risk by doing all we can to prevent or reduce the risk of common technical issues blindsiding us in the first place. Mitigation starts well before virtual class day, and there are several strategies we can use.

Take Preventive Action

One of the best ways to mitigate is through preventive action. This involves taking steps to alleviate risk for you and your learners in advance. For example, it is important to send pre-class communications to learners to welcome them, set expectations, and include steps they can take now to ensure all works well for them technically. This can be accomplished by sending a welcome email or a welcome video. It is an opportunity to also request learners check their connection and their access to the technology to ensure a positive learning experience. In the earlier days of virtual training, the platforms we worked with often prompted participants to download plug-ins, which took some time. Ensuring this was done before class day made it less likely there would be hiccups at start time. Thankfully, platforms have greatly improved. However, in your preliminary communications, you should still ask learners to test their connections, audio, speakers, and access to the platform before class day. Many platforms provide ways to test connections ahead of time. There are even sites and apps you can visit to test your internet connection speed, such as speedtest.net.

Other preventive actions include communicating the expectation to log in five to 10 minutes early. This also provides valuable time for extra troubleshooting. As a facilitator, I always insist on connecting at least 30 minutes ahead of time with my producers. This gives us time to check audio, go over any last-minute arrangements, set up whiteboards if they're not completed already, pull up materials, place a welcome message in chat, and so on. It can be tempting for successive training programs that meet multiple times to forgo the half-hour minimum setup time, but I always advise this because surprises can still emerge.

One time I was tempted to log in only 15 minutes early because it was another session in a program where we had already met together as a class earlier in the week. Everyone had successfully been able to connect, and all had gone well. However, this turned out to be the day the producer accidentally sent the training link for a different date in the series, and to our great surprise, none of us were able to log in. The producer scrambled to correct the link and resend it quickly to all. After that, I reminded myself that I knew better. Even if you think it should be easy to log in because you've already worked with the same learners on the same platform with the same producer earlier that week or the week before, you still need to make time for last-minute troubleshooting just in case. When things go wrong, that time buffer is essential for resolving issues before learners join so you can start on time.

In another virtual training class, many learners were new to the technology platform. Because it was a small class, I met with them for scheduled, 10-minute tech checks the week before to check their system's compatibility with the platform. These sessions proved to be invaluable because two of the dozen or so participants discovered issues that we were then able to resolve before training day. One learner was not able to use his camera and had to enable it in settings on his device. Another had a very poor audio connection from her location, so I asked her to call in on the phone line instead, which worked much better. This way, on class day, she knew to call in for the audio and connected via internet for the visual portion, and all worked smoothly. If we hadn't troubleshooted ahead of time, it would have been very frustrating for her and everyone else and significantly delayed our start time.

When participants log in ahead of time for tech checks, this also increases their comfort level with the platform, and reduces their class-day anxiety (and mine). Above and beyond resolving technical issues ahead of time, the extra bonus is that they appreciate their facilitator spending individual time with them. I noticed how it helped build our working relationship, and some even spoke up more in class because they had already talked with their facilitator and felt more comfortable. Because we invested in mitigation strategies beforehand, we enjoyed a smooth first-day kickoff to our virtual training program.

Your perceived credibility and likability—whether we like it or not—can also play a role in whether participants choose to participate and listen. This is the power of relational building in learning. Although 10-minute tech checks are not practical for every class and topic, it may be appropriate based on several variables, such as learners' familiarity with the technology, level of expertise with online learning, your availability, and of course, class size. I usually use them if it's a robust virtual training program where we'll meet several times over several weeks and teach-backs or presentations are part of their assignments.

Make a List of What Could Go Wrong

It's also important to identify ready-made solutions to common technical issues ahead of time. The best way to mitigate technical challenges is to identify all the common issues that could go wrong and then plan—or research if you don't know—ways you could address them. As e-learning expert Bill Horton recommends, when you rehearse, write down all the things you can think of that can go wrong on index cards and then shuffle them. "Every five minutes during a rehearsal, draw a card and pretend that the problem on the card just occurred" (Horton 2006). This gives you the opportunity to calmly practice and think through what you could or should do, rather than waiting and hoping for the best during a live session. The hoping for the best strategy can certainly be tempting for some, but it is never best practice. Strategic planning will not only provide you with solutions in the moment, but give you the repetition needed to resolve issues with confidence. Table 9-1 lists 10 common technical issues I've encountered, actions to take to prevent them, and how my producers and I have addressed them when they did occur.

Table 9-1. Common Issues and How to Address Them

Common Tech Issues	Preventive Actions Before Class Day	How to Address
Cannot hear audio or cannot see slides	Mitigate with pre-class messaging (welcome video or email) to test their connection, speaker, mic, and platform link well beforehand.	Request they exit and rejoin session to reset everything (slides and audio). If audio issues only, request they call the phone option for audio instead.
"Never received" the handouts or participant guide	Send handouts or participant guides in the very same invite message that contained the link to the session a week before class and send another reminder the day of training.	If your platform allows, upload the PDF of your handouts or digital participant guides for learners to download. Alternatively, you can post the links in chat where they can access them.
Lost internet connection or lost power	After going over netiquette guidelines on front end, remind them what they can do if they lose power. Have mobile phone charged and nearby. In case it happens to you, print out your slides and all materials, so you could have your producer share materials and you could train via phone audio if necessary.	Have learners join via audio from their mobile phones and if the session is being recorded, offer to send them the recording later.
Session link not working	In pre-communications, strongly encourage participants to log in five to 10 minutes early to allow for extra troubleshooting if needed. Send a reminder link the day of training.	Request producer resend the link or remind them of the phone number they could use to call in for the audio portion.
Audio distortions with echoes or feedback	In pre-class communications, encourage them to use an external mic, headset, or earbuds. Sometimes when using a built-in mic, their audio input can be picked up through their speakers and create a feedback loop. Remind them of netiquette guidelines upfront.	Exit session and login to reset. Producer or virtual trainer can check the participant panel to locate the source of the active audio, and then mute the individual. Alternatively, facilitator can mute everyone at once, and unmute them later after reminding them to mute themselves if they're in a noisy environment.

Table 9-1 (cont'd)

Common Tech Issues	Preventive Actions Before Class Day	How to Address
Hear other people talking in the background	In pre-communication email or video, encourage all to find a quiet space to attend class. Communicate netiquette expectations early in the session.	Correct the behavior as soon as it begins, as this can become distracting to all participants. Politely remind all to mute if they are in a noisy environment.
Unable to hear the audio from the recorded video clip, audio not synced with video, video screen frozen, or video won't play	Assign videos to be watched before class day as a pre-class assignment. As you go over netiquette, remind participants to close all applications not needed for class to conserve bandwidth.	Stop sharing video. Enable system audio before re-sharing video for learners to view. Or post the link in chat for them to go off and view on their own and request all return in 10 minutes. If learners are still unable to view, offer to send them the link to the video after class for async viewing.
Webcam not working	In pre-class communications, set the expectation to "be camera ready." Also explain they should test their webcam with the respective platform ahead of time.	Ensure that on their device they have checked the settings to allow webcam use. Ensure their sliding cover is open on a laptop camera. Check to make sure the desktop computer's camera isn't open, so their webcam can connect with the virtual training platform. Suggest they try exiting the platform and rejoining to reset.
Polls won't launch	Print or have all poll questions and potential options ready to go nearby as plan B.	Ask the question verbally and have learners chat in their answers of A, B, C, or D, or have backup slides of poll questions open and ready to go for a quick pivot. Or use the whiteboard to type each question and A, B, C, and D, which learners can circle with annotation tools.
Breakouts not working	Facilitator should rehearse breakouts with a few colleagues before class day to iron out bugs. If using Zoom, ensure you have enabled breakouts. If using Microsoft Teams, ensure the person managing breakouts is the organizer who created the session link (this requirement may change in the future). If you wish to share whiteboards or PDFs with all breakout groups, practice this ahead of time.	Consider moving the breakout activity to later in the class and troubleshoot during a break with your producer before trying again. Consider using paired chats for discussion or debriefs. Alternatively, conduct the activity as one large group.

I realize it is tempting for some learning professionals to rationalize, "It'll be OK" or "I'll figure it out" the day of virtual training. However, those who initially think that way usually admit later to a change of heart. If you fly by the seat of your pants and think, "I'll just throw in a poll here" while you're training and you've not used them before on a specific platform, you may discover your account is not enabled to use forms for polls or you need a different role as the organizer or host with more rights. As one of my learners succinctly put it, "This type of venue really doesn't work for winging it." She's right!

A client of mine wanted to show a video through a virtual platform training session and assumed it would work fine because he could hear the audio through his own headset. He assumed his learners could hear it too. However, we could not hear the video because he had forgotten to enable the system audio on that specific platform before screen sharing. These are the common types of issues that are helpful to practice ahead of time, so you can prevent them from happening during your live event. One of the best ways to do this is to invite a trusted colleague or your producer to test it with you ahead of time. It takes two to test both the learner's and the facilitator's experiences, because displays will look different depending on your role.

Practice as You'll Train

When I assign teach-backs or presentations to learners so they can apply what they've learned in my virtual training programs, I sometimes hold virtual office hours. These are optional, scheduled drop-ins where learners can individually practice their teach-back with me in the same platform we'll be using. They are encouraged to practice on their own as well, if they have access to the platform, but it also gives them the chance to play with the technology and feel more comfortable.

One of my learners scheduled a time to practice with the technology in one of these optional office hours. She connected to the platform from her office, and we worked through some minor fixes. At the end, she said she felt ready to go for her teach-back the following week. When the day came, she surprised me by logging in from a cabin up north because her family decided to begin their holiday weekend early. She was now facilitating from a laptop instead of her desktop computer and had forgotten to bring her mouse. As a result, she struggled to use the annotation toolbar because using the trackpad instead of a mouse made clearing annotations more challenging. Her bandwidth connection was also sketchy, her room lighting through her live webcam no longer optimal, and it was difficult to hear her audio at times. However, the lesson learned that she shared with me later was priceless: "I've learned to practice exactly how I'll deliver it."

One key mitigation strategy is to rehearse in the same environment and with the same hardware and software you'll use for your live session, so you eliminate any new variables and can find solutions to issues that emerge during practice.

In virtual training, we try to recreate an environment offline where we can rehearse, make mistakes, and figure out ways to address them before class day. Going through this explorative preparation phase provides you with experience and confidence so you are no longer worried about what could or might happen.

PRO TIP 68
Rehearse with the same hardware and software, at the same location, around the same time of day as your live event to allow any surprises to emerge so you can resolve them ahead of time.

Try Out All the Platform Features

As my father used to say about some things, learn it "forward and backward, and inside and out." We can also apply this sage advice to learning a virtual training platform. When you can confidently say you know what every button does, then you know you're ready to train on the platform. One of the best ways to determine this is to schedule a technical rehearsal with your producer. You can also familiarize yourself with the platform by clicking every button, see if you can get stuck, and then figure out how to get unstuck. This way you remember it more. For example, on some platforms where it may not be as intuitive to clear the annotations, play around with every annotation tool so you know your way around the toolbar backward and forward. Where is the eraser? Does it clear all drawings or just the last one? Will the drawings stay on your slides when you advance, or do they not carry over to the next slides? When there are issues you cannot resolve or you need specific answers, feel free to access online user discussions, use the technical chat with your vendor, or reach out to product technical support to get answers well before your live session.

Learning what all the functionality on the platform does and how to use it also boosts your confidence. Not only will you speak with aplomb, but your learners will pick up on the natural confidence and authority in your voice, which boosts credibility. More important, when you deeply know the ins and outs of your platform and what all the tools do, you are better prepared to remedy a tricky situation. This way, you are equipped to make quick decisions in the moment and move more smoothly from a roadblock to an alternate route.

It's also important to plan for troubleshooting when using different virtual training platforms. More than a decade ago, a colleague of mine was instructing a virtual class using a virtual platform. The client provided a producer for the event and my business partner was using the annotation tools with his slides. On this event, he used some annotation tools to circle and highlight where learners should focus. He then cleared annotations and clicked to advance his slides. But the slides would not advance. As you can imagine, this was a moment of panic. In this platform, the facilitator needed to click an arrow icon to regain mouse control after using the drawing tools and then click once more on the slides before they would advance. Rehearsing this ahead of time would have eliminated this moment of panic and feeling stuck in the middle of a live session.

Many common virtual training platforms like Adobe Connect, Webex, GoToTraining, Blackboard Collaborate, and Zoom share common features, just as most makes and models of cars share similarities in features and functionality. I drove many kinds of rental cars over the years when traveling across the US to train clients in person. Even though the cruise control or the headlights may have been in a slightly different location on each rental car, I still had a mental model for where I generally might find them. In the same way, although there might be slight differences with platform tools and where to find them, most platforms share general commonality in their features and functionality. Because of your prior knowledge from working on other platforms, you can acclimate more easily to additional virtual training platforms.

Testing everything ahead of time can also spare you from embarrassing moments. Once I used a live review game for my virtual training session. I wanted to gamify our content review and add a level of fun. I tested the system audio and visuals with a colleague ahead of time to see if I could speak over some music for the duration of the game. However, we discovered in this test that I could not talk over the music in the virtual training platform my customer used. Because the music level needed to be loud, my spoken audio was soft. Therefore, I decided to play a few opening seconds of the music to set the tone for the live event, but then fade it out so my learners and I could still talk and be heard by each other during the review game.

▬ ▬ ▬

So, mitigation is doing what we can before the actual event to minimize the risk. And even though I mentioned things can go wrong, it doesn't always mean they will. Once I was contracted as a trainer to run four virtual training sessions on the same topic in a one-week period for a large company. I did not have a producer to assist me back then, so it was much more stressful to realize it was all resting on my shoulders. I worked repeatedly with my client contact, and we had multiple technical rehearsals and abbreviated run-throughs. As we met for tech rehearsals in the weeks leading up to the live events, we encountered several technical issues. But because we discovered these issues early, we were able to work through them all beforehand. What is so memorable about this for me is that when it came time for the live virtual sessions, everything worked perfectly! All four virtual training sessions went smoothly and we didn't experience any issues. So, it is possible. Again, I attribute this to the work we'd done ahead of time and the mitigation efforts that paved the way for these successful live events.

 PRO TIP 69
Know your technical platform better than the back of your hand.

Manage

The second M in the 3 Ms Method is manage. This addresses what to do when both predictable and unpredictable challenges occur. Predictable issues require flexibility, while unpredictable issues require agility. We will explore both and identify prescriptive tips to help you be flexible and agile. But there is one tip that applies to both the expected and unexpected technical challenges that occur, and that is to keep backstage items backstage.

For example, if you lost your printout of your slides, or your new microphone won't work even though you previously tested it, or you accidentally just spilled your water glass all over your notes, or your cat just threw up in your home office, or there's a huge spider crawling up your wall, or your computer almost launched a big update, learners don't need to know these things.

Many of these treasured memories have happened to me, and I'm sure many of you have your own thrilling stories to share. Whatever it is, your customers (who are your learners) don't need to know all these behind-the-scenes details. It can distract them from where they should be focused, which is on what they're learning. Once when I was teaching a virtual training class, I must have said something that sounded close to the name Siri. Suddenly my mobile phone started talking aloud. I was using a USB external mic for that class, so I knew learners could probably hear my phone talking. Because I was also speaking at the time, I didn't have the luxury of turning Siri off in settings, so I threw my phone into a desk drawer quickly and closed it while I continued to talk. As soon as I gave my learners the opportunity to work on something, I muted myself, opened the drawer and turned off my phone. Later on the recording, I could hear a muffled voice in the background but there was no need to share that with learners. It would have been a distraction. Now when I have my phone nearby for training, I always turn Siri off. Regardless of what you might experience, carry on professionally, and keep backstage items backstage to ensure learners stay focused and have an overall positive experience.

The exception to this, of course, is if you can tie what just happened to the topic at hand, and on the fly. For example, if you accidentally spilled water over your notes right before class began and your training topic was emotional intelligence (EQ), you could share what happened as an illustrative story later in the training session. For example, it might sound something like, "Let's talk next about how we can apply this to our professional lives. You know when right before our training began today, I accidentally spilled water all over my notes." You could then go on to share how you had to dig deep to manage your emotions: You were immediately flooded with frustration and anger. Then you had to remind yourself to reframe the situation with compassion toward yourself because accidents are a part of life. This helped you calm down and even laugh about it later. By reframing, you were able to avoid carrying anger and negative energy into the training session. In this example, the vulnerability you demonstrate by sharing this can even inspire learners to open up and share EQ stories of their own. So, if you can tie what just happened to your topic at hand, this is the exception.

Another way to keep items backstage is to share things or discuss what you're observing through the back channel via private chat with your producer. For example, my producers always ask me in private chat if I'm ready to go before they kick off a session. Sometimes, they'll remind me that we're getting close to the end, or I'll share an issue that came up and they'll let me know if it's resolved. All of this is done through private chat via the platform. Backstage items and backstage communication don't always need to be heard or seen by the customer. Instead, we ensure participants' experiences are positive, productive, and professional.

PRO TIP 70
Keep backstage items backstage.

Managing the Predictable

The good news is that many of the things that can go wrong in a live session are predictable. Referencing the premade list of potential things that could go wrong from your mitigation efforts (plan B, C and sometimes D) can save the day. These are the issues that most commonly occur. By going through the steps in the mitigation phase, you'll already determine the things you could do, and your knowledge and pre-work will help you manage them live in the moment. For example, slides may not advance, learners may not hear audio, or you may think you're sharing and advancing slides when learners can't see them. Have your list nearby during live virtual training events so you are ready with a solution to try.

PRO TIP 71
Over-prepare and be ready with multiple solutions for the most common technical issues so you can be agile and creatively problem solve as challenges arise.

Know, too, that multiple solutions exist in any given moment for any given problem. Past experience and remaining calm can help you see them. If you are accidentally muted, your producer or learners will let you know, and you'll just summarize what you said when you were on mute. Or if someone else is sharing by the time you figure it out, you can type in the chat what you shared while you were muted. Most importantly, if you remain calm, alert, and attentive, you will be better able to think of solutions.

When major difficulties happen and you need more time to troubleshoot, you can send people to take a brief refresher or stand-up break. I like to remind them to use this time to "get a beverage, walk around your environment, take a bio break, spend some time in mindful stillness, or whatever they need to refresh and come back to the virtual space." I try to encourage time away from screens during these breaks, such as avoiding checking email. Blood flow to the brain increases just by standing and moving. So, definitely remind learners to stand up and move around during all breaks if possible. Then, while they're on break, you can work on more extensive troubleshooting. This helps you remain calm knowing everyone is not waiting for you to resolve an issue. If you train without a producer, learners may have to wait for you to complete certain tasks. So, it is a best practice to partner with a producer if you can.

PRO TIP 72
If you need extra time to troubleshoot, give everyone a longer refresh break.

Once, when I was presenting to a remote client through a virtual training platform, I did not realize my internet connection started going in and out and my audio was getting muffled, but my producer came off mute and let me know. This also let learners know it was being brought to my attention, because they were experiencing difficulties hearing me too. I asked my producer to send them on a short break while I left the platform and logged back in to reset everything.

I also like to have an independent, short assignment ready to give to learners at any time just in case we need more troubleshooting time. I sometimes share this with my producers ahead of time. This way, if my connection goes down, my producer could assign the short work assignment, which always relates to the topic we're learning about that day and keep things moving. This gives learners something to do, allowing them to reflect on the topic through an assignment. More important, you can troubleshoot and partner with your producer while learners are working on their assignment.

 PRO TIP 73
If you encounter a complex technical issue, give learners something to do by assigning a pre-made, topic-relevant assignment to work on while you troubleshoot. Share this assignment with your producer ahead of time, so they can use it too, in case you lose connection.

Managing the Unpredictable

In addition to managing the predictable, one intermediate skill for virtual facilitators is being able to manage the unexpected. According to a research study of the skills synchronous facilitators need to support virtual learners, "developing critical thinking skills" and being able to "manage unexpected issues calmly and efficiently with little disruption to the class" were identified as necessary advanced skills (Phelps and Vlachopoulos 2020).

We described earlier that predictable, common issues can be addressed with flexibility, and ideally, by working in tandem with a producer. However, when the unpredictable comes along—and there will be surprises—these are managed with agility. Agility is being able to deviate from the plan swiftly when the unexpected happens. In addition to agility, we need to maintain poise and professionalism. According to virtual training expert Jennifer Hofmann (2004), "Lots of last-minute, unanticipated problems can occur when working remotely via web technology. Synchronous trainers must be able to maintain the course flow and manage high-stress situations with grace."

One of my clients in her teach-back suddenly couldn't find her chat, as she informed me later. I watched her face on camera, noticed the pregnant pause, and could tell she was panicking inside. But outwardly, she said very calmly, "Great, thank you for those responses. Let's move on now." When we had the opportunity to debrief privately afterward, she said, "I couldn't find my chat panel. It was open and then it went away." This can happen to the best of us. You can sometimes use alt/tab to find all the open screens and this can be a way to find the chat pane again if it is undocked. Sometimes the chat function can be found in different locations depending on whether you are a participant or a host. Of course, if you have a producer, you can task them to assist with reading or summarizing responses if needed. And if you have a seasoned producer, you can let them know via private chat and they can manage the chat, or you could avoid using chat until after the next break, which you can use to relocate what you need.

The good that comes from successfully managing the unpredictable is that after you've experienced so much that can go wrong and resolved or figured out ways to keep moving, it no longer has a grip on you. You stop being afraid of what could happen or what could go wrong, because you've already experienced so many things that have gone wrong in the past and learned that the world didn't end. This experience then fills you with the quiet confidence of knowing that whatever comes your way, your producer or you will likely be able to find something workable. Of course, there will be a few times when you may not be able to fix something, so you instead have to minimize the disruption as best you can.

Another time I was scheduled to train with a co-facilitator many years ago on an earlier web conferencing platform. We thought we were being proactive by logging in an hour early, because that was the earliest we could access the link. We tested everything, including all our tools, uploaded our materials, and checked our connections before the training class began. Then we closed the session, because we were so early that we still had quite a bit of time to grab a drink and take care of some other work-related items. However, back then on this particular platform, the session link could only be used once (drum roll, please), but we didn't know that yet. So, when the time came for us to log back in, the link was closed and we were all locked out, including our learners! Naturally we were horrified, and of course, had to scramble to create a new session link we could email to everyone asking them to please use the new link to join the session instead. But life went on and it was a lesson learned.

Growth comes from making mistakes because mistakes are how we learn. One of the best troubleshooters I know is from Germany. He has experienced more technical issues than you could ever imagine in a lifetime. But this is exactly what makes him so skilled as a troubleshooter. It's because he has been exposed to so many technical issues and problems, and has successfully worked through them, that he is a true expert who demonstrates mastery solving technical problems. So, the silver lining to experiencing technical issues during virtual training is that you are building your troubleshooting expertise and learning from each lesson. This is how skill is built—one technical issue at a time.

Partner With a Producer

Partnering with a producer is one of the best ways to manage both the predictable and unpredictable. It is so effective because there are too many tasks to manage concurrently when we teach live online. When you add technology to the mix, many things can go wrong and there are more tasks and jobs to complete.

The physical body provides a helpful metaphor here. Several jobs must be done inside the physical body—too many for just one organ to do alone. So, each organ has a job—the liver, the stomach, the bladder, the spleen. In virtual training, there are also too many jobs for one person to manage smoothly. You can accomplish more when you partner with a producer to manage the technical side, while you focus on facilitating and connecting with learners. One of my clients said it best, "I wish I could just teach and not have to worry about the technology." We are so grateful for producers and their partnership in live online learning to help us do this more effectively.

PRO TIP 74
Partner with a producer to manage the event so you can focus on facilitating more effectively.

Back in the early 2000s, I was preparing to deliver my local ATD chapter's first ever virtual program using web conferencing tools. Naturally, the organizers were a bit nervous because they had only held in-person events up to that point. At the time, the field was so new that the term producer in the context of virtual training was nonexistent. I knew there was a lot to manage while delivering it myself from a remote training room. We also had a full roster of attendees. So, I asked my business partner if he would join me in person from where I was connecting remotely to help watch the chat in case I missed anything important, assist with technical issues, and of course, provide moral support. This was the early makings of a producer role.

That said, you might be thinking that adding another resource to your training event is not feasible, or your manager would never approve, or you are a training department of one. But there is still creative sourcing you can do. You may need to do a bit more persuading to make your case for the improved benefit or find a colleague in another department who is technically savvy, but it can be done.

You can also work with your producer ahead of time to agree on shared responsibilities and delegate tasks like technical troubleshooting. When training customers virtually using Adobe Connect at SkillPath, our producers set up a separate chat pod for technical issues and another chat pod for training content discussion. At the beginning of the training, producers let participants know which chat pod was for what and both were always visible to learners. This way, the producer managed technical issues in the technical chat, and as facilitator, I monitored posts related to the training topic in content chat. Sometimes the wisdom of the group can also prove to be an asset. Your learners will help each other in the chat and answer some of their questions. When one facilitator was attempting to show a video and no one could hear the audio, a learner in the audience said, "I know how to fix that," and they were able to resolve the issue and move on.

As another alternative, you might consider a producer who can at least assist when attendees first log in. In her book *Producing Virtual Training, Meetings, and Webinars*, Kassy LaBorie (2021) identifies three types of producers: technical producers, facilitative producers, and start-time producers. According to her, a start-time producer assists in the beginning. They do not stay with the trainer for the entire session, although they can remain available. For example, when one of my producers at SkillPath was managing multiple sessions in a day, she would log in with me 30 minutes before the session began, stay on until everyone had joined, and once everything was working well, left to produce other sessions. She also let me know how to privately get a hold of her if I required assistance after she left. LaBorie recommends having start-time producers stay on for the first 15 minutes because this is when most technical issues occur.

When another professional is paired with the facilitator and is responsible for owning the technical responsibilities, this really frees you to focus on providing effective instruction. There are just so many technical and logistical things to address otherwise. Two heads are always better than one, and the amount of stress relief and nonverbal support it provides is worth it, every time.

Move Forward

The final M in the 3 Ms Method is move forward. Just because we resolved or could not resolve something, we still need to move forward as productively as we can for the benefit of the class. This ties into resilience, which is our ability to come back from hardship, difficulty, and challenge without remaining stuck in what just happened. The quicker we bounce back, the more resilient we are. What can help you recover faster, of course, is if you know what to do.

When we encounter challenges or troubles during virtual training, we need to be agile, creative, and think on our feet to find a resolution. Afterward, this might leave you reeling or grieving what just happened. But the quicker we can place what happened behind us, the more likely we are to move forward in a positive way. In 2021, Team USA Olympian gymnast Jade Carey turned a disappointing performance one day into an Olympic gold-winning performance the next. The previous day, she missed the podium after a surprising stumble in the vault final. She told NBC's *TODAY Show* host Hoda Kotb that after her performance on the vault, "I needed to put it behind me." This enabled her to channel a fresh perspective into her floor exercise final to take home gold (Kotb 2021).

Recovery is about resetting yourself emotionally and mentally after frustrating events, disappointments, or even technical glitches. It means letting go of what just happened. Unquestionably, not allowing a recent disaster to throw you off kilter can be challenging. A starting point is becoming very aware of what your thoughts are telling you. Thoughts can trigger our emotions like fear, frustration, anger, or sadness, resulting in physiological responses in our bodies. However, thoughts are also just thoughts. They are neutral. We don't have to believe them. We don't have to act on them. We can allow them to just pass by.

Sometimes after a more challenging disruption, I send everyone on a break, ensure I am muted, and imagine while exhaling that I am breathing out negative energy. You can even visualize a color for it (red light). Then, on the inhale, I imagine breathing in positive energy (white light). Remember, negative energy (even frustration) can poison the energy of your training session. As the facilitator, you are still an influential leader. What you say, feel, and do sets the trajectory for what learners may say, feel, and do. Releasing negative energy helps you move into a more positive state that helps learners follow as well. You can, of course, simply apologize for any inconvenience. And if we do not make a big deal of it, learners won't either. So, if something goes wrong, apologize, correct it, and move on. Do not belabor it; this just keeps the problem alive, and sometimes can become what learners remember most and all they talk about on evaluations.

Another time, I was teaching for the first time on a new virtual training platform. It was also my first time working with this producer, and he was gracious to showed me all the tools and functionality when we met for a tech rehearsal before class day. During the live session, however, when it came time to look at learners' responses to polling questions, for the life of me, I could not find the poll results. I quickly scanned the panels on both my monitors and still could not find it. In that split second, I made the decision to not draw attention to this fact. What I heard come out of my mouth—even though I had no idea how they had all voted—was "Well, it looks like we were all over the board on that one. Thanks for voting everyone." This was certainly a way to call the activity to a close, keep backstage items backstage, and keep things moving, but I missed the opportunity to highlight the real results because I couldn't find them. As the popular adage claims, hindsight is always 20/20. Looking back, it would have been better if I asked my producer to come off mute and summarize the polling results for us. Regardless, I kept things moving without disruption or distraction, but afterward made a point to learn from what happened.

Recovery in the world of virtual training is about adapting and, yes, growth. Of course, we do everything we can before the point of live instruction to practice the technology, to rehearse, and to know the platform as best we can. What is in our control is how we prepare. We mitigate, manage, and move forward as we connect with others across time and space regardless of what interruption or glitch may occur.

Summary

As one of my clients beautifully summarized earlier, "I see that the virtual environment is not really a space where I can wing it." The added complexity of technology and the wide array of interdependencies only invite greater opportunity for challenge. To guide you through, use the 3 Ms Method. This means you minimize the risk of things going wrong by taking several steps before class day. Then, when common, predictable things go wrong, you follow ready-made solutions identified beforehand. If unpredictable things happen, you do your best to resolve them in the moment and ask, "What can I do instead? How can I pivot? What is another way I can accomplish this learning activity?" There are almost always things you can do. Then, once you've hopefully resolved any issue, put it behind you. Simply apologize and move on. Do not continue to bring it up, resurrect or mention the issue again at the end, or apologize repeatedly to taint learners' overall experience.

You might be wondering how the true story at the beginning of this chapter concluded. Since the virtual trainer had lost his internet connection and appeared unable to reestablish it, the producer initially waited and then tried to move through the beginning slides herself. She filled in for him by explaining and sharing what she could about the topic, while he continued to try to reconnect. When efforts to reconnect failed, he called in to the session through a separate audio line and asked the producer to advance his slides even though he couldn't see them. This way, he was able to explain them via phone audio. The producer also administered the polls and shared the results aloud so he could hear them. This is why having a printout of your slides nearby can be helpful. When the facilitator asked learners to comment in chat, the producer summarized what she was seeing and read a few aloud so he could hear them as well. Eventually, learners were given an extended break, and during this time, the trainer was at last able to fully reconnect and return to facilitate the remainder of the session.

Troubleshooting and recovery do not have to be scary. It is the disservice, as Marshall McLuhan said, that comes with the service of technology. Once we realize this, we accept both the convenience and inconvenience of digital technology. We help ourselves and our learners by mitigating what we can ahead of time, managing through the technical difficulties in tandem with producers, and leading the entire class forward.

As you grow in your agile troubleshooting capability, you will become more skilled at taking preventive action, managing expectations, and pivoting quickly. Because even in the most challenging of circumstances—when we or our producers are not able to fix something—we can always move to plan B, C, or D and keep moving forward.

In addition to skillfully resolving technical issues, it's also important to develop evaluation skills so you can determine whether your virtual training has met its goals. In the next chapter, we'll look at the importance of measuring value and how to evaluate the impact of your virtual training programs.

Pro Tips for Practicing your Agile Troubleshooting Skills

TIP 66	Accept that things can and will go wrong with technology; technical issues are part of virtual training.
TIP 67	Use humor to diffuse tension, infuse positive energy, and redirect learner attention.
TIP 68	Rehearse with the same hardware and software, at the same location, around the same time of day as your live event to allow any surprises to emerge so you can resolve them ahead of time.
TIP 69	Know your technical platform better than the back of your hand.
TIP 70	Keep backstage items backstage.
TIP 71	Over-prepare and be ready with multiple solutions for the most common technical issues so you can be agile and creatively problem solve as challenges arise.
TIP 72	If you need extra time to troubleshoot, give everyone a longer refresh break.
TIP 73	If you encounter a complex technical issue, give learners something to do by assigning a pre-made, topic-relevant assignment to work on while you troubleshoot. Share this assignment with your producer ahead of time, so they can use it too, in case you lose connection.
TIP 74	Partner with a producer to manage the event so you can focus on facilitating more effectively.

"Go to where the puck is going, not where it has been."

—Walter Gretzky, father of Canadian hockey star Wayne Gretzky

CHAPTER 10

Evaluating and Innovating in the Virtual Space

It feels like a world ago. As a young teen, my high school driving instructor left our class speechless when he asked a single question: "Where should your focus be when you're driving?" Our class eventually cobbled together an answer, which sounded something like "Where you are on the road?"

"No," was his response.

We were stunned, and I'll never forget his explanation. "Your focus shouldn't be where you are . . . but where you're going to be." Ah, a trick question! We certainly wanted to take issue with this, but as 16-year-olds, we intuitively knew better than to argue with the only in-room, adult authority on the subject.

If we apply the point of this story and the opening quotation to a broader context, we see that technology—and specifically, virtual training—is also a moving target. As the title of this chapter suggests, evaluation and innovation are dual points of focus for this movement. First, with evaluation, there is a need to focus on what virtual participants are going to do with what they've learned. You don't want to focus on where you are exclusively (participants' satisfaction with the training), but rather where you're going to be (learners' workplace application and the impact to the organization). Whether or not participants liked the virtual training—although this plays into motivation—is not the end-all be-all.

Second, with innovation, you want to be aware of new developments in the virtual training industry and stay abreast of current trends. New innovations can also inspire your own experimentation for the betterment of live online learning. You want to be careful not to limit your vision to only where you currently are, but also keep an eye on future developments in the field, especially as the pace of technological change accelerates. From the late 1990s through 2019, many web conferencing platforms entered and exited the market. The platforms that remained tended to stay relatively similar with a few exceptions. But the global, explosive expansion of the use of virtual training platforms during the COVID-19 pandemic prompted accelerated improvements, sometimes even weekly.

Evaluation and innovation go hand in hand. Each informs the other. For example, we evaluate something to identify what is and isn't working. Innovation then often emerges when something isn't working and there is a problem to solve. Evaluation is one of the more challenging tasks we do as learning and development practitioners. And, if we are honest, evaluation may be one of those things that we tend not to focus on or do as often as we should. After all, you may consider yourself a professional designer or trainer, not a professional evaluator. But our training solutions should always evaluate the effectiveness of what we do. We have a vested responsibility to identify—or at least delegate partners to identify—whether our virtual training programs are having an impact, large or small. Otherwise, how do we know whether we are hitting or missing the mark?

Evaluation also helps reduce uncertainty. Any data you collect helps you make decisions about what and where to improve, so we must measure the right things. In some organizations, attendance is the only metric passed on to executives regarding training. Although this is certainly one metric, it does not measure whether participants learned and applied what they learned or whether that had an impact on the organization. We need to be prepared to have data at the ready to show whether training is making a difference.

As previously established in this book, online learning is here to stay. Organizations around the globe are investing more learning and development resources in it. Executives also have higher expectations for L&D. LinkedIn Learning's *2021 Workplace Learning Report* surveyed more than 5,000 people (which included learning professionals, managers, and learners) from 27 countries. Accordingly, L&D professionals said they expected their budgets to increase and predict a continued shift away from ILT to online learning. "In early 2020, 38 percent of L&D pros expected to spend less on ILT and 57 percent expected to spend more on online learning. Today, those numbers are significantly higher: 73 percent of L&D pros expect to spend less on ILT and 79 percent expect to spend more on online learning" (Van Nuys 2021). The increasing allocation of additional resources for online learning is telling. We need to be evaluating the virtual training programs we create from these increased resources to demonstrate the resulting value.

In this chapter, we explore the final capability, evaluating impact. We will identify a virtual training approach for your consideration, highlight helpful evaluation frameworks, and offer examples for evaluating your virtual training. The second half of this chapter addresses innovation—because if something isn't working, we need to try something different. We should always be evaluating, because it shows us whether we're meeting our goals. And we should always be innovating so we can continuously improve. Both help us improve and both can take us to the next level.

 THE BIG IDEA
To continually improve, evaluate the effectiveness of your virtual training programs and push past the limits of what you've previously done to discover what could still be.

Evaluating Virtual Training

Clayton Christensen famously coined the Jobs to Be Done (JTBD) Theory. This theory stems from one central question, "What is the job a person is hiring a product to do?" (Christensen et al. 2016). This succinct, direct question can be useful for learning and development to ask. When virtual training—or training in general—is determined to be the best solution, you can use an adapted version of JTBD. For example, at the outset of a project, consider asking stakeholders, "What is the job you are hiring virtual training to do?" This question single-handedly drives to the heart of the workplace performance change needed. What is the job? How they answer can translate into your performance objectives for the course. From there, you can determine any knowledge or learning objectives to support the doing. It starts with a front-end analysis question like, "What should employees be able to do after completing this virtual training program?" In addition to asking stakeholders this question up front, you can also ask a few learners who will be in the training. As we explored in chapter 2, not only can you gather perspectives from a few sample learners early on for feedforward advice on designs, but you can also gather their perspective even earlier regarding the question, "What is the job you are hiring this virtual training program to do for you?" Learner responses are always insightful—because it's a different perspective—and this can guide your design trajectory.

Early on, when you first meet with stakeholders, internal customers, or external clients to conduct a front-end analysis, you ask questions to identify the workplace problem that needs to be solved. Yet often the "problem" may not be the real issue. If you dig a bit deeper, you'll discover that beneath the surface, there is sometimes a causal, underlying core problem.

Training is often identified too quickly as a solution when it may not be the most appropriate, depending on what the core problem is. Let's say, for example, a customer service team receives excellent ratings from customers, except for one staff person. Rather than deliver customer service training to the entire team "because it would be good for everyone any way," a more targeted strategy would be to offer customer-service coaching to the one employee who may not even realize their service skills are sub-par. In other workplace situations, all that may be needed is a type of workflow learning or performance support, like a job aid to support a procedural task or to illustrate how to use a system in the flow of work.

This book includes many recommendations from evidence-based practice and learning-science research. Pause and consider for a moment what science is at its essence. With science, we observe, take notes, and test our ideas to see if they hold weight by collecting data. We are empirical. If we look at it through this filter, this can also inform our definition of evaluation. We, too, want to observe the effects of the virtual training programs we create, so we can improve them and know whether they were effective. To be more rigorous about it, we can take measurements. These methods help us determine the overall impact of the virtual training programs we design and deliver.

A talented evaluator once taught me to always begin by asking an internal customer interested in evaluation, "What do you want to measure?" We can usually measure anything, but it's important to measure the right things. Our evaluations should be twofold: to assess the effectiveness of the program from the learners' perspective based on their experience, as discussed in chapter 2, and to evaluate it from the stakeholders' perspective in terms of the learner's ability to apply it to their jobs and have a larger impact on the organization.

So, in virtual training, where do we begin? We begin with the knowledge, learning, or performance objectives, which come from the front-end analysis you conduct with the internal customer, business area, or external client. Once the objectives are identified, it is at this early juncture that you want to create an evaluation plan for the training program. Consider the following elements as you develop your evaluation plan:

- What will you evaluate (up to what level)?
- Who will evaluate it?
- How often and when will you evaluate?
- What will you do with the evaluation data once it's available?
- With whom will the evaluation data be shared and why?

When you are considering what to do with the data, one of the best places to start is with the end in mind. Clarify how the data will be used to make decisions. Know what you're going to do with it before you collect it. According to Douglas Hubbard (2010) in *How to Measure Anything*, the goal is to reduce uncertainty. Any data you collect can help reduce the uncertainty about something and therefore inform future decisions about it.

For example, let's say you delivered a virtual training program to customer service staff on how to efficiently resolve customer issues via phone and reduce wait times. If your objectives are to give staff statement prompts they can use to quickly resolve an issue and close a call with courteous, polite service, you should convert these objectives to metrics you want to evaluate later (such as wait times, call length, and customer satisfaction). Then determine how you might collect this data. For example, to measure impact, you'll want to look at customer service surveys as well as wait time data to determine if callers are spending less time in the queue waiting for a representative. Lastly, determine with whom this data will be shared and how it can inform decision makers. This plan is determined on the front-end right after you identify learning objectives.

 PRO TIP 75
Create an evaluation plan in the design phase of your project, and evaluate learning based on the knowledge and performance objectives identified at the outset.

How Do You Evaluate?

Another way to think about evaluation is to look at it from the perspectives of the different audiences vested and determine who needs to know what. For example, when you train, you have multiple audience groupings who may be interested in the feedback: the learners, their managers, a design team, stakeholders, and your training delivery team (such as a producer or facilitator). The delivery team will want to know if learners found the virtual training valuable. Their managers should see the virtual training's worth because of their investment away from functional work. Executive leadership should see the overall impact to the organization, and in some cases, the ROI, especially for enterprise-wide virtual training programs or highly visible ones. Ideally, customers should experience the ripple impact as well. Be sure to capture your own perspective as a virtual trainer, and your producer's as well. Your perspective is also insightful. How did it go for you? Did it feel like you were connecting? Were people engaged?

Then, once you know who your target audience is for your evaluation data, you need to collect it. There are several ways to measure the effectiveness of virtual training programs. Some include direct observation, retention or turnover metrics, quality metrics, culture or employee satisfaction surveys, knowledge checks, skill assessments, interviews, key performance indicators, focus groups, learning management system test reporting, or competency assessments. Interviews, for example, are an opportunity to more deeply examine why learners may or may not have applied what was taught in virtual training to their jobs. You can use knowledge checks and assignments that gauge where people are and where they're struggling as pre-tests ahead of virtual training to ensure they're the right fit. After the training, you can conduct performance evaluations using rubrics to evaluate demonstrated competencies or abilities covered in virtual training. For example, once a learner demonstrates proficiency in competency-based virtual training, they then receive credit for course completion or competencies attained.

PRO TIP 76
Determine which levels of evaluation are most important to your customers, employees, their managers, and stakeholders to measure the effectiveness of your virtual training programs.

Collect Early Feedforward Advice: Evaluate As You Go

A type of evaluation that you can conduct during the design and prototyping phase of creating virtual training is called feedforward or formative assessment. This is what Michael Allen (2012) advocates in his Successive Approximations Model, leveraging continuous rapid prototyping in an iterative process through the creation and design of the training program. This early feedforward can be invaluable because input and feedback are collected on the initial program designs.

You can invite a few end recipients or staff who are in the target audience to be part of the design team. This way, you can run design ideas by them as you go. Who better to get feedback from than the ultimate end user? The reason this information is collected at the front end is because it saves time in the initial stages of design and allows for rapid prototyping and iteration. If feedback is collected at the backend, it's too late to adjust and too much time and resources have already been invested.

In contrast with formative assessment (which is part of the design process), summative evaluation comes at the end when you collect feedback from those who experienced and attended the virtual training. This is where learners might click a link to an online evaluation in the chat or receive an email that takes them to an online survey where they can evaluate the class.

Evaluation Frameworks to Guide You

There are a variety of influential frameworks for evaluation and measurement in the field of learning and development. Some include Katzell's Hierarchy of Steps, the Kirkpatrick Model's four levels of evaluation, and the ROI Institute's ROI Methodology, which also includes a process model. Let's review each and then connect back to virtual training.

Katzell's 4 Steps to Evaluating Training

In the early 1950s, prominent industrial-organizational psychologist Raymond Katzell originated the concept of a hierarchy of steps to evaluate training programs. This organizing structure laid a foundation for those who would later be inspired by his work. Step one identifies how "trainees feel" about the training. Step two identifies whether they learned through "knowledge and understanding." Step three identifies how much there were "on-the-job behavior changes" when they returned to their work. And step four looks at "any ripple effects" from these behavior changes like absenteeism or production (Kirkpatrick 1956; Smith 2008).

The Kirkpatrick Model

A model of measurement widely adopted across the talent development industry is the Kirkpatrick model. In 1959 and 1960, Donald L. Kirkpatrick first published articles based on his PhD dissertation about training evaluation in the *ASTD Journal*. The four words he identified in that article later became known worldwide as the four levels of evaluation: reaction, learning, behavior, and results (Kirkpatrick 1996).

According to the New World Kirkpatrick Model from the Kirkpatrick Partners (2021), the following are updated definitions of the original four levels:

- **Level 1:** Reaction evaluates "the degree to which participants find the training favorable, engaging, and relevant to their jobs."
- **Level 2:** Learning evaluates "the degree to which participants acquire the intended knowledge, skills, attitude, confidence, and commitment based on their participation in the training."
- **Level 3:** Behavior evaluates "the degree to which participants apply what they learned during training when they are back on the job."
- **Level 4:** Results evaluates "the degree to which targeted outcomes occur as a result of the training and the support and accountability package."

The ROI Process Model

Jack J. Phillips developed the ROI Methodology, which is a systematic approach to help organizations evaluate and improve programs and projects for greater impact. Just as chapter 2 discussed the influential role of design thinking, the ROI Methodology "uses design thinking principles to design for results needed" (Phillips, Phillips, and Ray 2020). This methodology helps organizations collect both qualitative and quantitative data to measure success for training programs like virtual training along a chain of impact from initial planning to requesting more funding. It also includes techniques to help isolate the effects of training programs for more credible data. In 1992, Jack Phillips founded the ROI Institute, which works with network partners in more than 70 countries around the world. Jack and Patti Phillips at the ROI Institute have also identified an ROI Process Model. This five-level model acknowledges an initial level for input and adds a fifth level for ROI, or return on investment:

- Level 0: Input
- Level 1: Reaction
- Level 2: Learning
- Level 3: Application
- Level 4: Impact
- Level 5: ROI

Level 0: Input

The input level acknowledges measures such as the number of people involved, their input of time into the process, types and number of programs, the scope, and costs. "Input is important but doesn't speak to the outcomes or results" (Phillips, Phillips, and Ray 2020).

Level 1: Reaction

The first level then is learner reaction. How are participants seeing the value in what you do? Is it relevant to them? Is it important to them? Would they recommend it to others? This reaction data from learners can be collected through surveys or evaluations that learners complete throughout the training in short spurts or near the end of a training program. It's a way to hear feedback about the training directly from the learners. For example, survey questions or online evaluations might ask if learners found the training valuable, if they thought it was engaging and relevant, how they might rate the facilitator's expertise, how they would rate the quality of the handouts or participant guide, if they would recommend the program to others and why or why not, how usable the technology was, and so on. It is at this level where you identify what participants think and feel (cognitive and emotional learning dimensions) about their overall learning experience.

Level 2: Learning

Level 2 evaluates participant learning and ideally new knowledge construction. This level looks at whether participants have created new schemas or mental models, retained new knowledge, and acquired new skills. It's a measure of not only knowledge acquisition but also skills attainment. Additionally, through reflection and learning from others in discussions, there may also be new insights, or participants may be more aware of things they were not previously aware of. The metrics at this level all measure the learning component. And learning is the foundation for using, which comes next.

Level 3: Application

The third level is the application. Learning must be applied; otherwise, our virtual training programs can be viewed as a waste of time from the perspective of executives. Was there a behavioral change? Was improvement noticeable and measurable? Did participants apply what they learned to their jobs based on the objectives? "This measure typically takes place at least 30 days after the training program ends" (Huggett 2017).

Level 4: Impact

Application is causal, and all causes have an effect. Application's effect in this context is the fourth level—the impact to the organization. Usually, these kinds of metrics are recorded in the system as productivity, waste or rework, the time it takes us to do something, sales, customer satisfaction, or customer complaints. For example, if learners consistently make performance changes at Level 3, this can affect results at an organizational level, such as raising customer satisfaction levels or reducing employee attrition metrics. Notably, the results in Level 4 are often the perceived value of the training for executive leadership.

Level 5: ROI

For this level, executives may be wondering if the expensive training programs are really working, especially if they're critical to the organization or connected to strategy that the executive team cares about. This can influence decisions about whether to devote more resources and continue the program. For this reason, executives may request ROI. In short, return on investment answers the question for every dollar invested in a training program, how many dollars were returned after the investment was recovered? The Phillips' formula for measuring the ROI percentage is:

$$\text{ROI (\%)} = \frac{\text{Program Benefits} - \text{Program Costs}}{\text{Program Costs}} \times 100$$

Alignment Model

The ROI Institute's Alignment Model brings it all together by visually depicting the alignment across stakeholders' needs (the why), the corresponding objectives for each (the how), and the results using the five levels (the what; Figure 10-1). "The objectives derived directly from these needs are defined, which makes a strong case for having multiple levels of objectives that correspond to different needs" (Phillips, Phillips, and Ray 2020). For virtual training, reference this model to best understand the needs driving target objectives and what the results will look like at each level. Implement your program keeping targeted results in mind.

Figure 10-1. The ROI Institute's Alignment Model

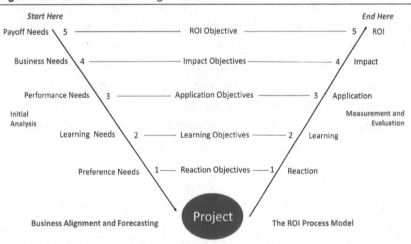

Reprinted with permission from the ROI Institute, Inc.

Evaluate Virtual Training to the Level Needed

Perhaps not surprisingly, the most common method of evaluation among many organizations who do virtual training boils down to tracking attendance. As ATD's 2021 report, *Virtual Classrooms: Leveraging Technology for Impact* attests, the clear majority (88 percent of the hundreds of organizations surveyed) evaluate training based on attendance and completion.

As you are aware, just because an employee logs in to a virtual training class and remains online for the duration does not guarantee they learned anything, not to mention demonstrated competency. Nor does it prove that they will apply what they have learned to their functional work. This is why virtual training should be evaluated above and beyond attendance. We also need to take a closer look at our reward system. When we award a certificate for attendance or a digital badge for logging in at the right time and logging out at the right time, aren't we rewarding the wrong things? Wouldn't it be better to test for competency and then, once they have demonstrated proficiency, award the digital badge or certificate?

In the rest of this section, we'll look at some ways to ensure your evaluation efforts for virtual training are a success.

The Manager's Critical Role to Aid Learning

We have long known that managers play a crucial role in the effectiveness of their employees' learning. But did you realize how crucial they are? "Research has consistently shown that the managers of a group of participants are the most influential group in helping participants achieve application and impact objectives, apart from their own motivation, desire, and determination. No other group can influence participants as much as their immediate managers" (Elkeles, Phillips, and Phillips 2014). To take this a step further, organizations who shared concept card reminders, reinforcement aids, follow-up activities, or other resources with learners' managers after the training were significantly more likely to be high performing (ATD 2021).

The number-one most crucial factor in whether participants apply what they learn after attending a training session is if the manager sets expectations with the employee before they attend the training (Elkeles, Phillips, and Phillips 2014). This level setting is also important for virtual training. With live online learning, this pre-training session could be a brief on-camera online meeting or quick phone call to reiterate why the manager thinks the training topic is important for their direct report, tying it into organizational goals, what they expect from them after completing the training, and how excited they are to hear how it goes afterward.

The second most important factor in whether employees apply what they learn after training is if the managers follow up afterward as well (Elkeles, Phillips, and Phillips 2014). Managers need to be strategic—they aren't likely to have time to meet with every direct report before and after on every training topic. However, for the more robust virtual training programs and where it makes sense, they should. Either remotely or on-site and in person, managers could ask their direct reports what they learned from their virtual training class, try to incorporate key action items from the training into performance appraisal goals, or observe their demonstration of the competency on the job and provide data back to the virtual trainer.

 PRO TIP 77
Communicate to managers the important role they play evaluating and reinforcing what participants learn in training.

When my virtual training programs span several weeks, I email managers before the virtual training begins about what their employees will be learning and what the expectations are for the program. I also let them know that after the virtual training, employees will have a completed action plan to share with their manager. I give managers a heads up and ask that they have a conversation with their employees within one week after the program is complete to discuss their action plan. Likewise, I make certain that all participants are aware that their managers are there to support them and their action plans will hold them accountable to applying the learning to their work.

To aid the post-training discussion between managers and virtual participants, I send managers a sample email with suggestions for conversation starters and prompts. Figure 10-2 shows one example of an email prompt I have sent. Sometimes managers will even respond in kind with a thank you email or reach out to let me know they will soon be meeting with staff or that they did meet with them. Either way, we know managers are most influential in learners' application in the workplace and we need their support.

Figure 10-2. Example of Email Request for Manager Follow-Up

RE: Manager Action Requested

Good morning,

As you are aware, one of your employees recently completed the XX Virtual Training Program. This course was created for employees who XX as part of their job function or role.

At the end of this program, participants completed an action plan and were informed that copies would be shared with their managers. Therefore, please find a digital copy of your employee's action plan attached.

To support their application, please schedule a time to meet with your direct report over the next week so you can have a conversation about how you can support them and their action plan. For accountability, you might consider asking what they've already started applying, or how you can support them in these efforts. If helpful, feel free to also consider the following prompts to aid your conversation:

- I'm interested in hearing your top takeaways from the virtual program. Tell me more about what you identified as things to do in your action plan and why.
- What results have you observed so far?
- What will you not do anymore because of this training? How is that going?
- How can I support you with this action plan? What else do you need from me?
- It's OK to set functional work aside periodically to review your online workbook and training materials, because this is important.
- Think about setting a few, smaller goals with a timeline to help you implement your action plan long-term, and then let's revisit it occasionally during our one-on-ones.
- Keep up the great work!

Thank you for your professional development support,
Diana

Next, let's look specifically at how you might use the ROI Process Model, for example, to evaluate virtual training. Hopefully, these examples will inspire and spark ideas for you to use in your virtual training programs.

Level 1: Evaluating Learners' Reaction to Virtual Training

While organizations most often track virtual training by attendance and completion, the second most common evaluation method is Level 1 evaluations. According to ATD's 2021 virtual training report, 68 percent of respondents consistently evaluate with Level 1 evaluations, or "smile sheets" as they are commonly called. This method is simple and much quicker to implement than some of the other levels. The goal is to gather data to inform decisions about whether to continue offering the class or what parts to tweak and improve. "The challenge is to keep it simple, limit the number of questions, and use forced choice questions with space for comments" (Phillips, Phillips, and Ray 2020). Additionally, there may be questions to collect demographic or marketing data like how you heard about the offering and what other courses you would like to see, as well as a place for comments about what they might recommend for course improvements. Level 1 evaluation sheets often ask about criteria like:

- Whether the class met course objectives
- Perception of value and if it was worth their time
- Did they like it, and if so how much or how little and why?
- Appropriate class or program length
- Organization of materials
- Instructor credibility, knowledge, and preparedness
- Whether the virtual training platform and tools were easy to navigate
- If the links to course materials were simple to find
- If the digital participant guide was helpful
- Did the assignments have clear instructions?

The vast majority of my virtual training programs are measured at this level. It's easy to do and you can get a quick pulse on what learners thought of the training. The secret to getting returned and completed survey data is to keep your evaluations short. Just ask the critical questions.

In training classes that span several weeks, I'll give participants a two to three question survey at the end of each live online session to take a quick pulse check on where people are and what they think of the class so far. You can also use the whiteboard to have them type two to four words describing their experience that day or use a quick online poll from the platform to gauge how their virtual experience went. This way you're collecting feedback as you go. If I learn about integral improvements that need to be quickly addressed, I can pivot as needed in the middle of the program and genuinely thank participants for their feedback. I always use some type of short Level 1 evaluation at the end too and express verbally that we love to hear feedback from learners so we can make the program better.

Learning expert Bill Horton recommends asking online learners to contribute as many suggestions as possible for improving the course to generate an abundant supply of ideas (Kirkpatrick and Kirkpatrick 2006). This helps to improve the likelihood that you will receive more qualitative recommendations out of a larger sample. As we learned in chapter 2, the best ideas often come from the learners themselves. One of my favorite things to do with Level 1 feedback throughout is to encourage learners to use emojis, animated gestures like thumbs up, or applause to provide feedback on how things are going for them. As with everything, use this measure judiciously; you don't want to over-use it and weaken its effectiveness.

Sometimes, you can even incent learners to complete their virtual training program evaluations by offering a drawing with a prize at the end. Make it clear that participants will be eligible for the drawing if they complete the evaluation. Once they have all submitted their evaluations online—still during class—ask them to raise their virtual hands or click the green check so you can know when they're done. Then use the randomizer tool (if available on your platform) or use an online app to scramble their names and select one for the prize.

To provide your virtual learners access to more official Level 1 evaluations, you can include a link in the chat or provide a prompt follow-up email containing the evaluation. It's a best practice to request learners open the link and complete the evaluation while they are still in class and submit it digitally. To ensure a higher response rate, I try to carve out the time for learners to complete their evaluations during the virtual training. Make it the second to last activity you do—not the last activity, because sometimes learners have an online meeting right after your virtual class and have to jump out early and then are not able to complete it. This is important because the likelihood someone will complete the evaluation decreases once they leave the class. We also want to end on a high note leveraging the peak-end rule as discussed in chapter 2. For this reason, it's best to complete evaluations in-class right before your final, closing activity.

Keep in mind it's all well and good to track participant responses for Level 1. But what you do with the data is even more important. Do you save it in a file never to be looked at again? Do you share it with managers? Do you share it with L&D directors, the chief learning officer, or the executive team? Clearly, the virtual trainer needs to review response summaries to collect feedback and input for improving the class. The virtual trainer's manager also needs to see a summary of responses to inform their decisions about whether to offer the class again.

In the past, I've isolated some of the best comments and used them as marketing testimonials for promoting future class offerings. On your evaluation, you can include a phrase that says signing this document gives approval for your name and comments to be used for marketing promotions. Or if they wish to maintain anonymity (and for more honest responses), include an option that consents to using their comments without their name. Sometimes digitally checking a box with a typed name or leaving the name line blank to remain anonymous is sufficient. It's also better to avoid participants emailing evaluations back from an efficiency standpoint. Instead, all results are automatically tabulated by your LMS, a survey provider like SurveyMonkey, or other online means.

Level 2: Evaluating Learning From Virtual Training

For Level 2, virtual trainers or novice online instructors may forget the importance of including knowledge checks along the way. This should be part of the built-in design of virtual training. Instructors can include creative, fun, or feedback opportunities where the learners may not even realize they are being checked for new knowledge acquired in the course. Adapted online games can work, or you can use polls for quizzes or other apps for surveys, quizzes, and tests. Regardless, it is an opportunity to assess the readiness of your learners and determine if anything needs to be reviewed. In the 2021 ATD study *Virtual Classrooms: Leveraging Technology for Impact*, 57 percent of organizations said they measured the effectiveness of their virtual training programs at this learning level with quiz scores and knowledge checks.

In my virtual training classes, I like to incorporate quizzes as polls to check knowledge at this level. Most platforms have polling features you can use, and some even allow you to create and store tests that you can reuse. For example, in GoToTraining you can create tests ahead of time and then use them to assess competency knowledge before participants can earn a certificate or digital badge within their LMS. MS Teams also has the ability to link to surveys. This way you can request learners take pre-tests and post-tests to measure any knowledge gains by comparing pre and post scores. It's important to note that in writing your quiz questions, you should emphasize what should be done versus what should not be done. This is a clearer takeaway for the learner and more readily aids their adoption of the knowledge and behavior you want to see.

As we illustrated in chapter 7, another way to check learning and understanding is by requesting learners annotate a slide depicting imagery in which they need to correctly diagnose something. In our example, it was medical imaging. Annotation is also a way for learners to show you they understood something or know where to look. In my virtual training, I also like to leverage chat questions to check participants' knowledge to see if they're tracking with me or if we need to go back and review anything (I'll look for gaps in their chat answers or an extended slowness in their responses.) As online learning expert Bill Horton explains in *Evaluating Training Programs*, "you can embed evaluation events among the learning experiences" but as an ongoing practice for check-ins, keep them short (Kirkpatrick and Kirkpatrick 2006).

However, you cannot stop there. According to Aaron Horwath (2021), head of learning at Creative Force, "Only being concerned with measuring Levels 1 and 2 dooms any hopes of measuring meaningful impact from the start." As the authors of *Proving the Value of Soft Skills* remind us, "It's not effective unless you have an impact" (Phillips, Phillips, and Ray 2020). People might attend, but training success should never be based on attendance. People may or may not enjoy it, but this is no guarantee the organization will improve or grow. It may contribute to retention because staff relish the opportunity to professionally develop and enjoy time spent away from their desks. And learners might be learning, but there's no guarantee they're applying what they've learned. Let's advance to the next level and see how you might evaluate Level 3.

Level 3: Evaluating Application From Virtual Training

In the same spirt as the popular book title *Telling Ain't Training*, I contend that knowing ain't doing. Just because participants have learned how to do something in virtual training does not guarantee they will use it. As chairman and CEO of Allen Interactions, Michael Allen (2007), articulates, "Education is focused on acquisition of knowledge while training is focused on application of knowledge; in other words, education is about knowing and training is about doing."

In short, Level 3 is all about application of the learning to one's work. Often, the impetus for training in the workplace is some type of performance gap. So, when we measure at this level, we are following up to see if learners were able to close the gap. In this way, Level 3 also measures participants' willingness and ability to improve workplace performance through behavior change. This often requires investing more resources in Level 3 (time and money) to observe and measure any improvements. According to ATD's 2021 report *Virtual Classrooms*, only "slightly less than half of the over 300 organizations surveyed tracked how virtual training influenced their on-the-job behavior." A great example of evaluating application is a virtual training course on cyber security. Imagine that the course taught learners how to identify phishing attempts that come into their email inbox and how to recognize those suspicious emails that may be malicious. Learners are taught to be on the lookout for multiple spelling errors and urgency in an email message, for example. Then two to three weeks later, the organization might send a few fictitious emails that are indeed phishing attempts to employees to test those who were trained. This is a way to evaluate whether learners were able to correctly apply what they learned by identifying each phishing attempt and correctly reporting them to their IT department.

I recommend partnering with employees' managers for this level of evaluation. In the end, it is the manager who is evaluating them for performance quarterly, semi-annually, or annually. When I have partnered with managers for Level 3 evaluations of virtual training programs, I have provided them with aids like conversation prompts for their action plans and checklists for follow-up in their observation of skills, and talked with them about incorporating key principles or action items into their employee's performance appraisal goals to keep them accountable. The manager is the obvious choice as the key contact to observe and ensure that virtual learners are applying what they've learned, but our partnership of support with managers means that we can provide resources to help them. These aids, rubrics, key items learned, and other performance support tools then help them measure performance.

Partnering with an internal or external professional evaluator for Levels 3, 4, and 5 may also be useful. We are learning and development professionals, but not necessarily professional evaluators. By working in partnership with an evaluator, we can capture more data on these higher levels more efficiently and effectively.

There are also other steps we can take to ensure behavior change in the workplace. We discussed previously how managers' expectation setting with participants has the biggest impact on learners' application. In addition to managers setting expectations before and after virtual training, you can also invite virtual learners to share with their peers what they learned afterward. This, too, can also make a difference. According to Dorna Eriksson Shafiei, VP of Talent Management at Atlas Copco in Stockholm, Sweden, "In China, we developed a peer-to-peer learning approach, where learners present what they've learned to their wider team. Having discussions about how you can apply learning to your working environment is a critical part of changing behavior" (Van Nuys 2021). Remember, the more virtual learners talk about it, write about it, reflect on it, or use it, the more likely they are to apply their new knowledge on the job.

PRO TIP 78
Partner with managers to transfer ownership to them to observe and measure application in the workplace while you support them with aids or evaluation rubrics.

Level 4: Evaluating Impact in Virtual Training

Once you arrive at Level 3 as a way of measuring evaluation, you will be able to assess Level 4. I mentioned earlier about partnering with an internal or external professional evaluator for the higher levels (3, 4, and 5) if needed. You can also consider partnering with stakeholders to collect Level 4 and 5 data. You support the work and guide the process, but transfer the collection, analysis, and summary work to stakeholders or other partners.

The advantage of Level 4 data is that much of it already exists somewhere in the organization because these metrics are often tracked on an ongoing basis through other means. These could include customer satisfaction ratings, performance data, employee engagement surveys, sales numbers, efficiency, retention, costs, quality improvement, or employee satisfaction. For example, if you conducted a virtual training program about how to apply privacy laws in the context of your organization's work, you could use the number of privacy incidents at your organization before and after the training as a comparison metric. Remember to allow some time after the training before measuring the impact; 30 to 90 days is recommended. Be aware that the seeds of change can take a while to grow before you can reap results. As learning expert Bill Horton advises, "the kinds of business and institutional changes you want to measure for Level 4 seldom have only one cause. And they may take years to manifest" (Kirkpatrick and Kirkpatrick 2006).

When I consulted with an internal department on customer service training skills to be delivered virtually, we discussed the regular customer service surveys they already had in place with their external customers. As a way of measuring how effectively the service staff were able to apply what they learned from the customer service virtual training program, the director and supervisors could review the data from customer service surveys before the training as a baseline, and then, after 30 to 90 days, review the customer service surveys again to compare any changes to the data. In this case, the metrics consisted of both quantitative and qualitative data.

PRO TIP 79
Partner with stakeholders or an internal or external professional evaluator to collect organization-wide impact data when appropriate.

Level 5: Evaluating ROI in Virtual Training

For most virtual training programs, you will likely not need to measure to Level 5. Because of the time-intensive nature of collecting and calculating ROI, it may be prudent to reserve this level of evaluation for higher visibility, top-priority projects. Sometimes we need to ask ourselves, what's the ROI on ROI?

However, if the C-suite requests ROI data to review, you'll need to provide it. They may want to see ROI on projects that are part of the organization's strategic goals or enterprise-wide initiatives, for example. Additionally, Level 5 may be appropriate for virtual training when it's a robust program like leadership development that is required for all leaders in the organization and is offered multiple times per year. Executives may be interested in seeing the ROI to ensure their investment in this ongoing virtual training program is paying off. According to ATD's 2021 report *Virtual Classrooms*, only 25 percent of the more than 300 organizations surveyed evaluated ROI or business results.

If you do evaluate ROI, it's important for everyone who is part of the project (such as designers, developers, producers, and facilitators) to track their time and expenses from the outset, including material costs. Later, you can make the conversion to money where possible. When I've been part of measuring ROI for virtual training programs everyone on the project has tracked their time through an online project management software.

This made it easier for us and was also a more reliable way to track time. It also meant that all my time on the project, including project management meetings, gathering feedforward advice from a few learners early on, design and development, coordination meetings with virtual co-facilitators, and virtual delivery were tracked accordingly.

Another example of when ROI evaluation may be appropriate for virtual training programs is when executives are interested in a cost comparison between traditional classroom training converted to online delivery. Saving expenditures on flights, facilities, food, and hotel accommodations could be contrasted with the ROI once converted to virtual training programs.

Overall, evaluation is important to all training. Not only is it essential to evaluate the success of virtual training programs, but to also provide the data we need so we know where change is required. As discussed in chapter 2, we look to the learning sciences as an interdisciplinary field to inform our profession about how to improve effectiveness. At its core, science is about observation and collecting and reviewing data to examine the effects of something. Isn't this what we're also doing when we evaluate virtual training programs? We are collecting data to examine the effects of our training programs. We are ensuring the virtual training programs are "doing the job our customers hired it to do" (Christensen et al. 2016).

Future Innovative Trends in Virtual Training

The remainder of this chapter is devoted to exploring innovation for virtual training and online adult education. This is an exciting time for live online learning. The explosive, widespread adoption of web conferencing, video conferencing, and virtual training platforms in the wake of the COVID-19 pandemic have left an indelible mark. Consistent, global usage will continue to drive technology improvements, enhancements, and market competition. According to Pew Research and Larry Irving, the former head of the National Telecommunications & Information Administration, more extensive use of technology will be used for remote learning and education and this has potentially great benefits for reskilling and upskilling staff (Anderson, Rainie, and Vogels 2021).

According to the *2021 EDUCAUSE Horizon Report, Teaching and Learning Edition*, "Learning technology stands to become even more widely adopted on the road ahead, and the discovery of new needs and uses for these and other course-related tools will lead to ongoing innovations and entirely new learning technologies" (Pelletier et al. 2021). Let's look next at our role as innovators in the live online learning field. Specifically, we'll focus on immersive technologies, increasing global connections, and artificial intelligence.

Immersive Technologies

One trend to watch for in synchronous virtual training is XR (extended reality) immersive technologies. This is the umbrella term for VR (virtual reality), AR (augmented reality), and MR (mixed reality). These innovations, like the so-called metaverse, can help improve trainers' abilities to deliver learning virtually. As part of these experiences, facilitators can interact with learners in meaningful ways.

Virtual reality is the full immersion, where a learner might wear a VR headset. Then, you as facilitator may lead them through a fully immersive virtual environment with a simulated lesson. You can see how VR might lend itself most to learning where the spatial dimension is critical. AR is when learners view the real world through a smartphone camera with some digital elements overlaid on top of the live view. MR also begins with a real-world environment, but then blends digital objects with the real world so both can interact together.

These immersive technologies can simulate role-play interaction so learners can to practice a variety of topics such as conversation skills, leadership, consulting, sales skills, or customer service. They can then be tested on these skills to help support behavioral change. For example, there's a VR simulation that allows HR professionals to practice firing an employee with unacceptable performance. Letting an employee go is obviously a very difficult, emotional, and delicate conversation. "The program uses a 3D scan of a real actor and recordings of a variety of gestures, facial expressions, and lines of dialogue. Artificial intelligence, speech recognition, and language processing features ensure that the simulated employee understands what is said and responds appropriately" (Phillips, Phillips, and Ray 2020). Mursion.com offers VR empathy simulations where digital actors react in the moment based on what a learner might do and say in the simulation.

Naturally, these experiences also benefit from debrief sessions. This is where the role of facilitator may expand in the future to debriefing more immersive experiences. When I designed an escape room for 300 sales staff, which they went through in small groups, the debrief led by the employees we trained was notably the most important part from a learning perspective. This was where they could connect their experience to their own work and learn from the insights of others as they discussed how to move forward in a new way.

Immersive technologies may also provide greater opportunity for learners to experience autonomy in their learning. Participants may be able to choose from several simulated scenarios and select the one that most interests them, perform scenes with characters of their choosing, or even customize the layout or context where the scene happens. As we discussed in chapters 2 and 4, one element of motivation we can leverage is the learner's sense of autonomy and self-directedness.

PRO TIP 80
Take risks in virtual training, experiment, and continue to innovate in new ways.

Opportunities for Increasing Global Connection

In his 1964 book *Understanding Media*, and in other publications, Marshall McLuhan brilliantly foresaw how electronic media would bring all human beings together, writing "This is the new world of the global village." Indeed, our world has become a global village, and the internet was just the beginning.

With 21st-century technology tools that are constantly evolving, we can connect with anyone, anywhere, at any time. For virtual training, this means that in-roads are wide open for greater collaboration across physical distances. For example, our virtual classes can include international participants in real time. Obviously, this requires careful coordination with time zones as well as thoughtful research regarding cultural differences, appropriate customs, and language translations as live captions (which some platforms already support). The technical services needed for a global village will only continue to grow and improve.

Virtual classes have few limits regarding where participants and speakers might join. For example, if there is an expert from across the globe who can speak on your training topic or answer live questions with your class, this is now possible. Virtual designers and facilitators can think broader and go beyond our former limits of what was possible and imagine what is now possible.

PRO TIP 81
Invite global experts to engage learners and address their questions in real time during your live online programs.

Artificial Intelligence in Virtual Training

One technology that is exploding is artificial intelligence (AI). Those steeped in machine learning and AI are careful to qualify that it is not intended to replace jobs, but rather assist humans to perform their jobs better. As David Gering, principal data scientist at Danaher told me, "AI is able to analyze people's interactions after quickly reviewing large amounts of data. It can learn from responses in the past, determine which are most important, and which are least important."

Conversational AI is also available. This is where an AI assistant's voice is trained on the context and conversational nuances to respond to humans in a way that sounds and feels natural. For example, during Google's 2018 developer conference, CEO Sundar Pichai unveiled and demonstrated how Google Duplex, an AI assistant could call and book appointments on your behalf, such as making a reservation for you at a restaurant or scheduling a haircut (Google 2018). These are examples of how AI technology can assist humans by handling simple transactions and saving our time.

AI can also help virtual trainers deliver better learning experiences. According to LinkedIn's *2020 Workplace Learning Report*, "Artificial intelligence (AI) and machine learning are expected to be the next big technologies to impact learning" (Van Nuys 2020). Examples of applied AI in education are rapidly expanding, including AI products that listen to class discussions and highlight areas of improvement for instructors (Fusco, Ruiz, and Roschelle 2021). There are also AI apps that give people feedback on their presentation skills. This service is akin to an instructional coach. Other uses include the ability to identify participation metrics. "In this Zoom era, we also have seen promising speech recognition technologies that can detect inequities in which students have a voice in classroom discussions over large samples of online verbal discourse" (Fusco, Ruiz, and Roschelle 2021).

There are many other ways AI could serve the virtual training field by searching for patterns in certain metrics. Following are some potential areas where AI may be able to specifically assist facilitators and producers in live online learning: producer tasks and chatbots.

Producer Tasks

For organizations or training departments of one where a producer is not available, an AI assistant could monitor chat while the facilitator is training the class. For example, while the facilitator is explaining concepts and annotating on slides, AI could be programmed to monitor texts from learners and respond in kind with brief, prescriptive answers to common questions. If deeper questions are typed in chat, an AI assistant could interject verbally when there's a pause in the facilitator's speech and say, "Excuse me, Diana, Mary is asking what the most important thing is to keep in mind when conducting an effective performance review." This way the facilitator does not need to constantly check chat, and the producer can assist with more major technical challenges.

AI would not replace the producer role, but it would assist with rote tasks so the producer could focus on resolving the more challenging issues. For example, at the outset of the training, a facilitator might say, "Our producer Tom, our support bot Eva, and I are all here to help you in this virtual training program." It's conceivable that some day a virtual instructor may be able to select a customized voice for their support bot from a palette of options and perhaps even a choice of accents. Producers would be able to offload some of the easier technical challenges to these supportive AI agents.

Chatbots

An AI-powered chatbot or agent could serve multiple purposes in virtual training. For one, chatbots could be programmed to respond to the most common technical requests from attendees in a dedicated queue and walk them through steps to troubleshoot. For example, if a learner joins a live online session and is not able to hear anything, they could type to the chatbot, "I can't hear the session, but I can see the slides." The chatbot would then respond with the protocol they should follow to resolve. It's like performance support. For example, it might type a response like "Thank you for letting us know. Our apologies. Please exit the platform and log in again to reset everything."

In the normal chat pod, AI could answer common questions on its own or certain questions that repeatedly get asked in a replicated virtual training class on the same topic. This would allow the trainer to continue facilitating and skip over chat questions for which the chatbot already posted a response. Future virtual platform chats may also be able to accept more than just text, like snippets of audio recordings or brief video messages from learners. Some time in the future, AI could even look at all responses in chat, summarize the ones that have commonality, and report aloud in a conversational voice, "Ms. Howles, 30 percent of participants today are asking about. . . . Would you care to respond?" Adaptive learning is when AI uniquely and intelligently adjusts accordingly after gathering more data. For example, David Gering explained to me, "AI observes the patterns of what you do and then re-calibrates. The more data you collect, the smarter AI becomes."

Another benefit of using an AI assistant and chatbots with virtual training participants from different countries is what they can offer for language services. If, for example, you were teaching a class with global attendees and a learner typed a question in their native tongue into the chat, AI can do an immediate translation to the facilitator's native language so they can understand the chat. Since chat is an immediate medium, this would mean learners didn't have to worry about translations as they would still be able to chat in their native language.

 PRO TIP 82
Be open to opportunities for conversational AI to assist with facilitation and producer roles in virtual training.

Challenges With AI

As is true with everything, there are benefits and challenges with AI. The major challenge is the expense. This is because AI requires large data collection to become smarter. This requires building sets of many questions and triaging them with decision trees, which takes time. According to Gering, this enables it to be better equipped to identify patterns and offer solutions. More likely, rather than individual companies developing AI to aid virtual training, leading virtual platforms will find ways to integrate AI into their products and services. This might lead to commonality in AI features, functions, and support across platforms.

Another drawback is that AI is not entirely free of bias. For example, it has been demonstrated that if AI analyzes data that itself embodies bias, AI will just continue that bias. And, of course, sometimes we just want to talk to another person. Right? But as AI improves and becomes more human-like in terms of responsiveness, conversational quality, and voice sound, this apprehension may diminish. That said, perhaps AI serves as frontline help, with more specific or thorny problems escalated to the virtual trainer or producer.

Be Forward Minded

Around the turn of the 20th century, my grandfather-in-law was a professional blacksmith. Soon there was talk that times were changing, and something new was coming down the road . . . literally. The new automobile was rumored to potentially change the landscape for the blacksmithing trade. But my husband's grandfather didn't believe it. He didn't think anything would significantly change, so he didn't adapt. He did not reskill. Instead, he continued to professionally shoe horses the way he always had. When automobiles eventually become popular enough that horse-drawn carriages disappeared, he found himself out of an occupation. He lost his job, and learned a valuable lesson the hard way. Don't limit your focus and your vision to where you are, look where things are headed too. By not looking ahead and adapting, we risk being left behind. We need to push past the limits of what we have known to discover what could still be.

As tools and technology continue to evolve, they will continue to bring improvements and more affordances. The uptick in online learning budgets will also encourage new virtual training vendors to enter the marketplace. Let's not get stuck doing what we've always done. We need to keep pushing ourselves to be better, learn better, and train better using evolving technology. By allowing where we've been to guide us, observing where we are to inform us, and imagining what can still be to inspire us, together we can push the boundaries to take virtual training to the next level.

 PRO TIP 83
Keep abreast of where the virtual training industry is headed next.

Summary

You now have a blueprint for upskilling through evaluation and innovation. In this chapter, we explored evaluating impact, which is just one of eight essential core capabilities. Strive to consistently evaluate the impact of your virtual training programs. Dedicate time to assess their value, and review and analyze data so you can continue improving program offerings.

We also explored the potential future landscape for virtual training. Live online training is here to stay and it's brimming with opportunity. More evidence-based research is still needed to inform our practice though, especially as the technologies that support what we do rapidly evolve and change. Continued innovation will open the door to new ways of training and learning in the virtual space.

The challenge will be to approach virtual training in such a way that we give ourselves permission to move past older paradigms, thinking patterns, tools, and the status quo. Virtual training is a different medium with different opportunities. As such, it necessitates a fresh perspective and mindset. It may be a shared virtual space, but it is no longer a self-contained, four-walled room. I prefer not to use the term *virtual classroom* because *room* is outdated and can limit forward thinking about what is possible. In past presentations, Bill Horton has referred to thinking that gets stuck in the old paradigms as "horseless carriage thinking." The reason for this is because people called the first automobile a "horseless carriage." In other words, people used old terminology to describe something entirely new. It's interesting that we still say "horsepower" to measure a car engine's power! However, old terminology is no longer applicable and can limit our thinking with new tools. It is my hope that you, too, are inspired to think in new ways beyond the traditional classroom and see the potential for greater opportunity in virtual space.

After attending and congratulating my niece on her vocal recital at a liberal arts college, I was fortunate to also meet her voice professor. Clearly, the professor was a very accomplished vocalist herself. What I was surprised to discover, however, was that she was still taking private voice lessons herself. Here she was at a prestigious college of music teaching vocal majors, and yet, she was still honing her craft and developing professionally.

I believe that following a path of ongoing improvement should be part of our journey as well. As learning professionals who develop others, we should also be developing ourselves. In this way, we walk our talk. Regardless of our current proficiency level as learning analysts, learning experience designers, developers, facilitators, trainers, online adult educators, producers, evaluators, managers, directors, or chief learning officers, we must continue to professionally develop. To do this, we need to evaluate and innovate.

As we evaluate and look for ways to improve virtual training, it's also important to capitalize on the benefits of incorporating virtual training into blended learning solutions. The next chapter examines how to use asynchronous (on demand) and synchronous (live online) as a combined training solution.

Pro Tips for Evaluating Impact Skills

TIP 75   Create an evaluation plan in the design phase of your project, and evaluate learning based on the knowledge and performance objectives identified at the outset.

TIP 76   Determine which levels of evaluation are most important to your customers, employees, their managers, and stakeholders to measure the effectiveness of your virtual training programs.

TIP 77   Communicate to managers the important role they play evaluating and reinforcing what participants learn in training.

TIP 78   Partner with managers to transfer ownership to them to observe and measure application in the workplace while you support them with aids or evaluation rubrics.

TIP 79   Partner with stakeholders or an internal or external professional evaluator to collect organization-wide impact data when appropriate.

TIP 80   Take risks in virtual training, experiment, and continue to innovate in new ways.

TIP 81   Invite global experts to engage learners and address their questions in real time during your live online programs.

TIP 82   Be open to opportunities for conversational AI to assist with facilitation and producer roles in virtual training.

TIP 83   Keep abreast of where the virtual training industry is headed next.

"Rather than asking which technology is best for learning, you will find more fertile ground by using a blend of media that allows you to space out learning events, provide post-training performance support, and foster synchronous and asynchronous forms of collaboration."

—Ruth Colvin Clark, author, *Evidence-Based Training Methods*

CHAPTER 11

Flipping Virtual Training With Blended Learning

It's a classic story, and it's likely happened in your organization or perhaps one you know. Leadership decides to transition some traditional in-person offerings to live online delivery. They recognize the significant savings to be gained by reducing travel costs and time away from work, while accommodating a remote and hybrid workforce. In this example, let's say one of the traditional in-person classes is on effective teamwork. The instructional goal is for leaders to build high-performance teams and refine their people leadership skills. Because the traditional, in-person training was six hours of daily instruction over the course of two days, they decide to retain the same structure for the virtual training delivery. Essentially, this means virtual learners would now spend six hours onscreen over the course of two days. As you might imagine, this is actually a recipe for a snooze fest.

Although this situation may be quite common, it is not ideal. Converting traditional classroom instruction to live online learning is not an apples-to-apples exchange. Let's explore why. For example, the in-person classroom is more controlled and there's a variety of sensory stimuli available for nonverbal interpretation. In contrast, virtual training lacks access to full nonverbal cues for correct interpretation and there is greater opportunity for distraction. Moreover, screen time alone can be exhausting after more than two hours. We have all experienced the fatigue that can come from long stints of online work.

During the COVID-19 pandemic, virtual training expert Jennifer Hofmann commented on several occasions that she felt like we had gone backward as a virtual training industry. I attribute this to the huge influx of many virtual newcomers who made the sudden switch to live online learning. For example, adopters retained the same slide deck from in-person training without modification. But in-person delivery and online delivery are completely different mediums. As such, we need to design and deliver differently. "Virtual instruction is different than in-person training because it requires even more interaction with participants, removing technical barriers, affirming participants' comments, frequent visual movement, more visuals, adding in additional breaks and shortening chunks of time online because everyone is looking at screens, participant prompting, frequent instructor feedback, and more" (Howles 2020).

Another lesson recent adopters have learned the hard way is that "less is more" in terms of how much time to schedule for a virtual class. It's a common mistake to think that a five-hour in-person training can be converted to a five-hour virtual training. As you have likely discovered, this does not work well. In virtual training, shorter is always better.

So, what is a virtual trainer to do? How do we transfer a robust in-person program from the traditional classroom to the online medium? Two words: blended learning. Blended learning solutions combine live, online instruction with independent activities learners complete on their own outside the live class (for example, as pre-work and post-work). It's also important to note that blended learning solutions combine all the virtual trainer capabilities we've discussed so far: experience design, environment shaping, online facilitation, facilitator presence, technical fluency, dynamic engagement, agile troubleshooting, and evaluating impact. To effectively deliver training programs with a blended approach, you must reach competence in each of these capabilities. This chapter takes a closer look at not only how to increase the effectiveness of this learning solution, but also how to create more productive, richer, and deeper learning experiences while doing so.

 THE BIG IDEA
Blend synchronous online instruction with asynchronous components to improve learning.

What Is a Flipped Classroom?

The flipped classroom inverts traditional instruction. Higher education experimented with the notion of the flipped classroom by re-examining which activities made the most sense to do when people were together versus when people were not. What was most profound about this shift was the widespread realization that lectures were a passive activity for students.

In traditional higher education, a professor would lecture to students inside the classroom, while students would work independently on homework outside the classroom. However, educators realized this in-person time was being wasted in a sense by activities that didn't require an instructor be present. So, flipping the classroom meant that you reversed what was traditionally taught in a classroom with what happens outside the classroom and vice versa.

In a flipped classroom, coursework that involves collaboration, synergy, and discussion among students and between students and the teacher can be completed during the live, in-person time. To maximize time spent together in class, there could also be group discussions, analysis, Q&A, and other activities that rely on and involve community. Meanwhile, instructors could then video record lectures that students could view on their own time. "Instead of passively receiving course content during class, students digest the information outside of class on their own time. They might read written materials, watch previously recorded lectures, or listen to a podcast. Once they are in class with their instructors, students spend time answering questions, discussing material, or working in groups" (Berrett 2015). Could some of these lessons also apply to adult professional development and virtual training? Let's examine this next.

What Is Blended Learning?

The flipped classroom helps us better understand the concept of blended learning, and some aspects of the flipped classroom can indeed transfer to virtual training programs. Although blended learning is traditionally defined as pairing a traditional in-person classroom with online modules or e-learning, a more conventional definition includes pairing live online training with a full variety of asynchronous activities or independent work. Across a broader context, Ruth Clark notes that blended learning uses "multiple instructional delivery media that may allow for a combination of instructional methods" (Clark and Kwinn 2007).

In the context of this book, I'll refer to blended learning as the combination of synchronous and asynchronous elements that together comprise a program or course. This way, there are gains for learners because they benefit from both types of instruction. Each supports the other. For example, a blended learning solution for a leadership development program might include class components where learners take behavioral assessments on their own, complete reflection activities, read online resources, or complete a standalone tutorial or e-learning course on leadership. All this independent study could then also be paired with live online virtual classes where learners have the benefit of group discussion, asking questions and receiving answers in real time, working collaboratively, or solving case scenario challenges in small online breakout groups. The asynchronous work can be spread out for leaders to complete on their own time over several weeks or months either before, during, or after the series of live online sessions. In sum, blended learning solutions are truly a blend of live online class components with independent, self-paced coursework.

What Does Asynchronous Learning Do Best?

It's important to carefully consider which course activities lend themselves best to asynchronous learning. Likewise, thoughtfully consider which activities lend themselves best to synchronous. With async, we want to strategically offload instructional components learners can complete on their own time, ensure they support key learning goals, and then set timelines and deadlines for learners to complete them.

If independent work or pre-work is a required portion of the whole program, you must make that clear to learners. In the past, some learners tended to think of pre-work assignments as a "nice to have" or "optional." So, this distinction must be clarified. I include this messaging in my welcome email to learners up front, in the course description, and in my welcome video for learners to view before class. Then repeat it verbally to all again during our first day of class. Other strategies include emphasizing that asynchronous work must be finished before the course will be marked complete in the LMS or to receive overall credit at all. If, however, you intend for assignments to truly be optional, simply state as such.

As discussed in chapter 2, it's important to look at your objectives and the type of content you're training on to determine opportunities to transfer content to asynchronous delivery. For example, if you're training technical content, some of the training could be offloaded to recorded demos of how to use a new system or software, along with a job aid or another type of performance support aid. Live class time can then be used to address challenges with the system or resolve issues they might have experienced. If, however, your content is more business soft skills or people skills like how to give constructive feedback, learners will need to practice during the training. Skill practices usually lend themselves more to breakout activities in the synchronous class unless you leverage on-demand interactive case scenarios as an async activity.

What's important about asynchronous activities is that they can also include community interaction, which supports the social dimension of learning. For example, in an online discussion forum through your LMS or a course management system, learners can interact asynchronously with ideas shared by posting insights, questions, and comments as they interact with peers in the class and the facilitator.

Another example of an async activity is an interactive scenario that contextualizes learning by placing it in a real-world situation. Here the learner is called upon to act and make choices on their own through an independent simulation or module. Afterward, learners can meet in a live online class to debrief the experience, taking advantage of what synchronous learning does best. These live discussions help learners connect what they've learned in the scenario to the real world; specifically, their contextual workplace. Ideally, you could even end the scenario with a cliff hanger like "What would you do now?" and then allow learners to think about it and discuss what actions could be taken during live online class time.

According to Bundy and Howles' 7 Cs Framework for Case Scenarios, a well-designed case scenario involves the interplay of seven Cs, wherein each reinforces and complements the others for deeper learning (Bundy and Howles 2017). When all these components are used to create case scenarios, participants will experience an interactive, compelling situation from which they can make decisions and learn. Integrate the 7 Cs when you create asynchronous interactive scenarios for your learners.

Bundy and Howles' 7 Cs Framework for Case Scenario Design:

1. **Challenges.** It's best to reframe learning objectives as challenges and place learners in a challenging situation from the beginning of the scenario. Clearly present them with the problem they need to tackle and resolve.

2. **Context.** The context places learners in an immersive, real-world situation. Include the location and setting to help learners become more immersed in an environment and trigger their imagination.

3. **Characters.** Every good story includes people. In scenarios, learners become agents who can actively make decisions and interact with other characters. This adds more complexity and depth. Some characters may guide learners toward different trajectories, provide information, or offer different perspectives. It's always helpful to personalize learning by giving characters names and job titles as well.

4. **Content.** You cautiously want to include only enough content to support learners' doing and decision making. Add what is needed to carry the narrative. Exposing learners to challenging decisions with multiple options is also more realistic for them.

5. **Choices.** The scenarios need realistic points for learners to gather information, make decisions, and then receive feedback on their choices.

6. **Consequences.** Results from a scenario can be consequential feedback. In other words, learners experience the impacts of their decision. Corrective, explanatory feedback should be strategically placed right after decision making.

7. **Connections.** This is something the facilitator begins beforehand by setting up the experience. This is called pre-briefing. It lets them know what to expect by priming them before the activity. The connection piece also includes the time after the live virtual training, where learners can debrief and discuss how to connect it to the real world. This gives learners the opportunity to reflect on their choices and benefit from hearing multiple viewpoints from others' learning experiences too.

At the end of this chapter, I've included an example of a learning simulation from Attensi, which also demonstrates how asynchronous case scenarios can be paired with live learning. These interactive scenarios allow for the rich discussion and deeper dive analysis within a context. If a learner is interacting with avatars in a contextual situation and asked to make decisions that affect where the scenario goes from there, this leverages the social dimension of learning through an interaction with the avatar. The cognitive dimension is also apparent because of the mental effort required throughout. There is also an abundance of emotional engagement built into scenarios (for example, motivation, tension, risk, curiosity, and arousal), which helps make it memorable. Finally, there's a behavioral dimension where you are doing things by drawing from what you you've learned in the past, finding the information you need to make decisions, and, ultimately, moving through the course.

Here are some asynchronous learning activities you can incorporate in your blended learning courses:

- Videos
- Podcasts
- On-demand interactive case scenarios
- Published articles
- Pre-class e-learning tutorials
- Pre- and post-tests or quizzes
- Reflection writing
- Independent assignments
- Job aids or other types of performance support

- Infographics
- Discussion forum threads
- Independent skill practices
- Review postings on a networking community of practice
- Post-class boosters (such as text messages, emails, quizzes, or learning nuggets sent from facilitator or an LMS)

 PRO TIP 84
Offload independent class activities as asynchronous course components instead.

Most of these async activities lend themselves best to independent study and assignments. They are a great way to support what learners discuss and practice during the live online sections. Thinking and reflection are great indicators for which activity might work better as asynchronous. As Ruth Clark and Ann Kwinn (2007) summarize, "When time and reflection will benefit learning, asynchronous self-paced media permit learners to work independently at their own rates to complete assignments."

What Does Synchronous Learning Do Best?

Next let's explore what synchronous does best. To begin, synchronous training is a natural conduit for deeper discussion, participatory activities, and social interaction. A guiding question is, "What instructional activities lend themselves best to online face-to-face interactions and real-time collaboration?" When we offload some of the learning that can be done asynchronously, "live class time is freed up for higher levels of learning such as analysis, discussion, application, example review, and evaluation. This approach primes the learner ahead of time" (Howles 2020). Blended learning expert Jennifer Hofmann (2004) adds, "synchronous classroom time should be used for clarification, questions, collaboration, and application—all based on the asynchronous work completed prior to the live event." Offloading some of this learning not only yields more prepared learners and richer discussions, but also invites lively interaction. According to global talent analyst Josh Bersin (2020), "Through the process of asking questions, providing advice, giving context, and explaining specific examples and solutions, an instructor brings learning to life for each individual in their own meaningful way."

Let's focus on how synchronous learning capitalizes on social interaction. This social learning then supports engagement. "In a live, instructor-led experience, employees can interact in a way that fosters collaboration, potentially increasing learner retention and employee engagement" (Bersin 2020). We want to leverage the activities in our sync time together that make the most of our shared community. It is the value-add a live vILT facilitator brings to a synchronous class and it requires thoughtful design. It is worth noting that there is an element of learning for all of us that is fundamentally social. For example, think about how you first learned language as a toddler. You likely learned your native tongue socially, from those who raised you. With synchronous learning, we leverage all four learning dimensions (cognitive, emotional, social, and behavioral), but especially the social dimension.

In terms of appropriate length for the synchronous component, I recommend 90 minutes as the sweet spot, but live synchronous time can be anywhere from one to two hours. In a 90-minute session, for example, we do not want to waste precious live time watching a 15-minute video. That video is best assigned as required pre-work for learners to do before class day. You can see how this frees up time for activities with real-time interaction. One of the best benefits of offloading these activities is that they can help prepare learners for the topic before the live class. I have found live group discussions to be much richer are as a result.

Activities that lend themselves best to the synchronous class include:
- Presenting and receiving corrective feedback
- Delivering a teach-back and receiving feedback
- Doing a skill practice and receiving feedback
- Practicing a role-play exercise
- Large-group discussion
- Small-group breakout discussions
- Critiquing good examples and non-examples as a group

- Analysis
- Brainstorming
- Live question and answer periods
- Applying what learners will do back on the job
- Collaboration activities
- Problem solving in small groups

PRO TIP 85
Leverage the dynamics of synchronous class time for live discussion, small group breakouts, collaboration, brainstorming, analysis, problem solving, or skill practices with feedback.

The Magic Is in the Mix

Blended learning solutions, then, combine the best of both worlds. There is the instructional benefit of a real-time facilitator, the heightened energy of live interaction, and the opportunity to interact with other learners in real time. This then can be coupled with asynchronous reflection, review, and independent work to support the overall learner goals. This "down time" also supports learning by allowing participants to go at their own pace, review as often as needed, complete activities when it works best with their schedule, and not be overwhelmed by all the competing stimuli in a synchronous class. As Ruth Clark and Ann Kwinn (2007) point out, "consider supplementing the virtual classroom with asynchronous events, which impose less cognitive load by allowing learners to review and reflect at their own pace. By bringing together both synchronous and asynchronous elements, learners benefit from the strengths of both.

So, what might your learning solution look like if you used a blended model? Figure 11-1 shows a sample blended learning solution. For example, you might follow this sequence:

- Require a welcome video to be viewed before class.
- Meet as a live class.
- Complete more assignments independently.
- Meet as a live class again.
- Assign post-work or execute action plans.

Figure 11-1. Blended Virtual Training Program

Regarding the welcome videos mentioned in chapter 3, a one- to two-minute welcome video is a great way to introduce yourself, set expectations, and emphasize that pre-work and all coursework must be completed as program requirements. For example, required pre-work you might highlight in such a video could include logging into the LMS to take a pre-test, complete a self-paced tutorial, take a brief e-learning module, view a Vyond animated video, complete a worksheet, or conduct a tech check of your hardware and software.

PRO TIP 86
Use blended learning to blend the best of both synchronous and asynchronous elements for a comprehensive virtual training program.

Benefits of Blended Learning

Many research studies have looked at blended learning over the years. Blended learning solutions not only combine the best of the live online delivery medium and asynchronous activities, but there is also empirical evidence to support its superiority for learning. The results suggest learners demonstrate improved outcomes with blended learning. As Ruth Clark (2020) explains, "Because not all media deliver all methods, evidence suggests that blended learning environments are more effective than pure classroom or pure digital learning." The US Department of Education discovered significant learning gains in courses with blended learning media contrasted with only traditional classroom or only online learning (Means et al. 2009). Let's explore some of the reasons behind why blended learning solutions are so beneficial.

Spaced Repetition

To begin, blended solutions aid learning because they are more conducive for spaced repetition. And spaced repetition helps learning. When participants complete pre-work, attend live class, do asynchronous assignments, attend another live class, and finish post work on their own, there are several review points for material spaced in intervals over time. Cognitive psychology has served us well by teaching us about the power of learning over spaced intervals. This means content material is reviewed again and again with spaces in between reviews. As educational neuroscientist Janet Zadina (2014)—explains, "Spaced repetition has been shown to be one of the most effective ways to encode information into long-term memory. We know that repetition is important, but there also needs to be some space—some time—between repetitions. The ideal amount of time is that the repetition occurs when we are about ready to forget the information." To better understand this, imagine you attended a virtual training session on negotiation skills. You learned several concepts about successful negotiation, but after leaving that session you don't do anything with them and do not apply or use them. How much of it would you remember? Very little. And the next time you had to negotiate something, which might be a month later, you likely went back to doing what you always did.

Spacing out content in your blended virtual training programs can be powerful. For example, you can have pre-work that introduces a topic, synchronous class time to model and discuss it, and then launch a discussion forum on your LMS for participants to continue the discussion outside the live class.

For knowledge to transfer from working memory to long-term memory, it needs to be worthy of reuse. In other words, our brains have a system that prioritizes everything we need to know by how often we use it (or how often we fire the brain neural pathways for the information). The more we do something with the content—think about it, talk about it, use it, write about it, and apply it—the more it becomes wired in our neural pathways and the more likely we are to then store it in long-term memory for later retrieval.

Testing Effect

Blended learning solutions not only allow for more spaced learning, but also more recall through quizzing or polling. The testing effect suggests that simply by being asked to recall information, we are wiring our brains to be able to recall it. The more we recall the information, the better we are at retrieving it.

When virtual learners are quizzed or tested, they are recalling and firing up those pathways again. For this reason, quizzing supports learning. To quiz, you can incorporate polls as knowledge checks or pull up an online survey in your virtual training platform. As we've discussed, quizzes can also be assigned as async components between live online classes. Learners might struggle to recall new concepts initially, but once they do, they'll be able to retrieve them more easily in succession. This is just one more opportunity to fire those new neuropathway connections and wire the new information to long-term memory.

PRO TIP 87
Quiz learners with review questions to practice recall and receive corrective feedback.

Reflection

Another reason why blended learning is beneficial is because it allows for more built-in opportunities for reflection. If you have the luxury of an LMS or course management system, you can leverage discussion threads as excellent platforms for learner reflection. They allow learners to step back from the live session and marinate on the topics discussed, concepts introduced, and, most important, their own application. Asynchronous discussion forums can be insightful venues for reflection on what participants learn and how they will use what they've learned in their functional role. It also facilitates space between learning events for increased processing time and repetitive review.

One thing we've learned over the years about discussion forums is that learners don't usually do them unless they're required. Always prompt learners with open-ended questions to spark discussion. It's also best to be specific in your instructions (Figure 11-2). Sometimes I'll write at the top of the thread, "Please add a comment of your own reflecting on the prompt above, as well as respond substantively to one of your colleagues' comments." This way expectations are clear. They can't just say "I agree," "not exactly," or "good point" to a colleague. They must reflect more deeply. In his book *Teaching Online,* William A. Draves (2000), president of the Learning Resources Network advises the following to help stimulate increased interaction in discussion threads: Make your expectations for participation clear, create door openers by asking learners to tell you more, look for connections among participants and comment on those connections to spark greater posted conversation, ensure there's always a response to every comment whether it be from peers or facilitators, and spend more time nurturing the discussion threads initially but then step aside once learners demonstrate more self-directed behavior).

Figure 11-2. Asynchronous Discussion Thread Example

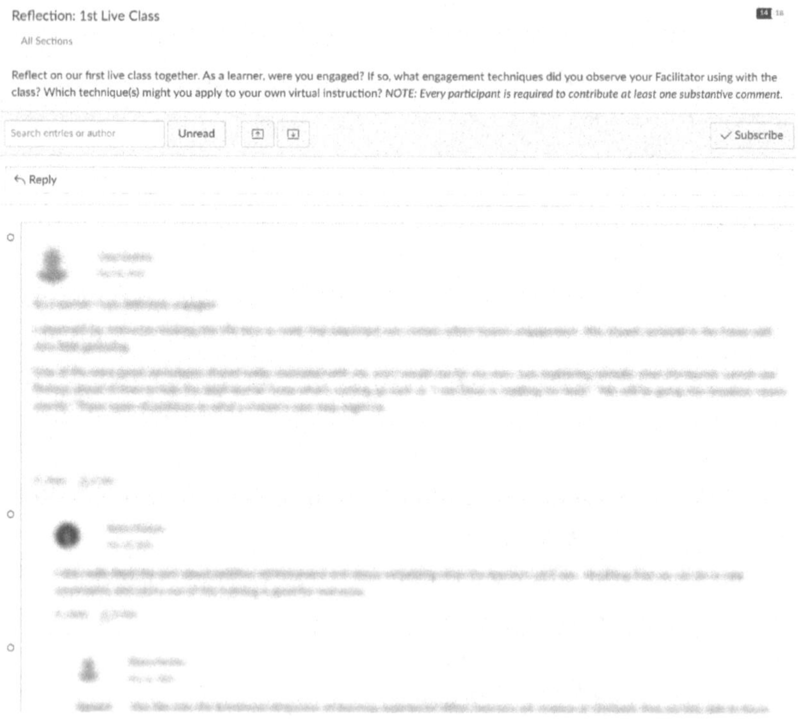

Printed with permission from the University of Wisconsin-Milwaukee.

Because reflection is so important for learning, let's look at some prompt questions to spark reflection in your learners. Some questions you might consider posting in a discussion thread, asking in a live session, or including on a digital worksheet assignment include: "What resonated most with you in the live session today?" or "Were you engaged during the session? If so, share your observations about why you were." According to author Carmen Simon (2016), when we use reflective attention, "we promote long-term memory because of a process called elaborate encoding." Elaborate encoding is when we try to make information that may be new to us more memorable. This way, memories can become stronger when activated again over time (Simon 2016). For this reason and for the sake of learning, it is always good to incorporate reflection into our virtual training programs, especially through asynchronous components.

I once attended a virtual training all about reflection. Quite ironically, the facilitators did not initiate any practice for us to stop and actively reflect—even though the training was on reflection and why we should incorporate it into our training. You see the blind spot, right? Our paradigm from traditional classroom education is to passively absorb information while an instructor speaks. This certainly has its place with foundational knowledge. Yet in the business world and in training and talent development, we must apply to see individual performance and organizational improvement. This is very different than knowing all about something. For instance, as a new driver, one might earn top scores in their driver's education class because they successfully learned all about driving content. But once they get behind the wheel, they may not be very skilled at the doing aspect. This is because knowing ain't doing. If learners don't apply what they've learned during a training, they are less likely to apply it on the job. Incorporate opportunities for your learners to reflect on their learning experience through the asynchronous activities of your blended learning programs.

■ ■ ■

Overall, blended learning offers many advantages. It allows for greater opportunity to boost learning by incorporating spaced repetition, the testing effect, and reflection. To put it into action, first examine your performance and knowledge objectives and determine which learning activities best achieve them, as discussed in chapter 2. Then determine whether these activities can be completed by learners independently or are best reserved for synchronous class time. Remember it's important to optimize higher levels of learning activities like analysis, discussion, application, example review, and evaluation for live online time. For example, you might "engage in group problem-solving activities that build upon concepts covered in the pre-work" (Howles 2015). Likewise, reading, viewing, and reflection activities are usually reserved for async-type activities.

Example of Blended Learning Components

Let's combine what we've discussed so far into a real example so you can see how this might be implemented. In a train-the-trainer virtual class I've taught, I communicate learning objectives to participants' managers ahead of time, and let them know that their employees will be creating action plans that will be shared with managers so they can help hold them accountable for application. Learners are then sent a simple initial activity right before the program begins. It is usually a welcome video of my talking head in which I welcome them, introduce myself, set expectations for the course, and convey I'm excited to meet them and work with them. In our first live class together, we engage in discussion activities and breakouts using the various tools we discussed in chapter 7.

On their own and before the next live class, they are given assignments like writing their own objectives, as well as independent e-learning tutorials to complete on the topic. The expectation is that this e-learning must be completed before our next live class. This continues again for the second class. After meeting for the second live class, they once again have some assignments to complete and a podcast to listen to or some articles to read. After meeting for the third live class, I send them booster email reminders summarizing the biggest takeaways one day, one week, and one month after the virtual program concludes (1x1x1). Additionally, all action plans are shared with managers, and managers are asked to have discussions with their employees within one week of completing the program. The employee does not receive a digital badge in the LMS for the program until all required pre-work, coursework, assignments, and action plans are complete. Next, let's look more specifically at how pre-work can assist on the front end and boosters can assist on the back end.

Pre-Work

Pre-work can be a great opportunity to whet learners' appetite for the training topic and trigger their curiosity and mental framework for the training. In my experience, they come to class with more questions and ready to discuss the topic when they were required to complete pre-work. I find that our live class discussions are richer because they invested effort ahead of time. According to a 2021 ATD research report, 65 percent of more than 430 professional talent development professionals said they included required pre-work before learners attend a live online session (ATD 2021). This might be a standalone e-learning tutorial learners must complete before the live class. After the live class, there might be another tutorial to complete with a few coursework assignments built in, which then prepares them for the next online class. Figures 11-3 and 11-4 show examples of tutorials and pre-work assignments I've used for some of my classes. Pre-work may include initial reading, videos, or self-paced e-learning modules. Figure 11-3 was published in The Learning Guild's *Learning Solutions* as an example of a self-paced asynchronous tutorial (Howles 2015).

Figure 11-3. Pre-Work Tutorial Example Using Articulate Storyline

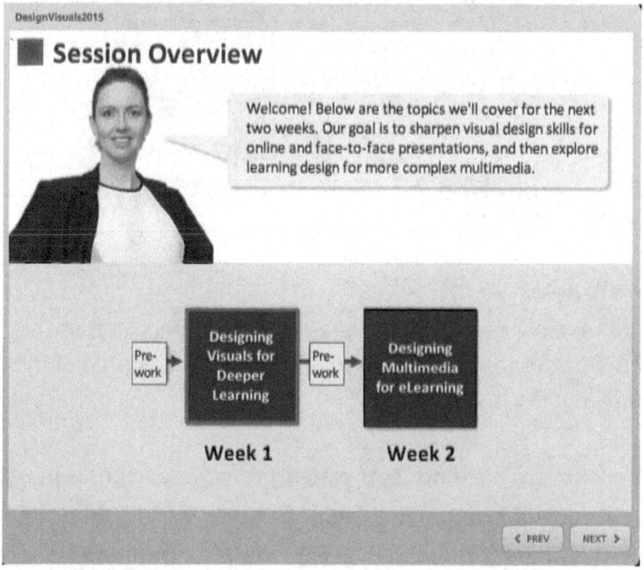

Reprinted with permission from Articulate Global, Inc.

Figure 11-4. Pre-Work Module Example Using Rise 360

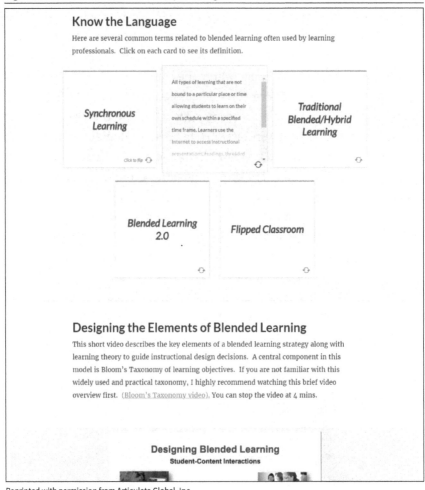

Reprinted with permission from Articulate Global, Inc.

PRO TIP 88

Assign required asynchronous pre-work to learners for them to complete prior to the live class to prime the pump and whet their appetite for the topic.

If some learners have not completed pre-work assignments, we do not reward them for not completing them. In other words, do not go over the pre-work in detail to fill them in. You can quickly summarize or discuss and analyze and then apply the content to worked examples for more learning, but do not fully explain them again. This teaches learners that they need to complete their pre-work or they will be lost during class. If you repeat and review everything in the pre-work, participants will learn they didn't have to do it anyway. Pre-work is designed to be pre-work.

PRO TIP 89
To ensure all learners complete pre-class assignments, track completions through your LMS or have learners submit something to you once they are done (such as a digital worksheet).

You may be thinking, "That sounds great, but my learners won't complete the pre-work because they never do." I've worked with clients on a coordinated approach to address this. In the welcome video, we clarify that all coursework (async and sync) and post-class action plans must be completed before receiving credit for completion of the program and their digital badge from the LMS.

But here is the real secret to ensuring learners complete the pre-work: Track completions for everyone, and individually follow up with those who don't complete it by the deadline, which should be two days before the live class. For example, if your first live class is April 10, your deadline would be April 8. Email whomever did not complete it on April 9. Surprisingly, they often apologize and thank you for reminding them. In my experience, they often get it to you the day before the session. You can also require them to send you something once they have completed it. Alternatively, you could track their completions with your LMS.

PRO TIP 90
As soon as the due date has passed, follow up individually with learners who have not yet completed their required pre-work.

Another key component of pre-work is the welcome video we discussed in chapter 3. Figure 11-5 is an example of an instructor welcome video script to give you an idea for what you might say. Notice the use of personal pronouns to leverage Richard Mayer's Personalization Principle as discussed in chapter 6, and the use of contractions to create the conversational feel. This can be sent to participants to view before your first live class.

Figure 11-5. Sample Script of a Trainer Welcome Video

"Welcome everyone! I'm Diana Howles and it's my pleasure to be your virtual trainer. I've been teaching online since 2000 and I've been in the learning and development field for 25 years. I know for some of you, this may be a brand-new experience. But regardless of where you are in your journey, we are committed to helping you be successful."

"This program will include four live online classes where we'll meet together live. For our first live session together, please be camera ready as it would be helpful to see everyone's faces online when we first introduce ourselves. There will also be assignments for you to complete on your own time in between each live session. Later in the program, you'll even have an opportunity to deliver your own teach-back. This is a great opportunity to practice what you've learned and to receive helpful feedback."

"In addition to watching this video to help you get oriented, there are also two required action items for you to complete before our first class. The first is to get comfortable with the learning management system we'll be using. In the week before class begins, get oriented by playing around in the system and locating the discussion thread forum and where the resources are so you are more comfortable with the interface. Your second action item is to identify a topic that you'll be training others on in the near future. You'll then use this topic as your teach-back when you apply the strategies and techniques we'll be talking about near the end of the course. I look forward to working with all of you, and we'll see you online real soon!"

Boosters

The best way to define a booster is with the help of a healthcare metaphor. Think about when you need to get a vaccine to prevent infection and disease from a virus. You were likely given your first shot, and then after a period of time passed, you likely received a second shot or a booster. Why? Because it bolstered and strengthened your overall immune system's readiness response if your body were ever to encounter that virus.

When we apply this concept to learning, it works in a similar fashion. After initially being exposed to new content, processes, procedures, and concepts, over a period we forget the information if we don't do something with it. A booster is something offered to us after an initial period has passed regarding something we were recently taught. Boosters are easy to do if you can leverage an automated LMS where you or your L&D colleagues can preset the messages and their dates and times. Email and even text messages can also work well for sending boosters.

My favorite booster format is 1x1x1. This means I summarize key content and push it to learners one day, one week, and one month after the last virtual training session in the program concludes. Sometimes this is through emails from me, or I've leveraged an LMS to automatically send booster messages to participants. There are also many digital apps available to support pushing booster reminders (sometimes, even through text messaging) to learners. In the first booster, I often summarize key takeaway points as a quick nugget summary for their review.

The second booster is a quiz of all the key points, where learners can test themselves. I also include an answer key at the very bottom in small print, so they can check their answers. Occasionally, I'll receive an email from a learner where they share excitedly that they "nailed it" and got them all correct. Not only does this motivate learners even more with the emotional dimension of learning, but it also leverages the testing effect where they are actively recalling the information.

The third booster features an example or testimonial of how a learner successfully applied what they learned so far, or a celebration of a learner who has already implemented a part of their action plan. Their success can motivate others, and this booster usually includes other ideas for application and additional resources related to the training topic that might be of interest to participants.

 PRO TIP 91
Send 1x1x1 boosters (one day, one week, and one month after a virtual training program concludes) to remind learners of key takeaways, or quiz them via emails, texts, or automated LMS messages.

Async Role Plays

One learning activity that is traditionally viewed as a synchronous activity is the role play. Ideally, a facilitator would model in abbreviated form what is expected, and then learners would follow by skill practicing themselves. When the facilitator models it first, they may use a seasoned producer to role play with them, a co-facilitator, or a learner volunteer or plant (who was asked and agreed to assist ahead of time) if you prep them appropriately. If we approach this by thinking out of the box, however, this activity could also be offloaded to an asynchronous format. Let's explore how that might work.

A facilitator could assign this activity as something to be completed out of class in partnership with other learners. Leveraging learner agency and participant choice as we discussed in chapter 4, you could also invite learners to sign up for slots, choose their own partners, and select from one of three role play topics themselves. The assignment could specify that learners would need to work together outside class with access to the virtual training platform, or leave it up to them to find a way to video record themselves. They would need to rehearse their role play and then do a final recording of their skill practice. It would then be up to the partners to upload their final role play video to a repository pre-designated by the facilitator for better organization and coordination. For example, it could be uploaded to a course management system, placed in a shared Dropbox folder, or uploaded to a private YouTube channel for the facilitator to then view and critique.

The facilitator then could email written or audio feedback of their comments to each duo, highlighting what went well and what could be improved for next time. This is just one idea for how you might offload an activity that is normally done during live class to asynchronous assignments. By offloading, we can capitalize more on the social, behavioral, and emotional dimensions of learning during synchronous class time.

Let's look at one more example of how you might consider taking something traditionally taught live and exploring why it might be beneficial to offer it asynchronously instead.

Videos

As mentioned previously, assigning videos for your learners to watch out of class before attending live online learning can be extremely valuable. It whets their appetite and prepares them for what's to come. If you do not have video resources, there are abundant resources on the web you can curate as well.

As you assign videos to your learners as asynchronous components, it's important to understand viewer habits when it comes to playing videos. This will help you edit a video, or direct learners to view only a certain portion, or position it better so they're motivated to watch all of it. TechSmith Corporation has conducted a fascinating study repeatedly on what keeps people's interest when they watch videos, and why people stop watching them (Figure 11-6). They discovered the sweet spot for ideal video length to be just a few minutes: "Across all countries in our most recent study, the majority of viewers prefer instructional and informational videos in the ranges of three to four and five to six minutes" (TechSmith 2018).

If you think that professional video quality is one of the main reasons people keep watching a video, TechSmith's research findings will surprise you. Instead, the top reasons viewers appear to keep watching is when they are genuinely interested in the topic, believe the content is relatable to them, and were drawn in by the speaker (TechSmith 2018). Less important variables included being required to watch it, whether it was humorous or unique, and the audio quality.

Figure 11-6. Why Viewers Keep Watching Videos

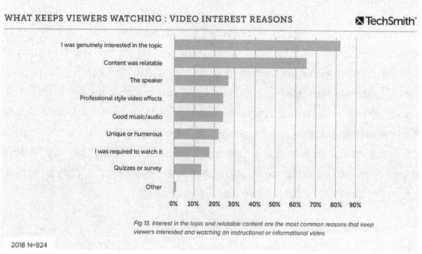

Reprinted with permission from TechSmith Corporation.

If we switch gears, what do you think might be the top reasons people stop watching videos? TechSmith's research study discovered that the biggest reasons why individuals stop watching is because they are not receiving the information they expected, they were bored or found the content uninteresting, or they needed to do something else (Figure 11-7; TechSmith 2018). Once again, poor professional quality didn't seem to matter as much, along with entertainment value or distractions.

Figure 11-7. Why Viewers Stop Watching Videos

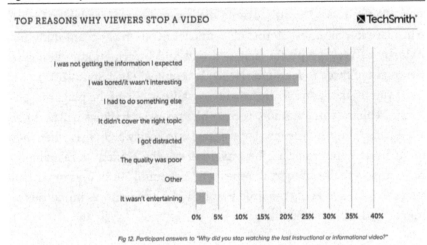

TOP REASONS WHY VIEWERS STOP A VIDEO   TechSmith

Fig 12. Participant answers to "Why did you stop watching the last instructional or informational video?"

2018 N=696

Reprinted with permission from TechSmith Corporation.

What does this tell us in terms of assigning videos as asynchronous activities with blended courses and live online learning? The takeaway is that we want to position the video and its content by tying it into participants' interests and setting accurate expectations upfront for how it will benefit them to view the video. We also want to tell participants what to focus on while viewing. For example, "when you watch this video, notice the cause of the problem and the result of each solution they try." These videos then can be assigned to learners to watch asynchronously in preparation for debriefing during live classes.

 PRO TIP 92
When you assign videos for learners to watch asynchronously, give a direction prompt for what to be watching for and how it will benefit them.

While some virtual trainers choose to show videos during the live class, there can be bandwidth issues resulting in freeze frames and quality issues for some participants. Despite troubleshooting ahead of time, inevitably at least one participant often seems unable to view the live video synchronously. The backup plan for this is to place the link to the video in the chat. Then participants can independently view while their cameras and microphones are off. When they're done viewing the video, they can return to the platform and select feedback reaction like the green check or the animated thumb's up to signal they have returned. Playing a video during class certainly can be done, but I have found over the years that it doesn't always work smoothly. Therefore, I prefer to offload my videos as asynchronous pre-work or post-work assignments. I clarify they're required, and highlight the short runtime.

To foster rich discussions later, you can apply some of the following techniques. One technique is to capture key screenshots of the video to stimulate learners' memory, and display them as you begin the group discussion. Also, to prime discussion and help learners get over the inertia we talked about in chapter 4, you can ask a good, open-ended prompt question like "What surprised you most about this video?" Then answer the question first with an example to prompt discussion and get the ball rolling.

Business Use Cases of Blended Learning

Next let's look at two global organizations that have successfully paired asynchronous and synchronous components such as live virtual training into blended learning solutions. Attensi and Aon have both successfully combined live online components with on-demand elements.

Attensi

Attensi is a Norwegian company headquartered in Oslo with additional offices located around the world. Their expertise is gamified simulation training. They use advanced 3D modelling to train employees in custom workplace scenarios. These simulations allow employees to interact with their software. Their software's immersive design incents repetition with rewards reflected on leader boards. Although Attensi's software may be used as asynchronous on-demand modules, it can also be paired with live online training as a blended learning program. This way, learners debrief their simulated experiences, which helps them make connections through live discussion and analysis.

For example, a global management consultancy used Attensi's gamified simulation platform to enhance engagement during their live online sessions (Figure 11-8). Their training offerings focused on behavioral topics such as client engagement, professionalism, agile team management, and project management best practices.

Figure 11-8. Attensi Asynchronous Simulation

Reprinted with permission from Attensi. Unauthorized use not permitted.

"For behavioral topics, allowing a participant the opportunity to immerse in an engaging simulation, test out different approaches, and understand potential outcomes before discussing these experiences as part of a breakout group has been highly impactful," shared Huw Newton-Hill, sector leader for professional services at Attensi. "Taking one solution for example, 98 percent of participants felt better prepared for their role and we know the learning sticks, as 93 percent said that reflections and learning from the simulation helped them in their everyday life, according to a survey taken five months after the training. For skill-based topics, facilitators have focused on the competition features within the Attensi platform to host live battles to drive engagement in the training during a live session. This has proven to spill over into deeper engagement in the self-directed learning components of a program."

Aon

Aon is a professional firm that sells financial risk-mitigation products such as health insurance plans, insurance, and pension administration. They employ approximately 50,000 employees in 120 countries and are head-quartered in London, United Kingdom.

According to Kelly Eno, Aon learning leader with the business services global contact center, they are responsible for upscaling approximately 1,200 call center agents annually for Medicare open enrollment season. They use a blended learning approach that incorporates both live online training with digital, self-paced e-learning modules.

"Our focus is new hire agent training, which is a four-week onboarding program," Eno says. "The asynchronous modules are created with Vyond and Articulate 360, and trains agents to educate Medicare-eligible customers about their supplemental insurance options and ultimately match them with a Medicare supplement plan. When agents complete the on-demand modules, we find they are more engaged in their learning and appreciate the opportunity to review content at their own pace.

"In the live online classes, we use two facilitators per virtual class with no more than 25 participants," she continues. "One facilitator serves as online producer while the other facilitator delivers the training. We heavily use breakouts for small group work. For example, breakouts are used to help agents practice mock calls and problem solve potential customer situations. Breakouts are also used to form small study groups. We leverage online breakouts as a great way to build colleague relationships and increase colleague engagement."

Summary

Blended learning solutions offer many advantages. By combining live online training with asynchronous components, we create learning programs that extend beyond one-time training events. The benefits are numerous: improved learning outcomes based on evidence-based research reinforcement of material, built-in review and spaced repetition for improved memory encoding, less taxing on learners when they can do some work independently, and increased time for reflection, absorbing, and reinforcing over time. This mix is the best of both worlds, with on-demand and live, real-time opportunities to support deeper learning. As Ruth Clark (2020) summed up beautifully in this chapter's opening quotation, "Rather than asking which technology is best for learning, you will find more fertile ground by using a blend of media that allows you to space out learning events, provide post-training performance support, and foster synchronous and asynchronous forms of collaboration."

Ultimately, our goal is to make impactful change in our organizations. Folding virtual training into blending learning solutions is one way to do this. Blended learning also supports all four of the learning dimensions we discussed in chapter 2. With asynchronous components, participants can experience the cognitive, emotional, and behavioral dimensions of learning. Through synchronous class time, learners experience it socially with their peers and instructor, behaviorally through tasks and skill practices with feedback, and cognitively and emotionally.

In the next chapter, we'll explore another type of blend that incorporates the hybrid mix of both online and on-site participants learning together in real time.

Pro Tips for Applying Blended Learning

TIP 84	Offload independent class activities as asynchronous course components instead.
TIP 85	Leverage the dynamics of synchronous class time for live discussion, small group breakouts, collaboration, brainstorming, analysis, problem solving, or skill practices with feedback.
TIP 86	Use blended learning to blend the best of both synchronous and asynchronous elements for a comprehensive virtual training program.
TIP 87	Quiz learners with review questions to practice recall and receive corrective feedback.
TIP 88	Assign required asynchronous pre-work to learners for them to complete prior to live class to prime the pump and whet their appetite for the topic.
TIP 89	To ensure all learners complete pre-class assignments, track completions through your LMS or have learners submit something to you once they are done (such as a digital worksheet).
TIP 90	As soon as the due date has passed, follow-up individually with learners who have not yet completed their required pre-work.
TIP 91	Send 1x1x1 boosters (one day, one week, and one month after a virtual training program concludes) to remind learners of key takeaways, or quiz them via emails, texts, or automated LMS messages.
TIP 92	When you assign videos for learners to watch asynchronously, give a direction prompt for what to be watching for and how it will benefit them.

"The separation of functions, and the division of stages, spaces, and tasks are characteristic of literate and visual society . . . These divisions tend to dissolve through the action of the instant and organic interrelations of electricity."

—Marshall McLuhan, media professor, philosopher, and author

CHAPTER 12

Combining Online and On-Site Learners in Live Mixed Learning

The class was intentionally kept small. Today there would be a total of 14 learners. Antonio arrived early to the in-person classroom to allow for any last-minute tweaks to the setup. The week before he had met with an IT technician to test and check all the hardware and software. There were a few hiccups, like when the overhead speakers in the room created some sound system feedback. This reminded him that during the netiquette guidelines he'd need to ask on-site participants to keep their built-in microphones muted on their laptops if they logged into the virtual training platform from the physical classroom.

Learners had been given the option to choose how they wanted to attend the training. Registration for virtual spots filled up fast, which wasn't surprising because several employees were connecting from other parts of the country, and others chose to attend virtually because they were working remotely full time. However, six learners registered to attend in person, some of whom had shared that they missed real-time interaction and were really looking forward to being in the same room again. They normally worked on-site a few days a week and worked remotely the rest of the time.

Although Antonio was lead trainer today, he was partnering with Mishika, a colleague in his talent development department who would serve as the virtual co-facilitator. Mishika had just logged in to Microsoft Teams from her home office. Eddie also joined virtually as their IT technician and would stay on as a remote attendee for the duration. This way Eddie would be able to troubleshoot technical issues immediately if needed.

The technology they were using to facilitate class for both on-site and online learners was ClickShare Conference, a wireless conferencing system. Logitech cameras were installed in the front of the room to capture a view of the learners, and another camera was placed in the best location to capture Antonio. Both cameras were high-definition video and had roaming features, so they moved on their own to zoom in and follow whoever was speaking or pan out when multiple people spoke. Antonio wore a wireless microphone to ensure virtual participants could always hear him well, which also gave him more freedom and mobility in the room. Additionally, the physical training room was equipped with microphones and speakers in the ceiling to pick up the audio from in-room participants.

As learners began to physically enter the training room and join online, Antonio welcomed the in-room learners and Mishika greeted the virtual learners. Some logged in virtually and said they couldn't hear anything, so Eddie worked with them right away to resolve their issues by communicating via chat. Just knowing Eddie would be there to help them with technical issues helped Antonio and Mishika relax a lot more.

After a brief ice breaker, learners were asked to raise their physical or virtual hand if one of three statements related to the training topic was true for them. Then Antonio went over the netiquette guidelines for their time together. He displayed PowerPoint slides by sharing his screen through Microsoft Teams for virtual participants, while at the same time, projected them on the SMART board in the front of the room for on-site participants.

Participants had been asked to complete pre-class assignments, which included viewing a video and reading an article on the topic. Next, Mishika led the large group discussion about the pre-work video and the pre-assigned article. She had open-ended discussion questions prepared and typed in text on a slide. Both in-room and virtual participants could see her on camera. Some virtual learners seemed less willing to contribute aloud, so Mishika encouraged them to share via chat. Seeing several chat comments and questions come in, she alerted Antonio, who selected some of the key comments and questions for her to share with the entire group. Those in the physical room raised their hand when they had insights they wanted to share aloud. Mishika called on people both remotely and in-person.

Antonio used the physical whiteboard in the on-site room to capture their debriefing session, before moving on to group brainstorming, which virtual learners could see through the Microsoft Teams platform. When it was time to divide into small breakouts, the virtual learners were placed into online breakouts and Antonio divided the in-room participants into small groups of three people. He requested they spread out around the room so they could hear each other better. In their small groups both online and on-site, learners worked together on a role play, taking turns practicing the skills they had learned. When it came time to debrief, the in-room participants had not yet moved back to their original locations and as a result, some of the remote participants said they could not hear them as well. So, Antonio asked the in-room participants to move closer to the ceiling microphones. Antonio always checked in with virtual learners first when asking a question and then directed it to an in-room participant. Antonio and Mishika knew it was best to give online and on-site learners as equitable a learning experience as possible.

▬ ▬ ▬

This type of training or instruction has been called "here or there instruction" (Zydney et al. 2019), hybrid, blended synchronous learning, synchronous hybrid learning, concurrent classroom, blended programs, hybrid classes, or co-located learners. What exactly is this type of learning space? This combination of training brings learners together from a physical room and online locations. As mentioned above, some call this hybrid, but hybrid as a term can be confusing because it's overused and references a variety of combinations. In a nutshell, this type of learning is live and trains in real time with a mix of learners on-site and online. All are connected and learning together concurrently, regardless of where they are. I call it *live mixed learning*.

In chapter 11, we explored how blended learning pairs asynchronous or self-paced learning with synchronous or live online learning. These mediums work together to support synergistic learning. As we discovered, the magic is in the mix. In this chapter, we explore a different type of blend—live mixed learning. We'll examine what it is and how it works, the workplace context that now calls out for this type of blend and its advantages, the challenges with this nascent method of training delivery, considerations for facilitators, and what they need to be aware of to ensure success. Like chapter 11, this chapter is not tied to one specific capability, but rather requires all the capabilities to be successful.

 THE BIG IDEA
Determining whether live mixed learning may or may not be viable depends on your resources for the requisite technology, staffing co-facilitators, design flexibility, ability to keep total class size small, and access to additional IT support.

What Is Live Mixed Learning?

So, what is live mixed learning? Simply stated, it is live training facilitated in real-time to learners who are online and on-site (Figure 12-1). *Live* clearly communicates that this is not asynchronous, recorded, or on-demand. *Mixed* communicates the combination of both virtual and in-room participants. In this case, the training allows learners who are both physically present and virtually present to learn together. I call this comprehensive approach to training "live mixed learning" because it calls out for a simple, fresh term that captures its essence. As Marshall McLuhan's quotation references at the beginning of this chapter, electronic media has brought about the integration of all types of media, and the former divisions and boundaries are dissolving and blending.

Now that you know what it is, how does it work? Live mixed learning allows trainers, facilitators, and instructors who are either virtual or remote to train learners who are both virtual and remote. The live video stream of the facilitator's image can be broadcast to all virtual attendees. Likewise, it's better if all in-person attendees can also view remote participants on live video and vice versa. You would also need a virtual training platform or video conferencing platform to connect all participants (such as Zoom, Microsoft Teams, Webex, Adobe Connect, Blackboard Collaborate, or similar). The technological platform would facilitate the screen sharing of materials as well as chat and other interactive tool functionality.

Figure 12-1. Zoom Live Mixed (Hybrid) Class

© Zoom Video Communications, Inc. Reprinted with permission.

The Hybrid Workplace's Influence on Live Mixed Learning

Hybrid workplace models are the new normal. Going to work either means commuting to an office building, working remotely from anywhere, or some combination of both. Most employers are leading this charge. In this scenario, an employee may work from a home office a few times a week and then come into the office a few times a week or a few times a month. In the *2021 State of Remote Work*, which surveyed 2,300 employees, 94 percent of workers who started working remotely due to the pandemic said they wanted to continue working remotely—at least some of the time—for the remainder of their careers (Buffer 2021). According to one 2020 research survey, employees on average were interested in working from home approximately two days each week in the future (Barrero, Bloom, and Davis 2021). As Matthew Hollingsworth, head of operations at We Work Remotely, said, "We now have a workforce who understands that many jobs can be done from anywhere and will expect their employers to offer remote-friendly work environments. It is fundamentally shifting the way we think about work" (Buffer 2021).

Hybrid work is here to stay. Although remote work was certainly in place long before the COVID-19 pandemic, it wasn't until then that it became ubiquitous for health and safety reasons. Out of necessity, organizations around the world began to work fully remote for the first time. Other organizations adapted and offered employees the option to do a combination of both remote and in person. Although this can be disrupting, disruption also breeds innovation. As author Charles Duhigg (2016) points out in *Smarter, Faster, Better*, times of disruption are great times for innovation. According to LinkedIn Learning's report, workplaces with both remote employees and employees in the traditional office environment are "going to be the way we work for the foreseeable future" (Van Nuys 2021). In fact, according to the *2021 EDUCAUSE Horizon Report Teaching and Learning Edition*, widespread adoption of these live, mixed types of learning models were identified as one of the macro trends that will shape the future of learning in higher education (Pelletier et al. 2021). Facilitators need to be prepared to provide solutions that accommodate and embrace both on-site and online learners at the same time, as the geographical disbursement of their workforce may permanently require it.

As organizations explore ways to meet the needs of the hybrid workforce, some employers have redesigned facilities to accommodate shared, generic workspaces, while still others allow employees to work from anywhere, like a local coffee shop or an extended vacation spot. As a result of this shift, hybrid work has spawned a new challenge for learning and development and educational practitioners. They are exploring how to bring together on-site and remote staff and figuring out what that means for learning and development. Some are on-site and near company headquarters, while others live out-of-state or out-of-country. With workers either in-office or off-site on any given day, how do you manage, coordinate, schedule, and deliver training to staff? You could provide all virtual classes for some or all in-person training for others, but how do you accommodate schedules that vary and conflict with their co-workers? Hybrid work environments necessitate different workplace configurations and the need to adopt new technologies to help reach staff wherever they are. A greater need for flexibility has emerged so staff can be trained regardless of where they happen to be on training day.

The core need created by the hybrid workplace model is the need to be able to train staff from wherever they are. This is where live mixed learning may be able to offer multiple benefits that may outweigh the costs. This model of combined on-site and online learners has been pioneered in higher educational settings for years. As experienced hybrid educator Kim Huettl told me, "Learners can attend any class, anywhere, in any format." As program manager in the School of Continuing Education at the University of Wisconsin-Milwaukee, she emphasized that this model can foster community and connection for those in the classroom, as well as remote learners, but requires superior and solid technology. Let's take a look at some of the other advantages to live mixed learning.

Advantages of Live Mixed Learning

As you consider whether live mixed learning is viable for you and your organization, you may be wondering what, if anything, is the value add. Why not just consider an all in-person or all-virtual training? Here are some of the advantages to this approach:

- Fits hybrid workplaces
- Cost savings
- Flexibility and choice
- Global reach and access equity
- In-person dynamics
- Community building among remote and on-site learners
- Wellness and health safety
- Learner expectations of modern training

Fits Hybrid Workplaces

Live mixed learning best supports a hybrid work environment. In hybrid workplaces, there are some days when staff will be on-site and other days when they will be remote. Some staff will prefer the in-person experience on days they are in the office. Then there are other staff who will always be remote. Most importantly, it accommodates a hybrid workplace schedule. If your organization is in a fully hybrid workplace, live mixed learning may be the best way to accommodate those who are off-site and on-site.

Cost Savings

Perhaps one of the strongest advantages of the live mixed learning model is the cost savings. There are significant savings realized by not flying all employees in for the training in addition to not having to pay for their hotel accommodations, rental cars, and other travel-related expenses. There is also cost savings because of the improved efficiencies that come with reduced need for physical spaces, overhead costs like heating and air conditioning of unused spaces, and fewer rentals of training spaces. As live mixed learning expert Michael Sitte, director of academic operations at Milwaukee Area Technical College explained to me, "Over the years, you'll get an ROI on it many times over."

Flexibility and Choice

Another significant benefit is flexibility. Live mixed learning accommodates learners who want the in-classroom experience, as well as those who may not be able to attend in person because of work schedules, where they live, business travel, being abroad, or even being ill. If you give learners flexibility based on their needs, locations, and schedules, they're happier. This emotional appeal can influence their motivation for the class, which as we've explored previously can influence their overall learning experience. Live mixed learning also provides greater flexibility for those who are working in different locations. Instead of requiring all staff to attend a training in person when they do not normally work in an office building, a live mixed class allows them to attend remotely.

Greater learner choice is also more welcome. Live mixed instructor, Katherine Dalland, a language arts department chair and humanities teacher, told me she found herself increasing choice for learners within the classroom. She worked diligently to "make sure everyone had a voice."

Global Reach and Access Equity

Another benefit of live mixed learning is its global reach. Void of geographical limitations, some professionals who may be across the world or have demanding schedules that do not allow them to physically attend class can still participate. Because many organizations have embraced and are operating as hybrid workplaces, they can now hire more employees who may live out of state, in other provinces, or another country. In addition, thanks to technology, you also can leverage geographical reach for speakers too. If there is an expert on your training topic on the other side of the world, they can still be invited and then you would carefully coordinate language translation as needed and workable times across time zones.

In-Person Dynamics

Some people just want the in-person experience. Period. Think of when you have gathered with people with whom you have not been in the same room for a long time. There is excitement, energy, collaboration, an acute sense of physical presence, greater sensory stimulation, and comradery and connection. A live mixed class can anchor a session with a different dynamic by introducing a sense of the live, in-person feel. This way, remote participants can also feel like they're right there in the room. All the while, remote attendees can be accommodated as well. Training sessions are anchored in the naturally occurring high-energy dynamic of when people gather in person. The live mixed format allows for collaboration and in-person connection with staff.

Community Building Among Remote and On-Site Learners

Another benefit is the bridge these classes can forge as professionals work together. Field staff who are remote or employees who work out of state, province, or country may not be as well known. Allowing the two groups to work together can help build relationships and community between them.

Wellness and Health Safety

Another advantage to this instructional format is that it allows for physical distancing to avoid infection transmissions. During the COVID-19 pandemic, for example, those who were ill, exposed to others who were infected, or under quarantine could still attend class virtually. At the same time, this format still allows for those who prefer the in-room experience to attend in person.

Learner Expectations of Modern Training

As hybrid workplaces become more commonplace, a greater number of employees are hired out of state or country. Because staff are able to work from anywhere, hybrid formats for some training will become the expectation. To stay competitive, we need to be open to providing opportunities for learners to learn both online and on location (Figure 12-2). There is also a growing need for performance support such as workflow learning. This is true in higher education, as well as in private and public workplaces. In the future, spaces for in-room-only facilitation may become less necessary and less suitable for a remote and hybrid workforce.

Figure 12-2. Live Mixed Example from KU Leuven Campus Kulak Kortrijk in Belgium

Reprinted with permission from IMEC.

Challenges With Live Mixed Learning

Before moving ahead with live mixed learning, there are several challenges to weigh first. Maybe you've already heard from others who have experienced poor learning or it was too complex or challenging. As technology improves and facilitators gain more experience with this method, training with the live mixed learning method will eventually become easier. For now, let's examine some of the key challenges:

- Technical issues
- Learning experience inequities
- Facilitator cognitive overload
- Significant time investment

Technical Issues

With more technical complexity comes more technical issues. As a result, the number-one challenge with live mixed learning is the greater opportunity for hardware or software technical issues. One of the most common issues is virtual learners' inability to hear well. For example, they may not be able to hear the facilitator (when the facilitator wanders away from a stationary microphone) or in-room participants when they talk. At times, when using live mixed learning, you may experience poor audio quality and delays in video streaming because of limited bandwidth. There can also be delays getting everything operational and working as it should. Additionally, when in-room participants partner with online participants in small, collaborative groups, other technology issues can emerge. These technical difficulties create a less-than-optimal experience for virtual attendees and may frustrate in-person participants if the training is delayed to fix issues. As one mid-sized insurance carrier shared with me after their transition to live mixed training, they needed multiple backup plans for connections and activities (as we also explored in chapter 9).

From the learner's perspective, the greater number of technical issues can be very distracting to the flow of learning. There can be long lag times if facilitators have to attend to technical issues that must be resolved before continuing. Lags in audio can also derail a session and hinder its success. Because there is so much happening in the learning environment between all the individualized virtual spaces and the in-room participants, there are several opportunities for learners to lose sight of where their focus should be. Any of these issues could easily disrupt a learning environment or a learner's focus.

Learning Experience Inequities

With live mixed learning, you work with two cohorts, each of whom join class differently. The in-room participants are one cohort, and the virtual attendees are the other. The challenge is ensuring that the remote participants do not feel like second-class citizens. Whenever this blend exists, even in meeting environments, the virtual attendees—if not on camera—are often inadvertently forgotten, ignored, or treated as less important than the in-person participants. If you interview these individuals, they often admit to feeling overlooked or left out, as most of the attention is given to those in the physical room.

I have experienced some facilitators unknowingly focus solely on the in-person participants, which reduces the virtual attendees to spectators who then watch the event passively. As we know, this is not the best way to learn, because optimal learning is interactive and experiential. From the facilitator's perspective, we are trying to create an experience that is inclusive of both online and on-site participants. In a live mixed environment, some have also felt a loss of communication and that the collaborative dynamic is not quite the same.

Facilitator Cognitive Overload

As we established earlier in the book, virtual training requires facilitators to manage several cognitive tasks concurrently—sharing a slide, annotating content and explaining it at the same time, keeping an eye on chat, and noticing when someone raises their virtual hand, to name a few. This is especially taxing for novice facilitators.

When we introduce live mixed learning, the mental load for preparing and facilitating these classes can be all consuming. Because instructors can be distracted with many more things that demand their attention, cognitive overload can become evident (Bower et al. 2013). Facilitators are still engaged in the tasks to manage a virtual training environment in addition to now leading the in-person group. As a live mixed facilitator, you may glance at your notes to determine what to explain next on a projected slide, but then, perhaps, a virtual attendee says they're not able to see the slide, you lose connection with your online co-facilitator, and an in-person participant raises their hand with a question. This can be a lot. Our working memory has its limits, and just like everything in the natural world, we can't do everything all at once. Splitting attention in so many ways is taxing on the facilitator and can overload them mentally. As a result, facilitators can become exhausted, overwhelmed, and ultimately less effective.

At the Ascilite Conference in Sydney, Australia, researchers presented studies on using this approach and noted how the instructors said it was challenging to maintain awareness of both the online groups and the on-site groups (Bower et al. 2013). As one educator put it, "You've got a lot of stuff going on in the background that you either choose to ignore or that you respond to" (Bower et al. 2013).

As with any task, the more experienced we are at managing two different cohorts at the same time, the more automated some of the work can become. The more automated the task, the less effort required from our working memory and the more we are freed up to be able to spend our cognitive resources on other things in the learning environment. We'll talk later about some considerations for you to help mitigate this as you teach live.

Significant Time Investment

Under the status quo, live mixed learning requires much more investment of time to prepare, coordinate, and test equipment to ensure all is connected and that all parties can hear and see correctly. Experts concur that more time is required of facilitators to ensure everything is working well than when only facilitating virtual training.

Because of this, we need to creatively manage the cognitive overload on facilitators, minimize distractions for learners from online or on-site cohorts, and prepare for the extensive setup, testing, and rehearsals needed to coordinate all the moving parts. These steps lend themselves to successful implementation of live mixed learning.

What can you do to create an optimal experience for both groups? In the next section, we'll address some considerations to address these common challenges to live mixed learning.

Preparation Considerations Before Mixed Classes Go Live

There are many things to keep in mind as a facilitator prepares to deliver a live mixed class. These include ensuring the requisite technology is in place, the technical setup and room support is ready, planning and preparation has been uniquely adapted for both locations, and you have communicated you have clear expectations. Let's examine them all.

Required Technology

To support a successful live mixed learning environment, you'll need specific technology in place. Here are some key requirements:

- Two in-room cameras
- A wireless microphone for in-room facilitator
- High-quality audio mics and an in-room speaker system
- Virtual training platform or video conferencing platform
- TV displays, large screens, or SMART boards
- Virtual participants' software and hardware, including cameras

Two In-Room Cameras

For integrated classroom technology, the in-room cameras each have different coverage assignments. The first camera must be able to follow the facilitator as they move around the room, even though facilitators tend to stay primarily in the front of the room. This movement can be controlled by a facilitator with a remote clicker that allows them to move the camera themselves, or you can purchase a roaming camera that automatically pans and follows the audio and movement of whoever is speaking. Roaming cameras can even zoom in automatically on individuals when the speak. The purpose of the second camera is to show the in-room participants to virtual participants. When this camera isn't there, the virtual learner can feel left out, or they may be curious about what is happening in the room because they cannot see anything except the facilitator. When virtual participants are also on camera (and can see the room and the on-site participants), it satisfies their curiosity for what the space and the other learners look like.

Wireless Microphone for On-Site Facilitator

We look to higher education for their leadership and expertise in this type of hybrid format. One of their strong recommendations is to provide a wireless microphone for the in-room facilitator. Not only does this allow the in-room facilitator to be more mobile, it also enables the virtual learners to hear them, regardless of where they are in the room, which otherwise could be an issue. Avoid using a laptop's built-in microphone as this can often cause distortion, echos, and tinny audio like you're in a cave. By far, the most negative comments about this training approach almost always have to do with poor audio. It's worth the investment to ensure the rooms and the facilitators are appropriately amplified with high-quality audio equipment.

 PRO TIP 93
Ensure the in-room facilitator has either a wireless lavalier microphone or a quality omnidirectional, in-room mic to facilitate mobility and quality audio.

High-Quality, In-Room Audio System

The most important element for live mixed learning is to work with your IT department and audio engineers to ensure you have high quality audio. Employing echo cancellation is also necessary to curtail sound system feedback. As hybrid expert Michael J. Sitte recommends, "spend the majority of your budget resources on the audio." When video freezes or doesn't work as well, the class can still find a way to move forward. However, poor audio can derail a live mixed class. This cannot be understated. You must get the audio right.

There are many ways to ensure quality audio. Some organizations use conference unit systems with built-in conferencing speakers and microphones to better amplify spoken audio for virtual learners. Zoom Rooms, for example, is software-based and allows for audio and video conferencing for in-room participants. This way, they connect with other rooms, people at their desktops, or even mobile devices. Zoom Rooms allows you to select your own hardware, and their software provides HD video and audio, screen sharing, annotation, and whiteboarding controlled from a touch screen. Other organizations have used Poly Studio cameras paired with omnidirectional microphones (like an Orb microphone) to pick up audio in any direction.

Michael Sitte shared with me how, in one successful hybrid setup, he and others installed speakers and six hanging microphones in the physical training room's ceiling. It is also important to clarify with in-room participants that if they have devices that are logged into the shared video conferencing platform they need to turn down their audio or make sure their microphones are turned off; otherwise, this could create a sound feedback loop.

PRO TIP 94
Prioritize audio technology as your largest expense and use quality and ease of use as top criteria for selecting supporting technology.

Video Conferencing Platform, TV Displays, Learner Hardware and Software

Clearly, you'll also need a virtual training platform (like Adobe Connect or Zoom), TV displays or SMART boards to share visuals with in-person and virtual participants, and cameras, devices with access to internet, and external microphones, headsets, or earbuds for virtual participants.

Leverage technology to best meet your needs. Prioritize audio and then allow ease of use and quality to guide your purchasing decisions. Some organizations have paired stand-alone equipment like a Poly Studio Premium USB video bar as an all-in-one conferencing system or Logitech Rally Bar conferencing device with motorized cameras and HD zoom, which serve as the built-in microphone, speaker, and cameras for the entire room. This way, whoever is attending the meeting virtually can see all the participants in the physical training room as well as a floating, smaller window of themselves, like a picture-in-picture feature. The camera is smart enough to detect when someone talks and will pan or zoom in accordingly to the individual speaking. If multiple people share aloud, the camera knows to zoom out to show all participants again. There may be a slight second or two delay for the camera to transition, however it gently pans so it's not dizzying to those watching on camera. To project in-room participants and enable them to see the video and audio of online participants on any large screen display, ClickShare Conferencing is a wireless conferencing system that can also help facilitate the audio and video of live mixed environments.

Setup and Room Support

Technical setup is critical to successful live mixed learning. The physical room selected is ideally dedicated to support the mixed format. As Sitte advises, these rooms should be carpeted, quiet, and away from noisy hallways or traffic sounds from nearby highways. In your company, government agency, or educational institution, find rooms that are shielded from heavy noise. Doing everything you can to ensure quality audio is paramount.

Setup also means visiting your in-room site and testing all the equipment to determine if you have all the technology you need. Test and ensure the audio is always high-quality for all cohorts regardless of location. Many virtual learners complain about not being able to adequately hear the facilitator or in-person attendees when they share aloud. If you are delivering on-site, have a colleague, IT staff, your producer, or a virtual co-facilitator be online to test the quality of the audio. Test and adjust for potential delays on the recipient end. As you move around the room, ask them to tell you when your sound is no longer audible or if the quality diminishes. This shows you the range you need to stay within. This is also true for the camera. If you use a roaming camera, test it out to learn where in the room you can go and be seen, and likewise where virtual learners cannot see you.

Another pioneer educator with the hybrid model is Dean Stewart, executive director of the Center for Exceptional Leadership at St. Norbert College's School of Business and Economics. As Stewart shared with me, "class setup matters" for the hybrid type format. When determining how to include both virtual and in-person attendees in their leadership cohorts with client organizations, he and other strategic leaders and educators worked collaboratively to thoughtfully design the space. "In-person attendees are seated in a U-shaped table in the traditional, in-person classroom," explained Stewart. "Then we use a large 65-inch monitor, which is a Neat Board and is on wheels, where we project Zoom with virtual attendees and roll the board in to fill the open space at the end of the U-shaped table." Literally, "this way everyone has a seat at the table."

Here are some considerations to guide class setup for live mixed learning. Consider the influence of physical setup. Subtle classroom setup dynamics influence not only how participants interact with each other, but also how participants interact with the facilitator. Just as room layout from auditorium style versus table groups can make a dramatic difference on the type of interaction that takes place, this is also true for hybrid situations. Think about desk placement in the physical room and camera placement that is the most inclusive.

PRO TIP 95
Thoughtfully arrange the physical setup by recognizing its influence on sharing and discussion within the space.

Planning and Preparation for Live Mixed Learning

Planning and preparation for the live mixed approach cannot be understated. It often requires more prep than you would otherwise experience with other delivery methods. Complete as much prep work as possible before class day. This might include placing all handouts and resources on the LMS ahead of time, setting up breakouts with the activities already listed on whiteboards, and being crystal clear about any instructions by also providing these in writing in advance (Bower et al. 2013). Share technical requirements with all virtual attendees ahead of time.

When looking for feedforward advice in the design phase, collect input from a learner who will represent the remote experience and a learner who will represent the in-person experience. Let's explore some specific strategies to help ensure your live mixed class is successful.

Keep Total Class Size Small

It's best to keep the total number of participants small, to the tune of 15 or fewer, until you become comfortable with this format. This is because there is added complexity and more to manage. The exception to this is if you have a very seasoned, lead facilitator who can successfully manage a larger class. Keeping class size smaller is one of the things you have control over and will help keep your class more manageable overall.

Try to Meet in Person With Everyone for the First Class

When you first build a hybrid or remote work team, it may be the worth the investment to fly everybody in to meet in person. This can help build those foundational work relationships when people are in closer proximity. Over time, the teams' productivity, their ability to work well together, the synergy and health of the team (contrasted with dysfunction in a team), earned trust, and cohesive bonding can all stem from initial relationship building. However, clearly this may not be feasible with extenuating circumstances like a pandemic or budget limitations.

The same can also be said for robust training programs where learners will be learning together over multiple weeks or months. As Dean Stewart explained, his live mixed leadership classes invite all participants to attend the first class in person. This helps place everyone on even footing. He said this format works extremely well because the core relationships first established in person then carry through the entirety of the program.

Allow Learners to Choose Their Primary Location Venue

One of the advantages of this format is its flexibility. Give learners the option to be in-person or virtual. This gives them the freedom to opt in, and the autonomy empowers them. However, if they are in-person one day and virtual the next, it can create more complexity and technical surprises. For this reason, they should choose how they will join for the duration of the program and commit to that format. To make the live mixed training worth your time, set a minimum expectation for how many on-site attendees you'll need. For example, if only one or two learners choose to be on-site, you need to determine whether it is worth the investment or if the class would be better served as all virtual.

PRO TIP 96
Allow learners to choose whether to attend the training program virtually or in person to honor their preferences and accommodate their schedules.

Establish Clear Expectations

Setting clear expectations prior to the live online learning event is always a best practice, even with live mixed learning. Request online participants log in at least 10 minutes early to every class. In both your pre-session messaging and at the beginning of the session, encourage all learners to turn off mobile phones, find a quiet environment, let colleagues around them know they're in training, and minimize learning distractions in their own environments for the sake of themselves and others. Additionally, be crystal clear on your instructions for any activities. If you ask a volunteer learner to paraphrase back your instructions, this gives you an opportunity to clarify any gaps between what was said and what was heard. When training across time zones, reference the time zone most common to virtual participants as well as the time zone where the physical class is being held. This helps convert and call attention to their time. For example, you might say, "We'll take a 10 minute break. For those of you on-site, it's 1 p.m. Pacific; we'll see you back here at 1:10 p.m. For those of you on Eastern time, we'll see you at 4:10 p.m. Have a good break!" This adds a customized touch and reminds them you recognize where they are.

Considerations for Successful Facilitation During Live Mixed Classes

We've explored preparatory considerations before going live, now let's turn our attention to how to best facilitate during class. There are several strategies you can follow to contribute to the success of your live mixed sessions. They include using co-facilitators, partnering with IT, sharing netiquette, building interconnection, using the same learning activities regardless of learner location, and countering implicit in-room bias.

Use Co-Facilitators

For larger classes, it's best to use co-facilitators and position one facilitator remotely and one in the physical room. Select one person to be the lead facilitator, particularly an experienced facilitator for both in-person and virtual. This individual could lead the class from either location. Sourcing facilitators in both locations helps learners feel supported, knowing that there's a leader in the space that they're also in. This also provides a spokesperson to speak on their behalf as needed, troubleshoot issues, or respond to their questions. This way, the mental load and duties are shared among co-facilitators, which makes it more manageable.

This is also a way to reduce the high cognitive load associated with teaching a live mixed class by sharing the facilitator role, along with also having IT on board to help produce the event. When there are multiple instructors, learners get different perspectives and more variety. This can also aid the dynamic engagement discussed in chapter 8 and can also provide a richer experience overall, especially in terms of the social and emotional dimensions of learning. Keep in mind that based on how many learners there are in the class, the number of facilitators assisting can be appropriately scaled.

There can be variations of live mixed as well. For one of my clients, I was the lead facilitator virtually connecting from the US Midwest. My client was on the East Coast and everyone was on-site together in the same room. They could all see me virtually on a big screen in their room. I requested a client contact be the facilitator to serve as my eyes and ears in the room. I relied on this individual to be the point person for sharing learner comments and encouraging their interactions, which worked very well.

PRO TIP 97
Use co-facilitators with live mixed classes and designate a lead facilitator (either on-site or online). Place the other co-facilitator in the alternate location.

Partner With IT Technicians or Arrange for On-Call Technical Support

When things go wrong in the live mixed class, there usually isn't time to fix them. As discussed earlier, longer lag times can distract and interrupt the flow of learning. For this reason, immediate online support is essential to prevent derailing distractions and frustrating learning experiences. Here are some of the ways mixed learning pioneers have found success.

One option is to partner with IT or a technical specialist. Speak with your IT department to see if they can dedicate staff to specifically support the live mixed learning rooms. They may also attend to other technical support issues for the organization, but having dedicated IT staff can help resolve any issues immediately. Partnering with IT also provides learners with a responsive and credible IT hotline to help them quickly address and resolve technical issues with the connection or platform (Boyarsky 2020).

If possible, request an IT specialist be available for tech rehearsals and at the beginning of the session to troubleshoot any issues as needed. Better yet, invite them to attend remotely for the duration. Seasoned hybrid instructor Michael Sitte recommends having an IT staff person attend as a remote participant who stays on for the entire class to assist with any technical difficulties. This way they are right there and always ready to help resolve any issue.

If you have a tech-savvy facilitator, they could also serve as a technical producer. For your initial classes, especially those that span over time for a virtual program, invite IT to be present to assist with technology challenges. Alternatively, equip your co-facilitators to be technically savvy to troubleshoot as needed.

PRO TIP 98
Invite an IT technician to be present for tech checks before class day, attend class virtually to address issues, or be accessible on call.

Establish Netiquette Guidelines for Live Mixed Class

Part of the educational piece for the virtual learner is knowing when and how to communicate. To set them up for success, tee up learners with pre-class communications from both the LMS and the facilitators to clarify exactly what hardware, software, and equipment they need for a successful class and to optimize their experience and manage expectations about what they'll do and why they're doing it.

In addition to setting expectations ahead of time via pre-session communications, you also want to establish them very clearly up-front during the session. One of the best ways to establish expectations is to communicate them through netiquette. For example, encourage participants to take initiative and speak up if they cannot hear well, avoid in-room side conversations, mute themselves when not speaking online, and use a headset if remote. As experienced live mixed instructor Kim Huettl shared with me, "Etiquette is really important for hybrid."

Another netiquette guideline you might consider adding is a recommendation that emerged out of seven case studies from educators in New Zealand and Australia. Request all learners type "Q" first in chat before typing a question. This way facilitators can quickly scan, identify, and respond to the posted questions (Bower et al. 2013).

PRO TIP 99
Clarify netiquette guidelines relevant to live mixed interactions for all in-person and virtual learners.

Build in Opportunities for Interconnection and Collaboration Among the Two Cohorts

To build a hybrid learning culture at an organization, be on the lookout for opportunities where the two groups can interact with each other. For example, during group discussions, on-site learners can play off comments from virtual learners and vice versa. Leveraging paired learning is another example. Some organizations have found success creating a partnership between a remote learner and an in-room participant so that they have the opportunity for paired chat. They would need time, of course, to meet, greet, and connect with an opening activity to build that relationship pairing early on in class. The prerequisite is that in-room participants would also need their laptops or mobile phones for some class activities. The online and on-site partnership allows them to communicate and ask questions more comfortably among themselves because a pairing is less intimidating than raising a question or comment to the group at large. For example, if a virtual learner missed where the assignment was posted, they could chat with their partner about where it is rather than asking the facilitator. This creates a support system for the virtual attendees, who can sometimes feel slightly at a disadvantage compared with those attending in person.

To build an environment that encourages community and a unified class, language can also provide cues. Be sure to model by actions and your language that "it's not an 'us and them' mentality . . . but instead a 'we' dynamic" (Finegan 2021).

Use the Same Learning Activities for All

Participants do better when you weave uniform experiences in regardless of whether they're in person or virtual. Work to ensure learning activities can be completed by both regardless of location. Level the playing field for all as much as you can.

To maintain a similar experience for both in-person and virtual participants, use a SMART Board that all can see in-room and is also projected online. When you use a poll, ensure all can access it digitally to vote. When you ask them to chat, allow all to use the online chat if they wish. Allow for slight variances as needed, while ensuring an equitable experience. For both cohorts, you can leverage Q&A, rich group discussions, rotating presentations, feedback, group brainstorming, and small-group work.

Applying what we learned in chapter 2 about live mixed learning, gather perspectives from a few real virtual learners and in-room learners to inform the overall design. Designers needs to think carefully about which exercises can be done well in the classroom, and how to convert them so they are suitable for the virtual platform as well. For example, it's best to use the same medium for brainstorming and documenting ideas. Use online whiteboards to document for all to see. Be flexible. Another example of a learning activity designed to suit both audiences would be posing a discussion question for all to contribute to verbally, or assigning a challenging scenario for them to solve in their small breakout groups.

Breakouts

Higher education has been a leader in hybrid breakout activities as they have adopted best practices working with both on-site and online learners for years. Michael Sitte and his colleagues discovered it worked best to divide in-person attendees into small discussion groups within the physical room, while virtual attendees were divided into virtual breakout rooms. This way, there was less complication with technology issues and there wasn't a lot of talking over each other. The downside to this is that virtual will be working with the same group all the time, and they often feel slightly disadvantaged because they don't have eyes and ears in the room.

Experienced instructor Katherine Dalland mixes remote learners with in-person learners during breakouts so remote learners don't feel like a separate learning group. To make this feasible, she sends in-room learners into other areas (extending outside the original classroom as needed) and makes sure all are connected with their own headsets and laptops.

Whiteboarding

For collaborative whiteboarding, make sure all can participate equally on a shared whiteboard. For example, if you have a Zoom Room, all participants should be able to see the whiteboarding completed in-room and online. If you are using an in-room SMART Board, you can annotate on the whiteboard, which will then be displayed to virtual learners. Alternatively, in-room participants with laptops can contribute to the same whiteboard tool virtual participants use through the video conferencing platform.

Counter In-Room Implicit Bias

Without realizing it, we can demonstrate a preference for one group over another—typically the in-person cohort—without conscious knowledge. Be aware that facilitators can unknowingly attend more to in-person learners when they are also in person. This doesn't seem to be the case when a lead facilitator is virtual. In my experience, when I've been the lead facilitator virtually and had another facilitator at the on-site location, we were all able to equally participate. The on-site facilitator was the point person for on-site participants. As a counter strategy, cater to the virtual first, and then rotate back and forth.

If you include round robins, icebreakers, or question prompts, call on virtual attendees first. As this is the group most often forgotten (especially when they are not onscreen), disciplining yourself to always ask a remote learner first will help you be inclusive.

PRO TIP 100
Maintain an equitable experience in learning activities regardless of whether participants are remote or on-site.

Additional Considerations

As you weigh whether live mixed learning is viable for you or your organization, here are some additional considerations to help with your decision, approach, design, preparation, and implementation. Many lessons are pulled from higher education, as they more broadly apply this method. Lessons can also be drawn from corporate hybrid meetings, which also showcase the live mixed environment.

Train Facilitators for Live Mixed Format

One tip is to offer workshops and drop-in rehearsals so facilitators can learn how to use the equipment, IT support resources, and other considerations for being successful live mixed facilitators. Michael Sitte encourages new adopters to approach the process with patience, test it out first, and do their best to avoid getting frustrated. He recommends offering training for instructors ahead of time by beginning with early adopters. From there, mentor and coach others to use the new mixed approach to learning and continue to share best practices for the community of facilitators who use the space.

Selecting facilitators to lead live mixed classes who demonstrate competence in all the capabilities discussed in this book is ideal. These facilitators possess the knowledge and skills in the areas of experience design, environment shaping, online facilitation, facilitator presence, technical fluency, dynamic engagement, agile troubleshooting, and evaluating impact. The instructor's capabilities have been found in several studies to be one of the critical factors of success for live mixed sessions and their respective activities (Bower et al. 2013).

Record Sessions

Researchers have also discovered that recording sessions is important for live mixed learning. This is a way to capture all the combined interactions of the mixed learning experiences, which learners can reference later (Bower et al. 2013).

So far in the live mixed format, we've discussed two learner groups (your on-site and your online learners). However, if you plan to record your sessions, you also have a third audience: the on-demand, asynchronous learners. This is important because during your live sessions, you should also occasionally refer to this third group to customize it to them as well. For example, if I know that my live mixed class will be recorded and made available for asynchronous learners to view on demand, while I'm training I might say, "Welcome to those of you joining us online, in the room, and to those of you watching this recording" or "for those of you watching the recording, go ahead and do this exercise with us too." This way you grab the attention of all your learner groups and speak directly to them.

In a similar vein, as lead facilitator, I try to always make sure I am cognizant of being inclusive by describing what each group cannot see. This is imperative if learners are listening to audio playback while driving or perhaps don't have access to the video portion. This is similar to the prescriptive tip covered in chapter 4 about making the invisible audible. For example, if the camera that displays in-room participants is off or unavailable, virtual learners cannot see in-room learners. If this happens, I make a mental note to verbalize what they cannot see. In a leadership class, let's say I ask on-site learners to raise their hands if they've been a manager before. In-room learners would physically raise their hands and virtual learners would normally raise their hands using the platform's hand-raising prompts. If I know virtual learners cannot see their on-site peers, I might say "for those of you online, about 75 percent of the 12 of us here in the room just raised their hands, and it looks like all raised their virtual hands online." This way everyone feels included and part of the action.

Improve by Evaluating and Collecting Learner Feedback

In chapter 10, we learned the importance of evaluating the effectiveness of the training solutions you deliver. Be open to collecting feedback from both online and on-site learners to best determine how to improve your offering. Remember, some of the best ideas come directly from your learners. Apply the evaluating impact capability to evaluate the impact the program is having on your organization as well as the application, learning, and reaction of learners.

Deliver Live Mixed as a Blended Learning Program

As discussed in the previous chapter, blended learning solutions combine the best of both worlds. As we turn our focus to live mixed learning, we can optimize the benefits of this approach by designing blended learning programs. As Kim Huettl shared with me, you really want to maximize the time you're together in the hybrid environment for activities that lend themselves to being together. For example, peer feedback can be shared asynchronously so that synchronous class time can be devoted to collaborative-type activities. In live mixed, you can include "collaborative evaluation, group questioning, joint problem solving, role-play, whole-class discussions, and collaborative design tasks" (Bower et al. 2013). "By bringing together the two contexts and continuing to utilize the opportunities that remote learning has to offer—asynchronous learning, self-paced lessons, personalized pathways, additional one-on-one touch points—we can help students to continue to learn and grow together, as one class, no matter where they are physically" (Finegan 2021). Online exercises like viewing videos as supporting learning activities, for example, combine the benefits of in-person and virtual learning while providing access for all regardless of where they're located (Boyarsky 2020).

 PRO TIP 101
Leverage the benefits of blended learning by coupling asynchronous assignments with synchronous, live mixed learning.

Summary

Successful live mixed learning requires first and foremost, high-quality audio, supporting hardware and software technologies, extensive preparation, equitable learning activities, and skilled co-facilitators. This chapter outlined a variety of considerations for you and your organization so you can weigh whether live mixed learning is viable. We've explored what live mixed is, its advantages and challenges, and considerations before going live while facilitating.

We are currently in the middle of accelerated development in this area. Ease of use and quality should remain guiding criteria as you purchase technologies to support live mixed learning. As the modern workforce continues to adopt hybrid and remote work models, more organizations will use this delivery approach. As they do, the service technology will improve and perhaps one day the divisions between on-site and online will feel more united. More research, experimentation, observation, and best practices are still needed for this instructional approach.

Whether live mixed learning is appropriate for your organization depends on whether you have the supporting technology, need the location flexibility for your learners, have the ability to source multiple skilled facilitators, can provide design flexibility, are training topics that do not need to be hands on, can offer smaller class sizes, and have access to additional IT support. Although this solution may not be recommended for every virtual training class, do reflect on whether adopting live mixed learning makes sense for some of your training topics and programs. It may yet be another opportunity for training improvement. As Dean Stewart put it, we should explore what this venue opens up in terms of possibilities that could work even better.

As we embrace a global hybrid workforce, let's keep several things in mind. First, recognize that virtual training is here to stay. We know virtual learning can be effective across time, space, and distance. The need to upskill has never been greater. Second, remember that the eight core virtual trainer capabilities are meant to guide your development and your craft. The Virtual Trainer Capability Model provides a framework to help build your skills and advance the profession. Third, there is a plethora of knowledge and tips outlined for you in this book. Take the opportunity to digest, experiment, and reflect on each of the tips in the chapter summaries.

Because we are in a profession that helps others develop new knowledge and skills, my hope is that this book has helped you develop new knowledge and skills too. It is because you invest in others that this book has invested in you. As we rise to the challenge, let's set the bar high by pushing ourselves to be better virtual trainers and online facilitators. Why? Because worldwide learners and future generations deserve our best. Together we make an investment in the most precious commodity we have—the global workforce.

Ultimately, remember that as we eventually reach full competence in experience design, environment shaping, online facilitation, facilitator presence, technical fluency, dynamic engagement, agile troubleshooting, and evaluating impact, all of these interconnected capabilities will help us take our virtual training to the next level. I wish you continued success as you upskill, reskill, and innovate. I'm excited to see what you'll do next! Now let's go transform the L&D world . . . one virtual training program at a time.

Pro Tips for Training With Live Mixed Learning

TIP 93	Ensure the in-room facilitator has either a wireless lavalier microphone or a quality omnidirectional, in-room mic to facilitate mobility and quality audio.
TIP 94	Prioritize audio technology as your largest expense and use quality and ease of use as top criteria for selecting supporting technology.
TIP 95	Thoughtfully arrange the physical setup by recognizing its influence on sharing and discussion within the space.
TIP 96	Allow learners to choose whether to attend the training program virtually or in person to honor their preferences and accommodate their schedules.
TIP 97	Use co-facilitators with live mixed classes and designate a lead facilitator (either on-site or online) and place the other co-facilitator in the alternate location.
TIP 98	Invite an IT technician to be present for tech checks before class day, attend class virtually to address issues, or be accessible on call.
TIP 99	Clarify netiquette guidelines relevant to live mixed interactions for all in-person and virtual learners.
TIP 100	Maintain an equitable experience in learning activities regardless of whether participants are remote or on-site.
TIP 101	Leverage the benefits of blended learning by coupling asynchronous assignments with synchronous, live mixed learning.

References

Allen, M.W. 2007. *Designing Successful E-Learning: Forget What You Know About Instructional Design and Do Something Interesting.* San Francisco: Pfeiffer.

Allen, M.W. 2012. *Leaving ADDIE for SAM: An Agile Model for Developing the Best Learning Experiences.* Alexandria, VA: ATD Press.

Allen, M.W., J. Dirksen, C. Quinn, and W. Thalheimer. 2014. "A Serious E-Learning Manifesto." Chapter 22 in *ASTD Handbook: The Definitive Reference for Training and Development,* edited by E. Biech. Alexandria, VA: ATD Press.

Anderson, J., L. Rainie, and E.A. Vogels. 2021. "Experts Say the 'New Normal' in 2025 Will Be Far More Tech-Driven, Presenting More Big Challenges." Pew Research Center, February 18. pewresearch.org /internet/2021/02/18/experts-say-the-new-normal-in-2025-will-be -far-more-tech-driven-presenting-more-big-challenges.

Andreatta, B. 2018. *Wired To Connect: The Brain Science of Teams and a New Model for Creating Collaboration and Inclusion.* Santa Barbara, CA: 7th Mind Publishing.

APA (American Psychological Association). 2020. "Habituation." *APA Dictionary of Psychology.* dictionary.apa.org/habituation.

Aristotle. 1954. *The Rhetoric and The Poetics of Aristotle.* Translated by W. Rhys Roberts and I. Bywater. New York: Random House.

ATD (Association for Talent Development). 2020. *2020 State of the Industry: Talent Development Benchmarks and Trends.* Alexandria, VA: ATD.

ATD (Association for Talent Development). 2021. *Virtual Classrooms: Leveraging Technology for Impact.* Alexandria, VA: ATD Press.

Atkinson, C., and R.E. Mayer. 2004. "Five Ways to Reduce PowerPoint Overload." *Creative Commons* 1(1): 1–15.

Barrero, J.M., N. Bloom, and S.J. Davis. 2021. *Why Working From Home Will Stick*. Working paper no. 28731. Cambridge, MA: National Bureau of Economic Research.

Berrett, D. 2015. "How Flipping the Classroom Can Improve the Traditional Lecture." In *A Guide to the Flipped Classroom*. Washington, DC: Chronicle of Higher Education.

Bersin, J. 2020. "A Framework for Optimizing the Virtual Live Learning Experience." Whitepaper, Adobe Connect, 2–4. adobe.com/content /dam/cc/us/en/products/adobe-connect/resources/framework_for _optimizing_live_virtual_learning_experience_whitepaper_2020.pdf.

Biech, E. 2017. *The Art and Science of Training*. Alexandria, VA: ATD Press.

Bloom, B.S., M.D. Englehart, E.J. Furst, W.H. Hill, and D.R. Krathwohl. 1956. *Taxonomy of Educational Objectives: The Classification of Educational Goals, Handbook 1: The Cognitive Domain*. New York: David McKay Co.

Boller, S., and L. Fletcher. 2020. *Design Thinking for Training and Development: Creating Learning Journeys That Get Results*. Alexandria, VA: ATD Press.

Bower, M., J. Kenney, B. Dalgarno, M.J.W. Lee, and G.E. Kennedy. 2013. "Blended Synchronous Learning: Patterns and Principles for Simultaneously Engaging Co-Located and Distributed Learners." Presented at the 30th Ascilite Conference at Macquarie University, Sydney, Australia, December 1–4, 92–101.

Boyarsky, K. 2020. "What Is Hybrid Learning? Here's Everything You Need to Know." OWL LABS, June. resources.owllabs.com/blog /hybrid-learning.

Bozarth, J. 2016a. "Nuts and Bolts: How to Rock Your Virtual Classroom with Participant Chat." *Learning Solutions*, May 3. learningsolutionsmag.com/articles/1953/nuts-and-bolts-how-to -rock-your-virtual-classroom-with-participant-chat.

Bozarth, J. 2016b. "Nuts and Bolts: Rocking the Virtual Classroom— What About That Whiteboard?" *Learning Solutions*, April 5. learningsolutionsmag.com/articles/1938/nuts-and-bolts-rocking -the-virtual-classroomwhat-about-that-whiteboard.

Bozarth, J. 2020. *Less Content, More Learner: An Overview of Learning Experience Design.* The Learning Guild, May 13. learningguild.com /insights/250/less-content-more-learner-an-overview-of-learning -experience-design.

Buffer. 2021. "The 2021 State of Remote Work: Top Insights and Data from One of the Largest Remote Work Reports." Buffer. buffer.com /2021-state-of-remote-work.

Bundy, C.B., and L. Howles. 2017. "Interactive Case Scenarios: The 7 Cs Framework," *Educause,* October 23. library.educause.edu/resources /2017/10/interactive-case-scenarios-the-7cs-framework.

Burnison, G. 2019. "7 Years Ago, Google Set Out to Find What Makes the 'Perfect' Team—and What They Found Shocked Other Researchers." CNBC, February 28. cnbc.com/2019/02/28/what-google-learned-in -its-quest-to-build-the-perfect-team.html.

Christensen, C.M., T. Hall, K. Dillon, and D.S. Duncan. 2016. *Competing Against Luck: The Story of Innovation and Customer Choice.* New York: Harper Business.

Christopher, D. 2011. "Facilitating in the Global Virtual Classroom." *InfoLine.* Alexandria, VA: ASTD Press.

Christopher, D. 2015. *The Successful Virtual Classroom: How to Design and Facilitate Interactive and Engaging Live Online Learning.* New York: AMACOM.

Clark, R.E., and J. Elen. 2006. "When Less is More: Research and Theory Insights about Instruction for Complex Learning." *Handling Complexity in Learning Environments: Research and Theory.* Bingley, UK: Emerald Group Publishing.

Clark, R.C. 2020. *Evidence-Based Training Methods: A Guide for Training Professionals,* 3rd ed. Alexandria, VA: ATD Press.

Clark, R.C., and A. Kwinn. 2007. *The New Virtual Classroom: Evidence-Based Guidelines for Synchronous e-Learning.* San Francisco: John Wiley & Sons.

Clark, R.C., F. Nguyen, and J. Sweller. 2006. *Efficiency in Learning: Evidence-Based Guidelines to Manage Cognitive Load.* San Francisco: John Wiley & Sons.

Conceição, S.C.O., and L.L. Howles. 2021. *Designing the Online Learning Experience: Evidence-Based Principles and Strategies*. Sterling, VA: Stylus Publishing.

Cross, J. 2007. "What Is Informal Learning?" Informal Learning, November 27.

Cuddy, A. 2015. *Presence: Bringing your Boldest Self to your Biggest Challenges*. New York: Little, Brown Spark.

D'Mello, S., B. Lehman, R. Pekrun, and A. Graesser. 2014. "Confusion can be Beneficial for Learning." *Learning and Instruction* 29:153–170.

Dennen, V.P., K.D. Word, and Ö. Arslan. 2021. "Webcams at Work: A Survey of Learning Professionals' Practices and Perceptions." Research Brief, Instructional Systems & Learning Technologies, Florida State University. purl.flvc.org/fsu/fd/FSU_libsubv1 _scholarship_submission_1621457890_5284fd79.

Di Vesta, F.J., and D.A. Smith. 1979. "The Pausing Principle: Increasing the Efficiency of Memory for Ongoing Events." *Contemporary Educational Psychology* 4(3): 288–296.

Dirksen, J. 2012. *Design for How People Learn*. Berkeley, CA: New Riders.

DiSalvo, B., J. Yip, E. Bonsignore, and C. DiSalvo, eds. 2017. *Participatory Design for Learning: Perspectives from Research and Practice*. New York: Routledge.

Douglas, J., and S. McKenzie. 2016. *Let Them Choose: Cafeteria Learning Style for Adults*. Alexandria, VA: ATD Press.

Draves, W.A. 2000. *Teaching Online*. River Falls, WI: LERN Books.

Duarte, N. 2008. *Slide:ology: The Art and Science of Creating Great Presentations*. Sebastopol, CA: O'Reilly Media.

Duhigg, C. 2016. *Smarter Faster Better: The Transformative Power of Real Productivity*. New York: Random House.

Edmondson, A. 2019. *The Fearless Organization: Creating Psychological Safety in the Workplace for Learning, Innovation, and Growth*. Hoboken, NJ: John Wiley & Sons.

Edmondson, A. 2020. "Fearless—Creating Psychological Safety for Learning, Innovation, and Growth." The AAMC Annual Meeting, April 30. youtube.com/watch?v=_1Ub1xfSQ1s.

Edmondson, A.C., and G. Daley. 2020. "How to Foster Psychological Safety in Virtual Meetings." *Harvard Business Review,* August 25. hbr.org/2020/08/how-to-foster-psychological-safety-in-virtual-meetings.

Elkeles, T., P.P. Phillips, and J.J. Phillips. 2014. *Measuring the Success of Learning Through Technology.* Alexandria, VA: ATD Press.

Finegan, J. 2021. "5 Keys to Success in Hybrid Learning," Edutopia, May 12. edutopia.org/article/5-keys-success-hybrid-learning.

Finn, B. 2010. "Ending on a High Note: Adding a Better End to Effortful Study." *Journal of Experimental Psychology: Learning, Memory, and Cognition* 36(6): 1548.

Fusco, J., P. Ruiz, and J. Roschelle. 2021. "AI or Intelligence Augmentation for Education?" *Communications of the ACM,* July (12). cacm.acm.org/blogs/blog-cacm/251188-ai-or-intelligence-augmentation-for-education/fulltext.

Google. 2018. "Google Duplex: AI Assistant Calls Local Businesses to Make Appointments." Sundar Pichai presentation, May 8. youtube.com/watch?v=D5VN56jQMWM.

Hofmann, J. 2004. *Live and Online!: Tips, Techniques, and Ready-to-Use Activities for the Virtual Classroom.* San Francisco: Pfeiffer.

Hofmann, J. 2019. *The Modern Virtual Classroom Experience. Book 1: Facilitating the Experience: Developing Competence and Creating Engagement.* Portsmouth, NH: InSync Training.

Horn, R.E., E.H. Nicol, J.C. Kleinman, and M.G. Grace. 1969. *Information Mapping for Learning and Reference.* Cambridge, MA: Information Resources.

Horton, W. 2006. *E-Learning by Design.* San Francisco: John Wiley & Sons.

Horton, W. 2012. *E-Learning by Design,* 2nd ed. San Francisco: John Wiley & Sons.

Horwath, A. 2021. "Tailor-Made Evaluation." *TD,* April. td.org/magazines/td-magazine/tailor-made-evaluation.

Howles, D.L. 2015. "Design Tips for Flipping the Virtual Classroom." *Learning Solutions,* June. learningsolutionsmag.com/articles/1721/design-tips-for-flipping-the-virtual-classroom.

Howles, D.L. 2020. "Making the Shift to Virtual Training." *Learning Solutions*, May. learningsolutionsmag.com/articles/making-the -shift-to-virtual-training.

Howles, L. 2020. "Interview With Dr. Janet Zadina: Applying Educational Neuroscience Research to Instruction and elearning." *eLearn* 2020(5).

Hubbard, D.W. 2010. *How to Measure Anything: Finding the Value of Intangibles in Business,* 2nd ed. Hoboken, NJ: John Wiley & Sons.

Huggett, C. 2017. *Virtual Training Tools and Templates: An Action Guide to Live Online Learning,* Alexandria, VA: ATD Press.

Huggett, C. 2020. "The State of Virtual Training 2020." Cindy Huggett Blog, October 16. cindyhuggett.com/blog/2020sovt.

Immersive Learning News. 2020. "Understanding the Neuroscience of Learning." Immersive Learning News, March 14. immersivelearning .news/2020/03/14/learning-is-an-experience-everything-else-is-just -information-albert-einstein.

Interaction Design Foundation. 2021. "Design Thinking." interaction -design.org.

Jiang, M. 2020. "The Reason Zoom Calls Drain your Energy." Remote Control blog, April 22. bbc.com/worklife/article/20200421-why -zoom-video-chats-are-so-exhausting.

Kahneman, D., B.L. Fredrickson, C.A. Schreiber, and D.A. Redelmeier. 1993. "When More Pain Is Preferred to Less: Adding a Better End." *Psychological Science* 4(6): 401–405.

Kane, P. 2021. "The Great Resignation Is Here, and It's Real." *Inc.,* August 26. inc.com/phillip-kane/the-great-resignation-is-here-its -real.html.

Kang, S.H.K., K.B. McDermott, and H.L. Roediger III. 2007. "Test Format and Corrective Feedback Modify the Effect of Testing on Long-term Retention." *European Journal of Cognitive Psychology* 19(4–5): 528–558.

Kapp, K.M., L. Blair, and R. Mesch. 2014. *The Gamification of Learning and Instruction Fieldbook: Ideas Into Practice.* San Francisco: John Wiley & Sons.

Keller, J.M. 2009. *Motivational Design for Learning and Performance: The ARCS Model Approach.* New York: Springer Science & Business Media.

Kirkpatrick, D.L. 1956. "How to Start an Objective Evaluation of your Training Program." *Journal of the American Society of Training Directors* 10:18–22.

Kirkpatrick, D.L. 1996. *Evaluating Training Programs: The Four Levels.* Oakland, CA: Berrett-Koehler Publishers.

Kirkpatrick, D.L., and J.D. Kirkpatrick. 2006. *Evaluating Training Programs: The Four Levels,* 3rd ed. Oakland, CA: Berrett-Koehler Publishers.

Kirkpatrick Partners. 2021. "The Kirkpatrick Model." Kirkpatrick Partners. kirkpatrickpartners.com/the-kirkpatrick-model.

Kizilcec, R.F., J.N. Bailenson, and C.J. Gomez. 2015. "The Instructor's Face in Video Instruction: Evidence from Two Large-scale Field Studies." *Journal of Educational Psychology* 107(3): 724–739.

Kotb, H. 2021. "Jade Carey Talks About Winning Gold Medal in Floor Exercise." *Today Show,* August 2. today.com/video/jade-carey-talks -about-winning-gold-medal-in-floor-exercise-117751365509.

Krulwich, R. 2011. "A (Shockingly) Short History of Hello." NPR Wisconsin Public Radio, February 17. npr.org/sections/krulwich /2011/02/17/133785829/a-shockingly-short-history-of-hello.

LaBorie, K. 2021. *Producing Virtual Training, Meetings, and Webinars: Master the Technology to Engage Participants.* Alexandria, VA: ATD Press.

LibQuotes. 2021. "Isaac Newton Quote." libquotes.com/isaac-newton/ quote/lbk9b1x.

Liedtke, M. 2021. "Zoom's Boom Continues in 1Q, Raising Post-Pandemic Hopes." *US News & World Report,* June 1. usnews.com/news/business /articles/2021-06-01/zooms-boom-continues-in-1q-raising-post- pandemic-hopes.

MacLeod, E. 1999. *Alexander Graham Bell: An Inventive Life.* Toronto: Kids Can Press.

Masie, E. 2021. "My Post-Pandemic Learning List." *Chief Learning Officer Magazine,* June 4.

MasterClass. 2021. "How to Recognize the 5 Stages of Group Development." MasterClass Business. masterclass.com/articles /how-to-recognize-the-5-stages-of-group-development.

Mayer, R.E. 2014. "Principles Based on Social Cues in Multimedia Learning: Personalization, Voice, Image, and Embodiment Principles." In *The Cambridge Handbook of Multimedia Learning,* edited by Richard E. Mayer. New York: Cambridge University Press.

Mayer, R.E., and L. Fiorella. 2014. "Principles for Reducing Extraneous Processing in Multimedia Learning: Coherence, Signaling, Redundancy, Spatial Contiguity, and Temporal Contiguity Principles." In *The Cambridge Handbook of Multimedia Learning,* edited by Richard E. Mayer. New York: Cambridge University Press.

Mayer, R.E., and R. Moreno. 2003. "Nine Ways to Reduce Cognitive Load in Multimedia Learning." *Educational Psychologist* 38(1): 43-52.

McLuhan, M. 1964. *Understanding Media: The Extensions of Man.* New York: McGraw-Hill.

McLuhan, M., and B. Nevitt. 1972. *TAKE TODAY: The Executive as Dropout.* New York: Harcourt Brace Jovanovich.

Means, B., Y. Toyama, R. Murphy, M. Bakia, and K. Jones. 2009. "Evaluation of Evidence-based Practices in Online Learning: A Meta-analysis and Review of Online Learning Studies." Washington, DC: US Department of Education, Office of Planning, Evaluation, and Policy Development.

Merrill, M.D. 2017. "Using the First Principles of Instruction to Make Instruction Effective, Efficient, and Engaging." In *Foundations of Learning and Instructional Design Technology,* edited by R.E. West. Edtech Books.

Miller, M.D. 2014. *Minds Online: Teaching Effectively with Technology.* Cambridge, MA: Harvard University Press.

Moore, M.G. 2013. "The Theory of Transactional Distance." In *Handbook of Distance Education,* edited by M.C. Moore and W.C. Diehl. Abington, UK: Routledge.

Morgan, N. 2021. "Why You Need to Gesture on Zoom." Public Words, February 23. publicwords.com/2021/02/23/why-you-need-to -gesture-on-zoom.

Myers, D.G. 2014. *Myers' Psychology for AP*, 2nd ed. New York: Worth Publishers.

Paas, F., J.E. Tuovinen, J.J.G. Van Merrienboer, and A. Aubteen Darabi. 2005. "A Motivational Perspective on the Relation Between Mental Effort and Performance: Optimizing Learner Involvement in Instruction." *Educational Technology Research and Development* 53(3): 25–34.

Peck, M.S. 2003. *The Road Less Traveled: A New Psychology of Love, Traditional Values, and Spiritual Growth*, 25th anniversary ed. New York: Simon and Schuster.

Pelletier, K., M. Brown, D.C. Brooks, M. McCormack, J. Reeves, N. Arbino, A. Bozkurt, S. Crawford, L. Czerniewicz, R. Gibson, K. Linder, J. Mason, and V. Mondelli. 2021. *2021 EDUCAUSE Horizon Report® Teaching and Learning Edition*. Educause. library.educause.edu/resources/2021/4/2021-educause-horizon-report-teaching-and-learning-edition.

Petras, K., and R. Petras. 2014. *It Always Seems Impossible Until It's Done: Motivation for Dreamers and Doers*. New York: Workman Publishing Company.

Pfeffer, J., and R.I. Sutton. 2000. *The Knowing-Doing Gap: How Smart Companies Turn Knowledge Into Action*. Boston: Harvard Business School Press.

Phelps, A., and D. Vlachopoulos. 2020. "Successful Transition to Synchronous Learning Environments in Distance Education: A Research on Entry-level Synchronous Facilitator Competencies." *Education and Information Technologies* 25(3): 1511–1527.

Phillips, P.P., J.J. Phillips, and R. Ray. 2020. *Proving the Value of Soft Skills: Measuring Impact and Calculating ROI*. Alexandria, VA: ATD Press.

Pi, Z., J. Hong, and J. Yang. 2017. "Does Instructor's Image Size in Video Lectures Affect Learning Outcomes?" *Journal of Computer Assisted Learning* 33(4): 347–354.

Quinn, C.N. 2021. *Learning Science for Instructional Designers: From Cognition to Application*. Alexandria, VA: ATD Press.

Rice, G.T. 2018. *Hitting Pause: 65 Lecture Breaks to Refresh and Reinforce Learning*. Sterling, VA: Stylus Publishing.

Ross, L., D. Greene, and P. House. 1977. "The False Consensus Effect: An Egocentric Bias in Social Perception and Attribution Processes." *Journal of Experimental Social Psychology* 13(3): 279–301.

Rowe, M.B. 1986. "Wait Time: Slowing Down May Be a Way of Speeding Up!" *Journal of Teacher Education* 37(1): 43–50.

Ryan, R.M., and E.L. Deci. 2000. "Self-Determination Theory and the Facilitation of Intrinsic Motivation, Social Development, and Well-Being." *American Psychologist* 55(1): 68–78.

Schnotz, W. 2014. "Integrated Model of Text and Picture Comprehension." In *The Cambridge Handbook of Multimedia Learning*, edited by R.E. Mayer. New York: Cambridge University Press.

Schuett, D. 2016. "Skate to Where the Puck Is Going—Position for the Future to Achieve a Competitive Edge." Digital Realty, January 28.

Short, J., E. Williams, and B. Christie. 1976. *The Social Psychology of Telecommunications.* New York: John Wiley & Sons.

Simon, C. 2016. *Impossible to Ignore: Creating Memorable Content to Influence Decisions.* New York: McGraw-Hill Education.

Smith, K. 2020. "57 Fascinating and Incredible YouTube Statistics." Brandwatch, February 21. brandwatch.com/blog/youtube-stats.

Smith, S. 2008. "Why Follow Levels When You Can Build Bridges?" *Training & Development,* September, 58–62.

Sousa, D.A. 2011. *How The Brain Learns,* 4th ed. Thousand Oaks, CA: Corwin Press.

Stanier, M.B. 2021. "Humanizing the Virtual Experience." ATD-MAC Virtual Conference presentation, March 18.

Sweller, J., and J.J.G. van Merrienboer, and F.G.W.C. Paas. 1998. "Cognitive Architecture and Instructional Design." *Educational Psychology Review* 10(3): 251–296.

TechSmith. 2018. *Video Viewer Habits, Trends, and Statistics You Need to Know.* Okemos, MI: TechSmith Corporation.

ul Haq, F. 2021. "Five Reasons Online Learning Is the Future of Professional Development." *Forbes*, March 26. forbes.com/sites /forbestechcouncil/2021/03/26/five-reasons-online-learning-is-the -future-of-professional-development.

Van Nuys, A., ed. 2020. *2020 Workplace Learning Report*. LinkedIn Learning. learning.linkedin.com/content/dam/me/learning /resources/pdfs/LinkedIn-Learning-2020-Workplace-Learning -Report.pdf.

Van Nuys, A., ed. 2021. *Workplace Learning Report: Skill Building in the New World of Work*. LinkedIn Learning. learning.linkedin.com/content /dam/me/business/en-us/amp/learning-solutions/images/wlr21/pdf /LinkedIn-Learning_Workplace-Learning-Report-2021-EN-1.pdf.

Wang, Y., Q. Liu, W. Chen, Q. Wang, and D. Stein. 2018. "Effects of Instructor's Facial Expressions on Students' Learning with Video Lectures." *British Journal of Educational Technology* 50(3): 1381–1395.

Yang, J., F. Zhu, P. Guo, and Z. Pi. 2019. "Instructors' Gestures Enhance Their Teaching Experience and Performance While Recording Video Lectures." *Journal of Computer Assisted Learning* 36(2): 189–198.

Zadina, J.N. 2014. *Multiple Pathways to the Student Brain: Energizing and Enhancing Instruction*. San Francisco: John Wiley & Sons.

Zuckerman, M., J. Porac, D. Lathin, R. Smith, and E.L. Deci. 1978. "On the Importance of Self-Determination for Intrinsically-Motivated Behavior." *Personality and Social Psychology Bulletin* 4(3): 443–446.

Zydney, J.M., P. McKimmy, R. Lindberg, and M. Schmidt. 2019. "Here or There Instruction: Lessons Learned in Implementing Innovative Approaches to Blended Synchronous Learning." *TechTrends* 63(2): 123–132.

Index

Page numbers followed by *f* and *t* refer to figures and tables respectively.

M

manage (3 Ms Method), 254–261
  about, 254–255
  the predictable, 255–257
  with a producer, 259–261
  the unpredictable, 257–259
managers, critical role of, 278–280
Mayer, Richard, 163–164, 228, 230–231, 234, 317
McKenzie, Shannon, 104, 107
McLuhan, M., 240
McLuhan, Marshall, 290, 328
memory, working, 217–218, 340
Merrill, David, 30
messaging
  paraverbal (*See* paraverbal messaging)
  verbal (*See* verbal messaging)
  welcome, 67–68
microphones, 170–171, 343
Microsoft Teams
  background options on, 129
  breakout groups, 106
  screen sharing, 188
  self-view on, 71
  Together Mode, 121
  translations, 153
  welcome messages, 68
Miro, 200
mirroring, 168
mirror neurons, 168
mistakes, 77, 259
mitigate (3 Ms Method), 245–253
  about, 245
  with preventive action, 245–247
  with ready-made solutions, 247–250, 248*t*–249*t*
  by testing platform features, 251–253
  through practice, 250–251
mixed reality (MR), 289
Monet, Claude, 140
monotone, 167
Moreno, Roxana, 230
Morgan, Nick, 134

move forward (3 Ms Method), 261–263
movement
  with annotation, 229–230
  balanced, 220
  and "movement, rest, movement" strategy, 231–232
MR (mixed reality), 289
multiple facilitators, 223–227
multitasking, 111
Mural, 200
Murphy's Law, 245
Mursion.com, 289
music, 63, 236
mute, 64, 92
Myers, David, 215

N

Nature, 28
nervousness, 132, 165
netiquette guidelines, 70–72, 350
neurons, mirror, 168
Nevitt, B., 240
Newton, Isaac, 211
Newton-Hill, Huw, 324
The New Virtual Classroom (Clark and Kwinn), 218
New World Kirkpatrick Model, 274
noise-canceling headsets, 171
Norman, Donald, 20

O

objectives, performance, 36
on-camera facilitation, 117–119, 118*f*, 120*f*
  about, 117–118
  benefits of, 118–120
  BLEACH for (*See* BLEACH)
  challenges of, 120–122
  deciding when to use, 122–125
  to welcome learners, 67
on-camera fatigue, 120–121
on-camera participants, 142–145, 143*f*, 144*f*
on-demand learners, 354

About the Author

Diana L. Howles, MA, is an award-winning speaker, global virtual facilitator, and master trainer who brings 25 years of experience in the talent development industry. A virtual training expert, Diana has designed and facilitated live online and blended learning programs for clients since 2000. As a world-class online facilitator, she has trained organizations on a variety of professional business skills in more than a dozen countries, including Fortune 100 and 500 companies, government agencies, and educational institutions. Diana is CEO and co-founder of Howles Associates, a multimedia company that specializes in live online learning, and provides consulting, coaching, courses, and critiques to help professionals improve their effectiveness with virtual training programs and virtual presentations.

Diana has authored several learning and development articles over the years on trainingmag.com and in publications such as *TD, Learning Solutions,* and *Training*. She is a past president of the Association for Talent Development (ATD) Madison Area Chapter and was their first virtual presenter during the early 2000s showcasing and championing how web conferencing technologies could facilitate online training. Diana was also the first trainer to be certified through SkillPath's certification program for virtual trainers. In other past roles, she has worked as a learning and development manager, corporate senior trainer, learning designer, learning development consultant, leadership coach, systems trainer, and as a professional on-camera and voiceover talent. Diana also taught at Colorado State University and Edgewood College and has led and facilitated virtual classes for the University of Wisconsin-Madison and the University of Wisconsin-Milwaukee. As a seasoned professional, she is a respected thought leader in the field, and colleagues refer to her as a trainer's trainer. She is passionate about helping virtual learning professionals be successful, fascinated by learning technologies and multimedia, and committed to positively impacting the workplace.

Diana has a master of arts from Colorado State University and holds a bachelor's degree in communication and business administration. She is a frequent presenter at international and national in-person and virtual conferences. Diana also keynotes nationally.

As a lifelong learner, she enjoyed participating in an international exchange program in Germany and touring with singing ensembles across the UK and US. She lives in the Midwest in the United States with her family and very high-maintenance (but lovable) dog. You can connect with Diana at linkedin.com/in/dianahowles and @DianaHowles.